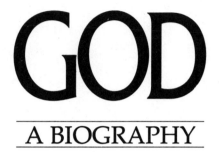

GOD

A BIOGRAPHY

GOD
A BIOGRAPHY

Steven R. Mosley

QUESTAR PUBLISHERS, INC.

PHOENIX

GOD: A BIOGRAPHY
© 1988 by Steven R. Mosley
Published by Questar Publishers, Inc.

Printed in the United States of America

ISBN 0-945564-03-1

to my parents
who first taught me to seek His face

|| CONTENTS ||

Introduction   11

I. SHIMMERING SWORD

Chapter 1   Elemental Force   17
Chapter 2   Victorious Warrior   27
Chapter 3   Skillful Creator   37

II. OMNIPOTENT RESTRAINT

Chapter 4   Altogether Absent   51
Chapter 5   Carefully Restrained   59
Chapter 6   The Saboteur   73

III. HOLY, HOLY, HOLY

Chapter 7   Consuming Fire   91
Chapter 8   Tender Heart   105
Chapter 9   Holy Encourager   117

IV. HERE BEYOND

Chapter 10   Most High   131
Chapter 11   Close Companion   145
Chapter 12   Surpassingly Present   159

V. SOVEREIGN SERVANT

Chapter 13   King of Kings   179
Chapter 14   Burden Bearer   195
Chapter 15   Lowly Lord   211

VI. ABSOLUTELY PERSONAL

Chapter 16   Ageless Rock   225
Chapter 17   A Thousand Faces   243
Chapter 18   Shepherd Wise   259

VII. CLEAR AND PRESENT PICTURE

Chapter 19   Manchild   279
Chapter 20   Fatherlove   293

Sources   311
Index   318

WE were out practicing how to get the collapsible stretcher into McDonough County Hospital Ambulance No. 2. I had finally figured out where the body bags and pneumatic splints were stowed away. The other orderlies and I were joking around on the green lawn in our stiff hospital white. Any excuse to get off Third Floor, with its bedpans and patients under restraint, was welcome.

And then I looked west.

The sun was setting with melodramatic farewell over the horizon, brushing magenta and vermilion over a swirl of clouds that seemed to form a corridor increasing in splendor toward a finely etched ball of fire. The colors splashed in counterpoint all across the expansive sky that loomed over our flat Illinois cornfields.

I had seen dramatic sunsets before. But this one seemed orchestrated to a thoughtful climax. It suggested something out there incalculably more than my life, and at the same time undeniably a part of it. It had an irresistible appeal.

I had been introduced to decay and death up close in our daily rounds at the hospital and on our wailing spins through the county. Yet here, simultaneously above it all, was this glory that, for me, swallowed up everything else.

This book is an attempt to put a face to that glory. It is a documentary of the personal qualities of the God of Heaven, showing (rather than just telling) what people have experienced of His holiness, power, compassion, patience, etcetera.

The book builds a series of pictures of God in action, in a way similar to film. Slices of contemporary life, biblical events, and personal experiences down through history combine to create a vignette of each divine attribute discussed.

Systematic theology often turns God into something of a math problem. His formal properties are divided, subdivided, and inserted into esoteric abstractions. You find fifty pages of densely packed exposition on "God's Incommunicable Attributes." The living, breathing Person disappears.

Building a consistent picture of God on the basis of experience has its problems too. The great variety of subjective data tends to blur His image. We could make God into anything from "Being" to a poached egg on the basis of what people feel.

So I've chosen what I believe to be a reliable framework for organizing the information of experience. My reference points are based on the Judeo-Christian Scriptures. I'm sure that others of the world's great spiritual writings could give us some suggestions on what God is like; there are plenty of upward reaches of the soul to respect and learn from. But at the same time I didn't want to make this picture a lowest common denominator of all religions. God defined by committee is quite uninspiring.

In this biography I propose to make the picture of God coherent, using the facts the Bible gives us, but also painting it in living colors through human experiences that flesh out those facts. I want to bridge the gap between a formal theology of God (objective but often meaningless) and the what-you-feel-in-your-heart conception of deity (meaningful but subjective).

In fleshing out Scripture, I've tried to gather evidence from a wide range of sources and from all periods of history. But because I restricted myself to those events verified by eye-witness testimony, contemporary accounts are more numerous. For example, there are an abundance of miracle stories associated with medieval saints, but firsthand reports are hard to come by.

This is, of course, *a* biography, one person's view. It would be extremely presumptuous to try to write *the* biography of the Almighty. Any portrait comes down to one personality interacting with that primary personality. I feel one can't just report external facts, but must also bear witness to what he has seen and heard and felt.

I've tried to translate the specs of a ponderous machine—immutable, inscrutable, omniscient—into the traits of an individual: intense, consistent, insightful. God is a compelling Person. Our descriptions of Him are too often as tedious and flat as computer manuals. This book molds the experiences and perceptions of Mexican Indians and Black Panthers, Chinese evangelists and romantic poets, L.A. commuters and medieval mystics into a full-color portrait of our Lord. I believe we can understand the Heavenly Father in a way that echoes both the system of theology and the depths of human experience.

PART
I

Shimmering
Sword

AS SOON AS I BECAME CONSCIOUS THAT
THERE IS SUCH A POWER OVER ME,
I FELT A POSSIBILITY OF LIVING.

Leo Tolstoy

1

ELEMENTAL
FORCE

A THUNDERSTORM rolls over the desert. In the predawn darkness a spotlight illuminates an isolated 100-foot-high steel tower. Two half-spheres of plutonium have been carefully hoisted to the top. Twenty miles away on Compania Hill scientists from Los Alamos peer toward "ground zero" through plates of welder's glass, eager to witness the birth of a new age.

At 4 A.M. the rain and lightning cease. At 5:30 the dark sky is suddenly, silently ignited. A yellow-reddish fireball, ten thousand times hotter than the sun, begins an eight-mile ascent into the heavens and turns night into day for more than a hundred miles.

Scientists who have spent three years preparing for this moment forget their assigned tasks and stare in shock at the awesome cloud.

Later one would recall, "It was a vision." He feared the boiling brightness would glare forever. Another felt for an instant that the ball of fire would never stop growing till it enveloped all heaven and earth. A *New York Times* reporter, lying on his belly, was reminded of God's command, "Let there be light."

An army general remembered "an awesome roar which warned of doomsday and made us feel that we puny things were blasphemous to dare tamper with the forces heretofore reserved to the Almighty." The brilliant physicist Robert Oppenheimer vividly recalled a passage from the Bhagavad Gita:

> If the radiance of a thousand suns
> were to burst into the sky,
> that would be like
> the splendor of the Mighty One . . .

Faced with an elemental force greater than anything seen before, these scientists, most of whom had no religious inclinations, described their experience in mythical and theological terms. It was as if they had come face to face with the power of God.

Tragically, the incredible amount of energy unleashed by the invisibly tiny atom would soon become "death, the shatterer of worlds." Human hands molded it into the ultimate weapon. But for a moment America's best and brightest were mesmerized by the sheer immensity of the force above them.

WHAT CAME AS A SURPRISING revelation to modern scientists was, in some ways, more familiar to ancient Hebrew prophets and poets. The God who revealed Himself to Abraham was, first of all, El Shaddai, the Almighty. The Old Testament pictures Him as a being who wields nature like a shimmering sword. His presence shakes things up.

In the Psalms, mountains melt like wax before Him, lightning flashes in a whirlwind, the depths of the sea convulse, its waters writhe, and the dry land trembles. When El Shaddai raises His voice the very earth melts away. At His command roaring wind, surging wave and quivering hill run errands.

When the Almighty made His definitive appearance to Moses and company on Mount Sinai, the elements became pyrotechnic with His presence. Lightning lit up Sinai's slopes. The whole mountain quaked violently and seemed to be ablaze, smoking like a furnace. When the priests pressed their trembling lips to ceremonial trumpets, God thundered back from an enormous dark cloud.

The Hebrews camped below Sinai had spent three days consecrating themselves in preparation for this encounter, but they were no match for Him whose voice threw the mountain into fiery convulsions. The people felt they would die if El Shaddai continued talking, so they begged Moses to speak to them instead.

Yet the encounter left a lasting impression. The Hebrews were able to celebrate their God in the very wildness of nature. Though aware that things had gone awry on this planet and that sin had deeply disturbed the cosmos, they still saw something of El Shaddai in the unbounded power of the elements.

Arkansas. c. 1930.

MY FATHER GREW UP on a small farm during the Depression. Life was pretty uneventful for him among the chickens and corn on a stingy plot of red soil near Texarkana. But one blustering, rainy day a dark cumulonimbus cloud began eating up the sky. From its menacing underside a black funnel spun toward the earth and began beating a path toward the Mosley homestead.

As the distant roar sent chills down little Ramon Mosley's spine the family scrambled into the cellar. There in the gloom he huddled with his terrified sister among the carrots and potatoes and listened as the tornado rampaged through their county, littering its wake indiscriminately with telephone poles, livestock and post offices. Ramon's gaping eyes were glued to the rattling cellar door. He thought any second the storm would plunge in and drag him away.

The tornado passed, however; the farm was repaired, and life resumed its slow, rhythmic pace. But the terror remained for the farm boy. After that day, the very earth, which had once been comfortingly solid, seemed to expose him helpless to the weather's violent whims. There was no place of safety. Every darkening of the sky, every strong breeze through the treetops, froze Ramon's pulse.

One Sunday in the white frame church two miles down the road, a visiting minister spoke about the power of prayer. He insisted that God is eager to meet our smallest and greatest needs. All we have to do is ask and He will answer. The power of God is right there at our fingertips.

For my father, these claims struck a resounding blow. He decided to try them out. Slipping off into the scrub oak woods by himself, Ramon looked into the immaculate sky which had recently gone berserk and told God he was awfully tired of this fear—would He, Sir, mind taking it away from him? The preacher had just said to ask, so Ramon just asked and went back to plowing the cornfield.

After a few days he became aware that he hadn't felt afraid since making his petition in the woods. A few gray clouds had gone by, the wind had picked up a few times, but that old acidy fear that gripped his stomach was gone. Apparently God had simply dissolved it, without benefit of progressive desensitization, positive thinking or any other mental exercise. (Ramon's sister would remain terrified of night breezes the rest of her life.)

It wasn't until many years later that my father realized how thoroughly God had changed his mind. He was somewhere in the Pacific, en route to the Mariana Islands in the middle of World War II. A fierce storm came up and quickly lashed the sea into wild gyrations. Thirty-foot waves exploded against the taut steel of his troop carrier. As the fury of the squall mounted and the ship swayed and pitched precariously, almost everyone except Chief Yeoman Ramon Mosley fled below deck. Only a few other sailors remained above on the bridge trying to hold the troop carrier on course.

Soaked with spray that shot high in the air from the roller-coastering bow, Ramon hung tightly to the upper deck railing. He found himself enjoying the storm immensely. His own youthful energies, cramped for so long aboard ship, expanded empathetically with the forces clashing from horizon to horizon. The untamed animation of sky, wind and water left him breathless.

Here, he felt, was God's majesty and omnipotence. In contrast to the false bravado of men below deck psyching themselves up for battle, Ramon felt awed and humbled before the titanic drama enacted around him.

THIS GOD OF THE STORM, whom my father and Hebrew psalmists knew how to celebrate, can seem pretty alien in a conventional religious setting. Amid lovely stained-glass windows, neat pews and orderly worship services one would expect Him to calm down a bit and speak in soothing, peaceful tones.

But there is more to our God than that. There is a part of Him that is raw power. He is an elemental force and on occasion flashes forth as such.

Cane Ridge, Kentucky. c. 1800.

TWO YOUNG PIONEER WOMEN decided one day to drop in on the Barton Stone camp meeting to see what his revivals were really like. They found thousands seated on rough planks inside a large circle of wagons. Standing on the edge of the assembly, they listened to the people sing simple folk hymns. The girls, known for their gaiety, giggled at the "runner" boys whose job it was to run off stray hogs and dogs during services.

In time Barton Stone, a Presbyterian pastor, stood

to his feet on the covered wooden platform and launched into his sermon. His words seemed to strike the people with physical force. After a while tearful penitents began filing toward a "seekers" pen set off by rails toward the front. Suddenly the two girls fell to the ground with shrieks. For more than an hour they lay there, pale and still as corpses. Some nearby began to fear they wouldn't revive.

Finally the girls stirred and began uttering pleas for God's mercy. Then, as Barton Stone recalled it, "The gloom on the face of one was succeeded by a heavenly smile, and she . . . rose up and spoke of the love of God—the preciousness of Jesus, and of the glory of the gospel, to the surrounding crowd, in language almost superhuman, and pathetically exhorted all to repentance. In a little while after, the other sister was similarly exercised. From that time they became remarkably pious members of the church."

BARTON STONE, like other revivalists on the American frontier, felt he was a witness to God's elemental force. The prostrated young women were two of many attending his meetings who came away believing that they had been struck down by the Almighty. Others would begin dancing or jerking violently during services.

These people encountered God as a force that had to be dealt with. He bowled them over. We can certainly assume that emotional fervor played a part in such phenomena. Revivals have had their share of fanaticism and sham. But still there is evidence in such gatherings for a powerful presence which converts participants in spite of their emotions.

Barton Stone wrote of one skeptical physician who visited his church to be amused by the wild proceedings. But he at length felt something powerful and strange come over him. The man ran out of the building and into the woods. "He was discovered running as for life," Stone wrote, "but did not proceed far till he fell down, and there lay till he submitted to the Lord, and afterwards became a zealous member of the church. Such cases were common."

The outburst of religious energy in the American colonies during the First Great Awakening seemed quite unexplainable to contemporaries, who termed it the "surprising work of God." For thousands listening to Jonathan Edwards and George Whitefield, God became an enormous weight flattening them with conviction and moving them through conversion.

Sinners were also prostrated decades later at Charles Finney revivals in the Midwest. In a typical journal entry Finney mentions speaking to conservative German settlers in a packed schoolhouse. Following his concluding remarks, "The sword of the Lord slew them on the right hand and on the left."

During the famed Azusa Street Revival in Los Angeles in 1906, people who came in were reported to "fall under God's power" and into ecstatic experiences.

Some of us are put off by such displays of overt power. But the history of revival amply testifies that God does sometimes come to people as elemental force. Perhaps many of those prostrated sinners were not that different from the erudite scientists in the New Mexico desert overcome by an awesome power above them.

THE CHURCHES IN WHICH I grew up were removed some distance from an untamed El Shaddai. We worshiped a quiet God on quiet Sabbaths in quiet small towns. In our conservative denomination, religion was not something to be noised about. And only quiet, unobtrusive miracles were acknowledged from the pulpit.

God was Almighty in theory. But the celebration of religion around me did not reflect that. I felt an obligation to witness. It hung over my head ominously. Yet I found it hard to speak to that huge, alien world out there from our isolated subculture. I believed sincerely, but in a corner. I never saw my faith echoed widely and was self-conscious about my peculiar beliefs.

Then I went to the Cotton Bowl.

Dallas, Texas. Summer, 1972.

EIGHTY THOUSAND high school and college kids filled the Cotton Bowl to the brim and buzzed with an excitement I shared. Campus Crusade's Explo '72 was turning us on to "sharing Jesus." We'd grown bold in the city that week—the world seemed to be opening up to faith. Now I looked out at a stadium filled with restive Jesus freaks. "Give me a J," a youthful announcer called. Eighty thousand voices roared back a "J!" that shook the vast circle of seats. This beat church all to pieces. I yelled with newfound gusto as Jesus cheers echoed back and forth from one bank of the stadium to the other.

Rain came one day and threatened to dampen the evening meeting. But no one wanted to leave. The songs went on. We huddled in the drizzle. The clouds bunched together and darkened. Then thunder roared across the sky above us. In an instant we were on our feet roaring back. Thunder echoed again. Again we cheered lustily. Everyone was happy now to be in the elements.

We carried on our boisterous dialogue for five minutes. Then the drizzle slackened, the lightning ceased, speakers came to the stage, and we settled down to listen to lesser voices.

Explo '72 broke all my inhibitions. God had busted out into the open. He no longer occupied a little corner of life. He thundered out over the whole world—and I could cheer back.

Yokohama, Japan. 1980.

THE WORLD OVER WHICH God thundered had enlarged considerably for me. I was seeing many oriental faces brighten in the light of His grace. I was also enjoying good fellowship with Scott, a missionary with whom I could share my struggles and joys.

One day a typhoon brought an unusual amount of rain and wind through our compound in Yokohama. I had become used to "typhoon warnings" as little more than forecasts of precipitation. But this time there was a real storm up. The rain poured down. The trees were jerking about like participants in a Barton Stone revival. The gale actually sheared off a few limbs.

I suggested to Scott that we go out and enjoy the weather. I had a football. We donned our worst clothing and ventured out. The wind rushed us; we had to lean and twirl through it and push through sheets of rain. But those elements were exhilarating. We felt caught up in the unbounded storm. The grass was slick with water. We slipped and slid through two-man tackle football until laughter sapped all our strength.

After resting in the pelting rain we rose to leap and shout our hallelujahs as the wind shook treetops above us. We were propelled by the same force. The whole earth was alive—every leaf, every blade of grass wildly animated. We could barely contain the life bursting inside us. I had never worshiped with such abandon.

PSALMS 96 AND 98 describe a similar type of worship. These two poems talk about the coming of the Lord to judge the earth. But there is no fear or foreboding in their description. There is exhilaration. The psalmist pictures this scene as the Almighty God comes to rescue His people: The sea roars, rivers clap their hands, the fields exult, the mountains and trees sing together for joy.

God is a force to be reckoned with, a wonderful

force of nuclear proportions. He wields nature in His hand as a shimmering sword and shouts to us in the storm.

I have heard deep in my bones the call of El Shaddai, the God of my father.

2

VICTORIOUS WARRIOR

ONCE GOD BROKE THROUGH to the Hebrews as an elemental force and they fixed their gaze in His direction, the chosen people began to make out a definite figure emerging from the storm clouds. It was the figure of a warrior.

In the Psalms we find a God who straps a sword to His thigh, rides to victory as a splendid fighter, and marches through Zion's gates a conquering hero, mighty in battle. He even takes on Leviathan, the embodiment of all that terrified the ancients, and crushes its head in the sea.

Isaiah gives us these words from the Lord:

> Yes, captives will be taken from warriors,
>   and plunder retrieved from the fierce;
> I will contend with those who contend with you,
>   and your children I will save.

This is the promise of a confident fighter. Zephaniah shows us God as excited rescuer:

> The Lord your God is in your midst,
>   a victorious warrior.
> He will exult over you with joy . . .

El Shaddai is aroused to the rescue of His people. He prevails over all opponents. But there is much more to the Warrior God than merely the destruction of His enemies. God characteristically displays His mighty arm in confrontations that result in enlightenment. He takes on evil powers, rulers and gods in order to expose their inadequacies and shatter their presumptuous claims. The Warrior God overpowers rivals. He forces them into situations where they cannot perform.

Mount Carmel, Israel. c. 860. B.C.

GROWING VERY WEARY of His people's chronic flirtation with other gods, Jehovah told His prophet, Elijah, to issue a challenge to the king who had presided over Israel's moral downfall. Elijah procured a meeting with infamous Baal-worshiping King Ahab and proposed the following: You gather your people from all over Israel and summon 450 prophets of Baal. We'll meet at the summit of Mount Carmel, each of us will prepare a bull for sacrifice, each of us will call to our God, and the one "who answers by fire—he is God."

Here was to be a great debate between ideologies. But in this case the cosmic protagonists themselves would be making the points.

Baal got first crack at sparking his sacrifice. The prophets called out their incantations and danced around their slaughtered bull for hours. Nothing happened. As noon approached, they worked themselves into a frenzy. Still there were no takers in the heavens.

Elijah made the most of their chagrin. "Shout louder," he taunted. "Maybe Baal has dozed off. Maybe he's out to lunch." Baal's prophets began slashing themselves with knives and called out more frantically. "But there was no response, no one answered, no one paid attention."

Then El Shaddai's prophet called the people near. He stacked twelve large stones on the ruins of an altar to the Most High, then laid on cords of wood and a sacrificial bull. Gutsy Elijah now made sure all the witnesses would know that it was God Himself who would set this fire. He had four large jars filled with water poured out on the wood and the offering—three times.

Then Elijah prayed to the God of his fathers Abraham, Isaac and Israel, and requested that He manifest Himself. Immediately fire flashed down and consumed bull, wood, altar, and the soil beneath it for good measure.

The people got the point—flat on their faces.

THIS IS THE Warrior God manifesting His power, discrediting His adversaries. We are perhaps not used to such an assertive God today. It is not often that we feel confident enough to call down fire from Heaven. But still, at strategic times in history, the Warrior God does spring forth.

Mei-hwa, China. 1925.

EARLY IN HIS CAREER, the great Chinese writer and preacher Watchman Nee spent a New Year's holiday with five other young believers trying to evangelize the village of Mei-hwa. The men had difficulty getting a hearing amid all the noisy celebrations. By the ninth day the farmers and fishermen still weren't listening. One of the frustrated evangelists asked, "What's wrong? Why won't you believe?"

He was informed that Mei-hwa already had a reliable deity, Ta-Wang. The day of his festival, made known by divination, was fixed for January 11. For the past 286 years, the villagers affirmed, Ta-Wang had provided unfailing sunshine for the day he chose.

The headstrong evangelist exclaimed, "Then I promise you that our God—who is the true God—will make it rain on the eleventh." His hearers seized the challenge. If Jesus could make it rain on the eleventh they would certainly listen to Him.

Watchman and the others with him were at first horrified by their brother's assertion. Was their God being presumptuously put on the spot? But after the men prayed very earnestly over the matter a phrase from Scripture flashed into Watchman's mind: "Where is the God of Elijah?" Watchman felt assured that rain would fall on the eleventh. So the evangelists spread the challenge widely.

That evening their host informed that half of the village natives were fishermen who spent months out at sea and could be relied on to forecast the weather accurately for days ahead. The odds for rain on the eleventh seemed bad indeed. But again Watchman was assured by the words, "Where is the God of Elijah?"

On the morning of the eleventh the evangelists were awakened by brilliant sunlight shining through their window. Quietly they gathered for breakfast. No sign of a cloud in the sky. As they bowed to say grace, Watchman observed, "I think the time is up. Rain must come now. We can bring it to the Lord's remembrance." They did so.

The first drops of rain hit the roof tiles before their "Amen." As the men ate their rice, the drizzle became a steady shower. On being served a second bowl, Watchman paused to give thanks and ask for even heavier rain. It began coming down by the bucketfuls. At the end of breakfast the street outside was deep in water.

A few faithful Ta-Wang supporters had carried their idol in a sedan chair outside, hoping his presence would stop the shower. But once it was in the street the downpour came. After a few yards the bearers stumbled in the flood. Ta-Wang fell and fractured his jaw and left arm.

Still they would not acknowledge defeat. The faithful repaired Ta-Wang and made fresh divination. A mistake had been made. The festival was supposed to be on the fourteenth.

Watchman and his men retired to pray. They asked for three sunny days and rain at 6 P.M. on the fourteenth, when Ta-Wang's procession would begin.

For the next few days the evangelists preached to large audiences under blue skies. The fourteenth began as another perfect day. When evening approached, Watchman and his friends brought their request to God and, not a minute late, His answer came with torrential rains and floods.

THE WARRIOR GOD SPEAKS through fire and rain. He confronts evil and turns foes into a footstool. His battles are not just confined to "primitive mission lands." There are violent struggles taking place right under our affluent Western noses.

We most clearly see the Warrior God in what is known as "spiritual warfare," or confrontations with the demonic. Things can get rather bizarre in cases of demonic possession. The battles are very traumatic at times. But people also witness decisive victories wrought by the Warrior.

The head of the department of psychiatry at a West Coast university described to me (rather reticently) one interesting case he had witnessed. A young woman at their medical center was experiencing seizures which left neurologists and psychiatrists baffled. After numerous tests they still didn't know what was going on.

The family of the patient asked in two pastors to perform an exorcism. The ministers called on "the Name of Jesus," the woman was "delivered," and her seizures ceased. This disturbed a great many of the faculty, but the woman's neurological problem did not return.

I recently interviewed a pastor, Robert Gale, with long experience in the "deliverance ministry." He described what were, to me, almost unbelievable victories over everything from chronic mental illness to anorexia—conditions in which, as he saw it, the demonic was somehow involved. The man has heard coarse masculine voices emerge out of petite women and seen people froth at the mouth and hiss like snakes. He has been in hand-to-hand combat. But in all these cases a "deliverance" resulted. It was simply prayer to Jesus, the Victor, which made the difference.

On another occasion I listened incredulously as a young woman named Dodie told me of the day a sinister force wrapped itself around her, tightening its hold until she couldn't move. Then it began choking her. Gasping for breath she struggled to say the Name. Dodie had to fight to pronounce each syllable: "Jesus, Jesus, Jesus." Slowly the force loosened its hold and moved away.

The Warrior God overpowers His adversaries; He is a fighter. Some of us may be put off by the more sensational aspects of these battles. Furniture flying about a room, people physically attacked, distorted faces—it can start to sound like *National Enquirer* material. But the confrontation these phenomena reflect is very real.

Let me give you a more modest example of "spiritual warfare." This particular event helped me to greatly appreciate the work of the Warrior God.

Southern Illinois. 1973.

ONE HOT, HUMID DAY in July I found myself guarding the boys' bathroom door at Little Grassy Lake Camp. Eight-year-old David kept flinging himself at me, tears rolling, nose running, mouth frothing with toothpaste. I, his cabin counselor, pushed him back again and again, trying in vain to calm the raging child.

It had started with "rest period." David, particularly gifted at misbehavior, was restricted to the cabin. Lying on his bed, he began to brush his teeth. After he spit on the floor a second time I lost my temper. Grabbing him from his bed I laid him down hard on the cement. I rubbed his body on the floor, wiping up the mess with his brightly colored shirt.

David exploded too. Crying and screaming, he wrenched loose from my hands and threw himself against his bed. Something broke inside him and an acidic anger cut across his face. After a few moments of aimless frenzy he started flinging clothes into his suitcase. Between sobs he shouted something about going home, not taking it anymore.

After five minutes of undiluted rage David still wasn't letting up. I decided to get the boy off by himself. David screamed and kicked all the way to the bathroom.

Isolated inside the cool cinder block room I thought he would spend his anger. But it grew, his rough cries looking for a climax, a way out, but not finding one.

In my alarm I used difficult words: "David, I love you. I want to help you." But he couldn't hear, sealed airtight in his blazing emotions. David was one of many kids bused down from a Chicago ghetto that week for a dose of civilization in nature. I could only guess at the passions his background had wedged deep inside him and at what children must endure growing up in the hands of sinners who don't know they are. At that moment it seemed as if all the lackings and longings of a cramped soul flared at me, screaming at the oppression, begging for restraint.

Finally after a fierce, helpless shove, David threw himself on the floor. He lay at my feet frothing and writhing, passion unabated. It was then that those old tales flashed into my mind. Those primitive, word-of-mouth tales. I saw flashes of Jesus on the field of battle, facing a naked, militant evil.

Reaching down, I picked up David by the shoulders. He stood facing away from me. A bit self-conscious and very desperate I said, "Get out in the Name of Jesus." Twice. I didn't sound to myself like one wielding authority. It was just a clean fling of faith. And David, I remember, couldn't hear me. He was still screaming so loudly.

But he stopped. Two or three seconds after my impulsive command he was supple in my hands, sobbing softly. I led David over to the sink and he let me wash his face.

"You feel better?" I asked, earnest and awed.

"I'm sorry," he whimpered, like a son made tender toward his father. Those were words I couldn't imagine David ever saying.

We talked for some time in that bathroom amid the graffiti. I wanted so badly for David to understand that there was Someone stronger than the passions running over him, that there was a Warrior who would fight on his behalf.

LOOKING BACK, I wouldn't want to diagnose David as demon-possessed. I don't understand the mechanics involved in demonic activity. I'm sure there is a good word in a psychology textbook for David's outburst. Perhaps just "temper tantrum" would do. But I think solutions are more important than labels. The point is, the Name of Jesus got results. That's what mattered. David's deliverance that day may only have been spiritual first aid, but for a moment the Victorious Warrior came close. I felt Him exulting over one He had snatched from the enemy.

All of us, of course, are in one way or another involved in a struggle with evil. The difference between losing your temper and wrestling with a demon is probably one of degree, not substance. I have seen the Warrior God act amid "ordinary" temptations. In fact it is in this area that His "extended arm" is the most helpful for the most people. I remember distinctly one occasion in which "the flesh" had me up against the wall. Temptation had attracted, bemused, and saturated my thoughts. I was on the edge of giving in.

It is almost impossible to extricate yourself once you have been sucked in that deeply. Once the temptation has you fixed, there is only one way out—sin. But this time I managed one last token gesture of resistance. I opened my Bible to Romans 8. Praying with desperate half-heartedness I tried to read. I called on the Mighty God to deliver me. (It's hard to do that while savoring sin at the same time.)

Somehow those familiar words of Paul about new life in the Spirit caught hold. I prayed more wholeheartedly. I continued to read, and then—my mind was changed. Thoughts hopelessly locked into sin bounced up to spiritual themes. God's principles became exciting. I got caught up in them.

And so I was freed. Right there in the same environment that had made me so vulnerable. Right there with the same sin available. I had been made strong and could turn away. I was, in fact, heady with strength.

For those who haven't scuffled in the dust with deeply rooted habits, the deliverance I have described may not sound like much. But for me it was remarkable. I had seen the Warrior God act on my behalf. He had lifted me out of a pit way over my head and I felt Him exulting over one He had snatched from the enemy.

3

SKILLFUL CREATOR

AFTER STROLLING through the Red Sea, watching Jericho's impervious walls crumble, and seeing the Lord of Hosts overwhelm vast invading armies, the Hebrews understandably got the idea that their God had more than ordinary power. They realized He was no mere regional deity with boundaries to His might. "Our God is in heaven," they shouted to the world. "He does whatever pleases him."

The psalmists are not content just to tell us that God is powerful; they are at pains to describe "the greatness of His power." Isaiah hints at the breadth of God's might. He pictures flies scurrying in from Egypt and bees from Assyria to do God's will in Judah—simply because the Lord whistled. Jeremiah is heard telling God simply, "Nothing is too hard for you."

The Hebrews rejoiced in their God's unlimited power. Centuries later theologians and philosophers began to analyze just what "omnipotence" might mean. Scholastic theologians like Thomas Aquinas seemed peculiarly preoccupied with the topic. If God could do anything, they wondered, could He change the past? Make two plus two equal five? Die? These kinds of queries have persisted down to the present. Wags are still fond of posing the trick question: Can God make a stone heavy enough for Him not to be able to lift?

A great many discourses on God's omnipotence

are devoted to unraveling the mental knots such questions create. People take pains to explain that God does not contradict Himself, can do anything logically possible, can do all that He wills.

These statements are probably helpful. Still there is something odd in both the questions and many of the answers. Omnipotence is often treated as a quantity—a part of an algebra equation that can be manipulated in relation to other factors. Many theological definitions seem like attempts to come up with some precise measurement of omnipotence. But we have a hard time measuring infinite quantity. It's unwieldy. How big do God's muscles have to be? For how many light years does His power extend?

Quantitative views of power become black holes collapsing under the weight of the infinite. Great quantities—taken to the limit—can leave us only cold or amused. How many megadeaths can one aircraft carrier pack into its warplanes? How much money can one trading company amass? How many freshmen can be inserted into a phone booth?

Such images are one reason it's hard for us to imagine infinite power—and why the prospect often leaves us feeling uneasy.

It's far more useful for us to view omnipotence in terms of a quality—the "greatness of His power." It is remarkable ability that the Bible celebrates, not some amorphous mass of potentiality. It is, in a word, *skill*. God is infinitely skillful.

Think of people with remarkable powers and you will see skill. An Olympic gymnast twirls above the parallel bars, every muscle in fluid sync. We watch amazed. How does he do it? His acrobatics are qualitatively far removed from what our own bodies can do.

We hear a singer express emotion in tones so full and rich that we think our ears will burst. How does she do it? Her vocal chords have somehow made a quantum leap above ours.

We listen as a poet reads his verse. He reveals depths of meaning we never thought possible in such few words. The whole fits together with such ingenuity. How does he do it? Somehow his ability with language has grown qualitatively far beyond ours.

That is power. That is skill. Specially gifted human beings who dedicate themselves to years of study and practice attain extraordinary abilities that excite others into using words like "genius."

That is the kind of excitement that animated the Hebrew poets. They were thrilled by the *quality* of God's power. Hidden in scores of psalms is the awed question: How does He do it? God's actions are qualitatively removed from ours. His skill boggles the mind.

In the Psalms God's power is most often associated with creation. Nature is a continual performance that inspires applause. As Creator, God displays His power for all to see. One can search endlessly into His skill.

Hebrew poets picture Him setting fast the mountains, stretching out the heavens like a canopy, clothing meadows with flocks and valleys with grain, filling the broad sea with swarms of animals great and small. Isaiah sees the Almighty leading a host of stars out of the night, calling each one by name. Jeremiah proclaims a God who made heaven and earth and all living creatures by the great power in His outstretched arm.

Again and again they all echo the theme: He made the earth by His power. One of the things that impresses us about the powerfully skillful is that they make their feats look easy. The gymnast, singer and poet performing at their peak seem to do it all so effortlessly. In a similar way the Creator makes it look easy: "He spoke, and it came to be; he commanded, and it stood firm." No lengthy incantations or complicated laboratory were required. Just a word of command. That is infinite skill.

Today most people are capable of admiring creation to a certain extent. We go out on picnics and comment on how nice the flowers are and how pretty the clouds look. And most of us have some idea that a Creator was somehow involved in all that. Still we haven't the vaguest notion of the performance we're actually beholding. The words "Skillful Creator" don't really sink in until we have observed nature carefully, up close.

Inside the Eye.

THE ACT OF SEEING is really an enormously complicated process. It begins when light strikes our eyes and is bent into focus at a precise angle by the transparent cornea. Next the blue, brown or green iris varies the amount of light passing through by changing the size of the pupil—actually a hole in its center which appears black. We don't have to think about any of this; nerve signals make the adjustments automatically.

After light passes through a colorless fluid called the aqueous humor (which is optically matched to the cornea and so keeps the rays bent at exactly the same angle) it reaches the tiny lens, made up of more than two thousand infinitely fine layers of transparent fiber.

This lens, unlike the lens in a camera, is pliable. It can bulge slightly or flatten out. This changes the way light is bent and thus helps us focus very sharply. Human vision is extraordinarily flexible. We can focus on objects a few inches from our nose and then switch instantly to a clear, sharp view of a distant star.

Next light travels (still on the same focused path) through a clear, jellylike substance that fills most of the interior of our eyes. Then it reaches the retina, a pink coating that covers the back of the eyeball. The retina corresponds roughly to film in a camera. Packed into the retina lie what are called rods and cones. These photoreceptors contain light-sensitive pigments.

The rods and cones are like two kinds of film. Plump cones are most active in bright light. They give us full-colored, sharp vision. The slender rods are for dim light. Like highly sensitive black-and-white film, they create a monochrome picture when little light is available. That is why color seems to disappear at night and we see basically different shades of gray.

These rods and cones are mixed together throughout the retina. About 130 million occupy an area the size of a postage stamp. Because of this we are able to switch with relative ease from vision in bright sunlight to vision in a very dim room.

Our photoreceptors, the rods and cones, also perform another vital function. They transform the light they receive into signals, partly electrical and partly chemical. Scientists are still trying to understand this complex process, but somehow a remarkable transformation takes place. The light that created an image disappears, and in its place coded signals appear.

To carry these signals, retinal fibers are required. These nerve fibers create a complex data-collection network that fans out over the retina. At a point in the back of the eye these fibers bunch together like a cable, becoming the optic nerve.

Now things are just beginning to get complicated. The optic nerves from each eye crisscross in the brain. They exchange information in some way so that the images from two eyes can be coordinated into one stereoscopic field of vision. Then more nerve fibers pick up the signals and carry them to the visual cortex in the back of the brain. The actual phenomenon of "seeing" takes place in this small mass of gray matter.

The billions of cells in our visual cortex are arranged in a number of layers. All these cells have highly specialized functions. Some send projections to other areas of the brain where memory and association occur. Most add up, combine, exchange and organize countless bits of visual data in some mysterious way yet to be fathomed. The result is the miracle of perception: A picture is produced in the mind through a process no high-tech computer can come close to duplicating.

Clearly, seeing is no simple matter. Vision is far more than just "taking a picture." The organs that produce sight are a marvel. Scientists tell us the delicate engineering of the eye's cornea and lens makes the most advanced camera seem like a child's toy by comparison.

THE EYE IS JUST one bit of performance in the vast theater of God's creation. There are countless other examples of God's outstretched arm in action one could cite: Monarch butterflies navigating two thousand miles south each autumn from the United States to central Mexico, riding thermals to favorable altitudes, exploiting wind currents, soaring so efficiently that they arrive at their destination fat and healthy. The human kidney taking blood cells apart, distilling some thirty chemicals, and putting them back together cleaned and precisely balanced—with each heartbeat. Farmer ants planting, fertilizing, cultivating and harvesting tiny plants underground.

When we stand close to creation, we are moved to ask the awed question, "How does He do it?" We begin to feel the qualitative greatness of God's power.

THE NEW TESTAMENT also speaks of God's power in qualitative terms. The apostles usually key on the "effectual working" of God's might. They admire His ability to fashion new abilities inside human beings. Believers receive power to become sons of God; they are strengthened with power in the inner man. We are promised more than we can think, or even imagine, according to the power that functions within us.

Just as the Skillful Creator produced dazzling works *ex nihilo*, out of nothing, so the Skillful Re- creator produces spiritual traits where none existed before. We observe His finesse most keenly in the quality of life He re-creates—in the most unlikely places. God's infinite skill takes on the cases we deem most hopeless.

The Bronx. 1958.

THERE WAS A THING inside Nicky that scared him. He couldn't understand it, or stop it. A feeling came over the boy every time he saw a cripple, a blind person, or a little kid—a feeling of hatred and revulsion. Nicky felt like killing anyone weak or hurt; for some reason he hated them.

It kept getting worse. He'd kick people on crutches, try to pull out old men's beards, rough up children. All the time Nicky would be scared and wanting to cry, but the thing inside kept pushing him on.

Then there was blood. The minute he saw blood, he'd start laughing and couldn't stop.

Nicky had grown up on the streets—fighting to stay alive. He became chief rumbler for the Mau Maus, adept at laying out bodies with a baseball bat. One day he and a few Mau Maus met up with boys from the rival Bishops gang in a candy store. They began taunting and shoving one another. One boy slashed open a Bishop's head with a butcher knife. Nicky saw the blood pour out and started laughing. He was horrified but couldn't stop laughing.

He lived for his gang. By the time he turned eighteen he'd knifed sixteen people and been to jail twelve times. The only truth he knew was the law of survival on the streets.

Then Nicky met the Re-creator. At a meeting for gang members led by David Wilkerson he was introduced to a God who loved and transformed people.

Nicky went up to the altar and prayed, "Dear God, I'm the dirtiest sinner in New York. I don't think You want me. If You do want me, You can have me."

He got a Bible from Wilkerson and went back to his apartment, wondering if he really had God, and how he would know. The first thing he noticed was that he wasn't scared as usual. A tough fighter in the daytime, Nicky was always scared at night, longing for the parents who were never there for him.

But this night he felt like there was company in the room, "the way I'd feel if my mother came back."

The next day two little kids came up and wanted him to see which was taller. Children had always run away from him before. Maybe he *was* a new person. Nicky put his arms around them.

A few weeks later a Dragon gang member, hearing he no longer carried weapons, tried to stab him. Nicky caught the knife in his hand. The Dragon ran. Nicky stood there looking at the blood. It had always made him crazy before, but now it didn't. He calmly ripped his shirt and tied up the wounded hand.

A short time after getting off the streets for good, the kid who'd been chief rumbler for the Mau Maus was studying to become a minister.

Ida Grove, Iowa. 1952.

THROUGH HIS ALCOHOLIC HAZE Harold thought of the men he'd seen shot in the war and realized he'd make a terrible mess in the bedroom. So, picking up his Remington 12-gauge shotgun, he stumbled down the hall to the bathroom. Stepping into the bathtub, Harold lay down and pointed the shotgun's muzzle into his mouth. This would be his final attempt to escape his broken promises, his web of lies, and the look of hurt in his children's eyes. This was his only way out of the bottle.

Harold had first taken a drink as a shy, tongue-tied

teenager. It made him feel like he was walking on air. Suddenly he could talk with the girls. He was confident and relaxed, the life of the party.

Soon he found he wanted three drinks for every one his buddies drank. Something inside urged him on and on. That drive persisted through his high school years and into college. After a year of study he dropped out and married a petite raven-haired girl named Eva. They were happy—when Harold wasn't drinking.

Then Harold's brother Jesse died in a car accident. The two had been very close and Harold drank more— to forget. World War II broke out and Harold served as an infantryman in bloody campaigns in North Africa and Italy. He had even more to forget when he returned home to Eva and his two small daughters.

He became a partner in a trucking business and did well. But his work often kept him out late drinking with business associates. When Eva tried to talk to him about his drinking problem Harold blew up. When sober he noticed dark circles under his wife's eyes. His girls sometimes hid in the closet when he came home.

Finally Eva and the children left the house. This shocked him into making a solemn promise. He swore, before a judge, that he would not touch liquor for a year. His family returned.

A few weeks later Harold traveled to a truckers' meeting in Ames, Iowa. One morning while he was away he woke up in a hotel in Des Moines with no idea how he'd gotten there. He stared at a neon sign flashing outside his window and then felt a familiar dry, stale taste in his mouth. As he stood up the room spinned. Staggering into the bathroom to wash his face, he saw vomit splattered on the toilet.

One more promise down the drain. After that he made no more pretense about trying to stop. He came home drunk more and more often.

Then on one fateful day in 1952, Harold promised

Eva he'd be home early for an important dinner date. He lingered after a business meeting for "just one drink." It turned into eleven before he knew it. He hurried home, but Eva and the kids were gone.

As he sat on his bed in the empty house that night his repeated failures overwhelmed him. Alcohol had dominated his life for ten years. He made promises, he prayed, but nothing could control his craving. Harold had failed everyone who meant anything to him. A nauseating feeling of self-hatred welled up inside.

There was only one way to end the hell his family was enduring. Eva was young and pretty, she could marry again. His girls would be able to forget, and they would be spared the disgrace of having a drunk for a father.

That's when he decided to end it all in the bathtub with his 12-gauge. The porcelain beneath him felt cold as he reached toward the trigger with his thumb.

Before he could press it down, it occurred to him that suicide is wrong in God's eyes and that he should explain to Him why he was doing this. He climbed out of the bathtub and knelt on the cold tile floor. "O God," Harold groaned, "I'm a failure, a drunk, a liar . . . I'm lost and hopeless and I want to die. Forgive me for doing this . . ."

Then he broke into sobs. "O Father," he continued, "Please take care of Eva and the girls. Please help them forget me."

He began shaking uncontrollably and slipped to the floor. He kept crying out to God until he lay still, exhausted. He began to feel a peace he'd never experienced. It seemed to drive out the emptiness, the self-hate, the condemnation. He felt a strange joy welling up inside.

As it turned out, Harold ran smack into El Shaddai's transforming power. He gave himself to the Victorious Warrior and began a regular program of prayer and Bible study. Harold made a commitment to stay away from alcohol altogether.

This time he had the spiritual strength to persevere. Harold Hughes kept his promise and went on to become governor of Iowa and later a distinguished member of the United States Senate.

But more important to Harold than all the public honors he would receive was one small incident that occurred shortly after his commitment to God.

Harold was studying the Bible alone in his living room one evening when he felt a nudge at his elbow. He looked up. It was his two small daughters, standing quietly in their nightgowns. He stared at them for a moment; they had changed so much, and he had missed so much.

Then Carol, the youngest, said, "Daddy, we've come to kiss you goodnight."

The father's eyes blurred. It had been so long since the children had come for his embrace. Now their beautiful clear eyes held no fear. Daddy had come home at last.

NICKY AND HAROLD give us a glimpse of the depth and height of God's ability. His is a power infinitely skillful. Most of us would have viewed those two men as terminal cases: the irredeemable delinquent and the hopeless alcoholic. It's hard to imagine any human leverage that could have moved those two people out of their deep ruts and into grace—a grace genuine enough for children to admire.

But the Skillful Re-creator took on those terminal cases, as He has taken on countless others. And in His re-creating, it is the quality of His power that stands out. These two people encountered the One who, as John Donne wrote,

> doth not alone dispose
> Leaden and iron wills to good, but is
> Of power to make even sinfull flesh like his.

47

Omnipotence is not some abstract equation in the sky, a number with too many zeroes for us to count. It is God's infinite ability. One senses that He takes great pleasure in His workmanship. He puts the finishing touches on His re-creations with elegant care: Kids run up to the former street fighter to be measured. Daughters kiss the former alcoholic goodnight. Imagine how good it must feel to have a dazzling skill that turns chemical/electrical signals into vision deep in our brains, and fashions love deep within calloused hearts.

ELEMENTAL FORCE. Victorious Warrior. Skillful Creator/Re-creator. These are all aspects of God's power, and there is a somewhat progressive relationship between them. Both in history as a whole and in individual lives, we first encounter God as a force to be reckoned with. His power overwhelms. We fall on our faces convicted of our frail sinfulness. Then we discover that the same God can rescue us. He swoops down in our midst as Victorious Warrior and we accept the redemption His outstretched arm brings. Finally we find that this God can renew, can create new life. He fashions hearts and minds into His image with infinite skill.

Martin Luther first met God as awesome force. A lightning bolt struck down young Martin on the road one day and terrified him into taking vows at a monastery. Later, however, Luther saw God's power in terms of a Mighty Fortress. That is our privilege as well. We may find refuge in the Almighty. He is always best pictured by those who celebrate the full dimensions of His power—awed by a force, heartened by rescue, captivated by skill.

PART
II

Omnipotent
Restraint

THIS DARKNESS IS THE SHADOW
OF THY WINGS.

Elizabeth Lloyd Howell

4

ALTOGETHER ABSENT

THIS CITY was always somewhat unsettling to me in its vastness. I first saw it as red and white lights spreading from horizon to horizon beneath a 707. We were descending to Haneda Airport at night. We flew for what seemed like half an hour and still more of Osaka glittered ahead. Coming straight from the cornfields of Illinois, I couldn't understand how one city could go on and on underneath us.

And it was full of people. Masses of people streaming through the train stations and department stores. People with blank commuter faces scurrying to work. Immeasurable multitudes who never seemed to turn their eyes heavenward.

Fresh from college, I had come with other "student missionaries" to teach English and Bible classes in Japan. I had visions of profound spiritual encounters with Buddhist sages and idealistic university students. What I discovered was a thoroughly secular society. The sheer volume of all that indifferent humanity was depressing.

We made friends. That helped. We had good Bible classes. That helped. But when we put on evangelistic meetings for the public, nobody came. We sent out effusive fliers, invitations far and wide—and one or two new faces would come in out of the crowd.

Time after time I would sit in our church as the

51

evangelist preached and stare out over a smattering of guests in a sea of empty chairs. The vacant seats spoke more loudly than the evangelist. I couldn't get them out of my mind. It was absurd. Wasn't Almighty God searching through this metropolis for potential children? Surely out of six million souls He could distill a few hundred seekers and bring them around to our meetings.

So one day in staff meeting I proposed that we ask God to pack the church at our next evangelistic series. The time seemed right. We student missionaries had grown close as a group. Having to make God real to people for whom He was a complete stranger had challenged and revitalized our faith. We had been claiming Bible promises to good effect. This was it. A godly momentum was building up our expectations.

We began praying, claiming promises, asking specifically that God would show His hand and fill all the seats. This was His work, winning people was His will, we were united in His Name.

We sent out our invitations, put up our signs. We kept praying. Opening night we swung back the doors, believing. The evangelist spoke. And his voice echoed back from hundreds of empty chairs.

It was a very long train ride home that night. At 10 P.M. the drunks were trying to make it back to studio apartments. The workaholics stared across the aisle more blankly than ever. Amid the monotonous clack of the rails, the whole world seemed terribly alone. I had to change trains at Nishinomiya station. While waiting for the local I walked out to the end of the platform. The city still spread its lights to the horizon. I looked up and pondered the dark, blank sky.

God had not shown His power. He hadn't acted at all. He hadn't answered our modest call. Where was the Almighty? Our efforts to speak for Him in the metropolis seemed painfully feeble. We hadn't even

made a ripple. God Himself had not made a ripple.
The millions just walked on by.

I AM NOT THE FIRST, of course, to wonder about the
apparent powerlessness of God. I could have found an
echo for my dejection that night in many of the Psalms.
The same poems that speak enthusiastically of God's
mighty acts also give voice to moments of anguish. Listen to David's tortured question in Psalm 13:

> How long, O Lord? Will you forget me forever?
> How long will you hide your face from me?

In Psalm 35 David is blunt:

> When my prayers returned to me unanswered,
> I went about mourning . . .

And he fairly shouts:

> O Lord, how long will you look on?

The Almighty seems to be just standing there—if He's
there at all. Why doesn't He DO something?

Other psalms eloquently express feelings of aban-
donment, rejection, and grim despair. These writers
obviously had experienced times when El Shaddai
seemed all but impotent.

But it's not just that God doesn't always do great
things for us that is troubling. We don't expect all our
prayers to be answered in the way we prescribe.
There's something more disturbing. There is a darker
side to God's powerlessness that has driven many people away from Him.

Riverside, California. 1970.

ONE BRIGHT SATURDAY afternoon I was persuaded to participate in a "Sunshine Band," a group from the college I
attended which visited local hospitals. They sang in the

halls and talked with patients. It seemed like a good idea.

So I went along and joined in cheerful choruses like, "Everything's Alright in My Father's House" and "I've Got Peace Like a River." We moved slowly down antiseptic hallways and smiled at the patients who glanced up curiously from their beds. It was a big place, full of institutional smells. Our voices echoed rather harshly amid the bare walls.

At the end of "Heavenly Sunshine" our procession halted and we dispersed into patients' rooms. I chatted with a black matron who seemed very afraid there but who warmed to the name of Jesus. Then I stepped into a large room with six beds. I started toward a patient who appeared about my age but then stopped cold. There were tubes running into his body from a cluster of machines. He seemed pretty banged up. What was I doing here? I began to feel faint.

Then I spotted the elderly man. He lay on the other side of the room, moaning. His body twitched as if trying to shake off an invisible blanket. I could not tell whether the man was asleep or awake. For a second I felt sure his pained jerking around would stop. But it went on. No one in the room was alarmed. No one seemed to notice.

Then it hit me hard—he's always like this. This is his existence. And that fact was as unfathomable as eternity. The poor man just lay there and moaned and writhed. Each day I went to breakfast, attended classes, lunched with friends, played tennis, goofed around, studied, watched TV. Each day he moaned and writhed. Dear God this is not some malfunctioning machine, I thought. This is a human being!

I swallowed hard. "Heavenly Sunshine" lay thick and gagging in my throat. The tubes, machines, soiled sheets and bare walls blurred into the elderly patient's convulsions and I had to rush outside for fresh air.

Suffering had always been an abstraction before that day at the hospital. You can maneuver abstractions into their proper place in the scheme of things. But afterward suffering had a face. You can't maneuver around a face; you can't forget it. Those contorted features embodied for me all the suffering I had ever read or heard about.

They also took me by surprise. In those few vulnerable moments in the hospital I felt pinned against the wall by the conviction that God Almighty and this poor man could not exist in the same universe. It was inescapable. The patient's spastic body was a constant witness against the faith I had cherished since childhood. It seemed to be wrestling to express an unpronounceable curse against Heaven. Everything was NOT all right in my Father's house. I didn't think I would ever have peace like a river again.

THIS IS THE DARKER SIDE of God's apparent powerlessness. It's not just a lack of heroic miracles that disturbs us. It's the Almighty's failure to stop suffering—something that surely basic decency requires. Evil abounds. People hurt. Tragedies multiply. Unspeakable crimes continue. And God seems idle. What dark accusations have passed through our minds!

What we probably don't realize is that our darkest thoughts find a mirror in Scripture. One of the most eloquent documents of grief over suffering is the book of Lamentations, written by the prophet Jeremiah. He sits amid the ruins of Jerusalem and recalls the slaughter of his people and the exile of the few survivors.

The prophet's eyes "fail because of tears." He stares benumbed at a tragedy "vast as the sea." He remembers a gruesome siege during which little children begged in vain for food and infants died on their mothers' bosoms. He recalls bodies clogging the streets of the city. It seems like the end of a nation, the end of all that Jeremiah has lived and labored for. There is no one to comfort the lonely city that was full of people.

The prophets understood suffering. They felt its keen edge every bit as much as contemporary writers. And they did not shrink from its loud testimony. In fact Scripture forces us to take one more painful step closer to the problem of evil in our world. It pushes us beyond the suffering of people in general, the suffering which humanity often brings on itself, to the darkest part of God's apparent powerlessness.

In the book of Job we find an outrageous case of suffering. Job is a good man who is systematically destroyed. Here virtue not only goes unrewarded, it is smashed into the ground. The book proceeds through a long series of speeches in which Job's friends try in vain to make what is manifestly unjust appear fair. They keep butting their arguments against the wall of undeserved suffering. Recently a friend helped me better understand the passion in the book of Job.

La Fox, Illinois. 1969.
Yucaipa, California. 1985.

BILL AND I SPENT our senior year together at a Christian high school in Illinois. Bill was a revelation to me. His amiable faith stood out in a world of stilted saints and comfortable sinners. I had begun to wonder whether you could be normal and religious at the same time. Bill was the only peer I had ever met who was on good terms with Christ and who made friendship with Him seem desirable.

Bill and I came to share a common bond. We actually prayed together in his room—door locked, lights out. We could talk about the Bible, even outside of church. And we could play flag football with gusto too. It was a good year.

A decade later Bill had become a pastor in Southern California and I had moved near L.A. to write for a Christian telecast. He invited me to speak at his church. My family and I had a great time visiting with him and his lovely wife. Bill took out his yearbook and we laughed about the good times.

We said goodby, promising to keep in touch. Yes, we should write. But we both got busy.

About a year later I got a call from the church secretary. Bill had gone out boating with his wife and a couple of friends. Several other weekenders were enjoying the lake. Bill was standing up in the boat when the driver suddenly swerved to avoid a downed skier. Bill flipped over and fell out. His head descended toward the water at precisely the right angle to strike the spinning propeller.

They swung back to pick up Bill but he had disappeared. He wasn't wearing a life-jacket. Frantically they began zig-zagging over the gray water. Not a trace. In one second he was lost forever.

Rescue boats were called in. They dragged the lake in vain. Bill's wife and friends were told that a thick underground forest lay under the area where he had gone down. Objects lost there were sometimes never found.

The first thing I thought of as I hung up the phone was what I might say to comfort Bill's wife. But I had no words. The faces from the yearbook came back. Why Bill? Out of all those people in the class of '70, why Bill? So many had wasted their lives. Bill was the one bright light. The best. How could such a life end so trivially? One little swerve of a boat and he lies irretrievably tangled in some underwater forest.

I imagined what it must have been like for the people in the boat, scanning the lake, terror gnawing at their stomachs, helplessly flailing their prayers against the cast-iron waves. Nothing could pry open the merciless deep.

In that frail little boat surely nothing was more certain than the utter absence of the Almighty. The meaningless destruction of the best must be the final argument that seals the case against omnipotence. As darkness gathered over the featureless lake and rescue boats kept scouring its waters—solely as a gesture toward the benumbed widow—El Shaddai Himself must have appeared irretrievably lost.

5

CAREFULLY
RESTRAINED

SOME YEARS AFTER I returned to the United States from my "student missionary" assignment, I made a surprising discovery. It related to that group of Christian teachers gathered in staff meeting to petition the Lord for a packed house. Those empty chairs at our evangelistic series still bothered me. I had found it quite unusual for such a highly motivated request to go so completely unanswered. Now I learned that two of the unmarried teachers had been sleeping together at the time.

I seemed to recall that those two had been less than enthusiastic about boldly claiming Bible promises for a soul in every seat. Now I realized why. There was a barrier there in their minds, an uneasiness about marching right up to the throne of grace.

Apparently, our petition as a group just couldn't go through. In that instance, sin short-circuited God's power. We were not fully grounded in grace. Sin (the transgression of God's Law) somehow prevented Him from doing what, according to Scripture, He was very eager to do.

Now I don't believe that only the prayers of the sinless are answered. If that were the case God would have hung up the phone after Jesus said His last Amen. But He is, according to wide testimony, still very much on the line.

The rest of us in that group did not expect an answer because of any special merit we possessed. Each of us had our imperfections and our obvious faults. But two people were involved in deliberate disobedience. With premeditation they regularly carried out something they knew was wrong.

I think that's what put up the barrier. It wasn't that God found their particular sin especially odious and so turned away in disgust. The problem was, the Almighty could not bless willful defiance.

Deliberate sin separates people from God. There's no getting around it. Sin is an insurmountable barrier (breached only by the heroic sacrifice of Christ). That might be hard for us to grasp in a world permeated by evil. Sin does not come to us as some hideous stranger. It's a warm, familiar tug. We tend to cozy up to it just as fast as we can.

But for God it is an outrage that cuts Him off from us. He cannot act, or more accurately, He cannot act and still be just. His power is short-circuited by sin. It can actually make Him appear powerless. Speaking to people who were openly corrupt and deliberately apostate, the prophet Isaiah explained:

> But your iniquities have separated
>   you from your God;
> your sins have hidden his face from you,
>   so that he will not hear.

Okay. So sometimes God cannot do great things for us because some deliberate sin gets in His way. It's not too hard to buy that. We're willing to give up on a few miracles. But then we get to the larger problem of misfortune and suffering in general. Jeremiah lamenting over a devastated city. The elderly patient writhing endlessly in his bed. That's harder to deal with. But let's try.

We need to go back a long way to get the big picture.

Creation.

THE ALMIGHTY HAD JUST fashioned a lovely blue and green planet bursting with flora and fauna, and he wanted people to inhabit it. He'd been very pleased with His work so far, everything seemed good to Him, and now He was ready for His crowning act of creation. Now what kind of people should He make?

Various options were open to Him. The Almighty could have programmed beings to wander contentedly about the Garden of Eden and raise their hands in adoration on cue. He could have created actors to play flawless parts for Him. But that would have been meaningless for God. From later portions of the Bible you get a strong impression He has always wanted beings He can have a loving relationship with. He wants to love and be loved. He has apparently filled the universe with that in mind.

Love, however, can't be compelled. It has to be given freely. Robots can smile, speak courteously, and do the dishes. But they can't love.

So God made His momentous decision. He said, "Let us make man in our image." God created Adam and Eve as free moral agents, beings with choice. They could make decisions independently of their Creator. They could choose their own fate.

FREEDOM IS A WONDERFUL thing to have, but it carries with it certain perils. Humans can decide to love God or to turn their backs on Him. They can follow the upward path or go off a cliff.

Sometimes when we complain about the state of the world we forget that God gave us free choice altogether. If the Almighty steps in and pushes us back on His path every time we make a wrong choice, then freedom doesn't really exist. Freedom means that we live with the consequences of our decisions. It means we can hurt ourselves and each other.

If we think this is too high a price to pay for freedom we should listen to the voices of those who have lost theirs. Some of the most eloquent voices have arisen out of the Soviet gulag. Aleksandr Solzhenitsyn recited verses of poetry over and over while laying bricks in brutal arctic weather. The lines he created in his head were his only freedom, and his greatest treasure. Andrei Sinyavski, another Soviet writer sentenced to a labor camp, kept a handwritten copy of the book of Revelation concealed in his boot. He was willing to risk his life for that tiny bit of freedom in a tundra of thought-control.

Without freedom you can forget about all that is most precious in human relationships, all that is most precious in life itself. Love can exist only where there is genuinely free choice.

Free and responsible people are capable of creating suffering. That point should help us understand a lot of the pain in our world and most of the tragedy.

But not all. There is still the darkest part of God's apparent powerlessness. We still have Job to deal with—and the gray lake that swallowed up my cherished friend.

Tomorrow's newspaper headlines will document the fact that suffering is not orderly. Life's tragedies are not simply a case of bad people getting their dues, reaping the results of their wrong choices. More than that is happening. Misfortune sometimes strikes with wild abandon. Suffering multiplies chaotically, out of proportion to any just deserts. There is a madness to the tragedies that strike down the best among us.

It's not easy to talk about this darkest part of divine powerlessness. Trying to express a credible answer is positively forbidding. But here we go. To get help we need to go back even farther, before the birth of our planet, for an even bigger picture.

Heaven. Eternity past.

LUCIFER, "son of the morning," occupied a privileged place near God's throne as an angel of light. But somehow he became discontented. Pride popped up. All this glorifying of the Almighty started getting under his skin. Why should He be the center of everything?

Lucifer started focusing on upward mobility. He fantasized about exalting his throne "above the stars of God." This archangel actually wanted to compete for glory with the Almighty Himself. Competition turned into open rebellion. War, of some kind, broke out in heaven, and Lucifer, along with the angels who sided with him, was thrown out.

Today we are inclined to think Lucifer a complete idiot for griping in heaven. How could he have turned away from that glorious place to outer darkness? But there is only one reason we believe him to be idiotic: We know what life is like apart from God. We know what outer darkness is.

Try to imagine what it must have been like for those angels who had known nothing but service to the Most High. They were happy to be sure. But then this Lucifer started wondering aloud why the Almighty wanted all the worship and honor to Himself. Why must everyone obey only Him? The archangel must have put on quite a campaign to win a third of the angels over to his side.

The one who later would earn a reputation as the great Accuser slandered God's government. Lucifer questioned His fairness. How did anyone really know God's way was best? No one had dared try an alternative.

All-powerful rulers usually react to those challenging their authority in one way: off with their heads. The opposition is destroyed and the status quo preserved. The Most High could have done the same of course: vaporize Lucifer at his first cry of defiance.

But that was not God's style. He let Lucifer have His say. If the Almighty had nipped dissent in the bud, the questions raised would not have been answered. Was God's way really best? Was there an alternative? Heaven's citizens would have wondered. The whole watching universe may have wondered.

Lucifer and his supporters were kicked out of heaven. But Lucifer, now degenerated into Satan, was permitted to make a bid for an alternative. He set up his booth in the Garden of Eden, a slick public relations operation alongside the Tree of the Knowledge of Good and Evil.

Eve, though cautioned, wandered over. She listened to Satan question God's trustworthiness. The good Lord's warnings about death, she was assured, were greatly exaggerated. Eve began to think maybe God was holding something back from her. Maybe she *could* be a god. In the end, Eve and Adam turned their backs on God's assurances and bought into Satan's alternative.

Again the Almighty faced a choice. He could have zapped Adam and Eve as soon as they betrayed Him by seizing the forbidden fruit. That would have prevented the cancer of sin from spreading. That would have prevented the holocaust of Earth's history. But again, it wouldn't have answered the questions Lucifer's protest had raised. No one had as yet seen how the alternative would work out—in human lives, in society, in history.

Nothing is more important to God than that those He has created be able to trust Him completely. He wants us to know, in our tiny corner of creation, how important the trustworthiness of His character is to the security of the universe. Without that everything falls apart.

So God permitted Satan to carry out his alternative program. Having found a willing partner in man, Satan could thoroughly develop his system—and unwittingly expose its horrors. The watching universe would be able to see the kind of world sin creates. And the question of the justice of God's government would be forever settled.

THAT'S THE STATE we're in. Sin is running its course. And that affects everything. Sin is much more than an isolated defect within man's soul. It is a malfunction of the entire created order. When Adam and Eve broke faith with God, the crack went very deep. Creation is much more interrelated than our contemporary age realizes. Man's fractured relationship with God threw everything else out of whack too. In our world, everything from aberrant DNA molecules to flash floods testifies to the true nature of Satan's alternative.

We often wish God would modify the alternative and subdue a few of its horrors. On occasion He certainly does that. But the Almighty must also permit sin to be exposed for what it is, and chaotic, arbitrary suffering is part of the picture. If God went around making sure that every tragedy fits an appropriate crime, that every pain is the meaningful result of some inappropriate action, then He would be guilty of a dreadful coverup. It would all be a terrible lie.

There is absolutely nothing fair about sin. It has no redeeming social value. That is precisely why Satan's alternative is so disastrous. In a world separated from God, innocent children bear the punishment their alcoholic parents deserve, calloused mobsters live to enjoy their grandchildren amid lavish estates, young missionaries are impaled by the natives they have come to help. That is what sin is all about. Horror. Madness. It is not a pretty picture. God will make sure it remains an unforgettable one.

He Himself absorbed its harsh colors and jagged lines while hanging as a human derelict on the cross. Christ did not go gently into the night. He writhed and agonized in the madness; He felt all the accumulated anguish of a world in which the innocent are brutalized and the best destroyed.

There is a good reason why we feel El Shaddai is irretrievably lost while we're circling in our pathetic little boat looking for a missing loved one. He is. In that moment we feel what it is like to live in a world which has abandoned God. In that moment we touch the outer darkness; we know what Satan's alternative means.

The nature of man, the nature of sin, the nature of God—all are involved and interrelated in the puzzle of God's apparent powerlessness:

Man is free to make real choices and live with the consequences.

Sin separates us from God; our planet is the theater in which Satan's alternative is fully exposed.

And God has restrained Himself—He is omnipotence under restraint, though the concept may be difficult for us. Semanticists could entertain themselves for quite some time with those two terms thrown together. What matters, though, is that we are given a clear picture in the Bible of the Almighty restraining His power. This is an aspect of God we have to deal with.

When God speaks as Elemental Force, His irresistible voice is said to thunder, melt mountains, convulse the sea, shake the Earth. But another quite different timbre to God's voice is also described in Scripture. The same prophet Elijah who saw God flash down decisively on Mount Carmel experienced a very different revelation in a cave on Mount Horeb. Elijah had fled there from the wrath of Queen Jezebel. Arriving on the scene, El Shaddai made it a point not to appear through a powerful wind that "tore the mountains apart and shattered the rocks," and not through an earthquake or a fire, but instead as a "gentle whisper." For a frazzled "servant of the Lord," the Omnipotent whispered.

That whisper is echoed in many parts of the Bible. Even the fiery prophets hear God speaking softly. Ezekiel quotes His plaintive cry over recalcitrant Israel: "Why, O Why will ye die?" Through Hosea He speaks as a wounded lover, pleading for idolatrous Israel to come back to Him. Such a voice coming from heaven is phenomenal. After all, why should the Almighty plead with anyone? What business does He have on His knees whispering promises in the ear of unfaithful Israel?

In page after page of the prophets you will hear the whisper of God, His heartfelt pleading. El Shaddai could compel allegiance with one thundering command. He could demand obedience, and get it. But He will not. He restrains His power. The thundering voice becomes a whisper.

Even as you look at the Victorious Warrior and His outstretched arm—the strong arm that is mighty in battle—you will find that it is attached to a gentle hand. "A bruised reed he will not break," Isaiah says of the Lord's Servant, "and a smoldering wick he will not snuff out."

How often in the up-and-down history of Israel we see God holding back His mighty arm just when we think He should stretch it out in judgment and strike the final blow of justice. Instead He hides His hand and waits for Israel to look His way again. (The next time you cry out to God and ask Him to wipe out injustice from the face of the earth, you had better add a request that He make an exception in your case and not wipe you out along with it.)

Auschwitz. 1941.

STARVING AND badly bruised, Father Maximillian Kolbe carried large stones toward the crematoriums where hundreds of thousands of people would be burned;

then he staggered through the mud carrying heavy planks under the lash of the infamous guard "Bloody Krott"—and all the while kept smiling.

That was the thing that stood out about this devout Franciscan. His fellow prisoners noticed it: God seemed to fill his whole being from top to bottom. One recalled, "Because they were trying to survive at any cost, all the prisoners had wildly roving eyes watching in every direction for trouble or the ready clubs. Kolbe, alone, had a calm straightforward look, the look of a thoughtful man . . . one not much concerned with protecting himself. . . . Spiritually, in spite of his physical suffering, he was completely healthy, serene and balanced in disposition, and extraordinary in character."

When the prisoners were served their pathetic morsels of food, everyone devoured the last microscopic crumb—everyone except Kolbe who frequently stepped aside and let others take his ration. After a while his companions asked incredulously, "Why do you let us take your food?" He answered, "Every man has an aim in life. Most of you men want to return to your wives, to your children, to your families. My part is to give my life for the good of all men."

Earlier, just after his arrest, Father Kolbe had been repeatedly beaten in a Warsaw prison. Guards would come into his cell and ask, "Are you a Christian?" Max would answer with a smile, "Yes I am."

The guards would pummel him to the ground and ask again, "Are you still a Christian?"

Just before losing consciousness Max usually managed to smile and murmur, "Yes I am."

In the midst of the brutality and terror of Auschwitz, Max felt the presence of his God. A fellow priest at the camp remembered Kolbe as one who "loved God more than himself. And he loved every man in God." Kolbe encouraged despairing prisoners with his fervent belief that God was still looking out for them and that His justice would eventually prevail. "Listening to him intently," one recalled, "we forgot for the time our hunger and degradation. He made us see that our souls were not dead." Another wrote: "Living day after day as he did hand in hand with God, he seemed to have inside him a kind of magnet by which he attracted us to himself, to God. . . ."

Kolbe's spiritual power had an effect on even the most hardened. A fellow inmate said, "Those eyes of his were always strangely penetrating. The SS men couldn't stand his glance, and used to yell at him, 'Look at the ground, not at us!'"

One day a prisoner escaped from the death camp. The commandant ordered everyone out on the parade grounds. According to the rule, for every prisoner who got away, ten other men must die. Ten names were announced. When the last one heard his name called, he sobbed agonizingly, "My wife and my children!"

Suddenly an older prisoner pushed his way toward the front, saying he wished to speak to the commandant. It was Maximillian Kolbe. Survivors later said it was a miracle no one shot him. The priest asked respectfully, "Herr Kommandant, please, sir, may I take his place? I have no wife; I have no children."

The dumbfounded SS officer actually took a step back in shock, then recovered enough to order Kolbe to join the other nine on their way to Block 13. In its dark, fetid basement they were to be starved to death.

Soon others in the block could hear songs of praise to God coming from the death cell. According to a prisoner named Borgowiec who worked there, "Every day . . . one heard the recitation of prayers, the rosary, and hymns. Father Kolbe led while the others responded as a group. As these fervent prayers and hymns resounded in all corners of the bunker, I had the impression I was in church."

For Kolbe and many other listening prisoners,

Block 13 had become a temple. Day by day the songs coming from it grew fainter, the prayers less audible. Soon there were only whispers. Then the first body was carried out. After two weeks only Kolbe and three others still clung to life.

The camp commandant decided they were taking too long to die and ordered the survivors killed by injection with carbolic acid. Borgowiec had to accompany the executioner to the death cell. He saw Kolbe murmur a prayer and hold out his arm. Borgowiec couldn't bear the sight and rushed away. When he returned he noticed Kolbe's naked body slumped against a wall. "His eyes were open. Serene and pure, his face was radiant."

In the midst of an overwhelming evil, God spoke with a whisper; He pierced calloused hearts with a smile. El Shaddai could have smashed those Nazi brutes with His outstretched arm; He could have forced them to submit to His ways. Instead He pleaded through this eloquent life just as He pleaded through corrupt Israel's prophets. He showed what He is like through a man totally possessed by Him. Instead of thundering down on those wielding their whips and clubs, He expressed Himself with a gentle grace.

THIS IS THE powerless God. The God who pleads and waits. It is a picture that should fill us with wonder. It is unlike anything we may expect to happen on earth. A great deal of our planet's history could be summed up with the aphorism: "Power corrupts and absolute power corrupts absolutely." Fortunately, God's absolute power is the marvelous exception to the rule. In place of the selfish manipulation we might expect, we discover a profound restraint. God is secure enough not to be possessive.

His restraint is what has created room for man's freedom. There are some who feel that an omnipotent deity inherently rules out freedom for human beings. Their emphasis on God's sovereign power swallows up the possibility of man as a truly free moral agent. But that position reflects a rather limited view of God's ability. It implies that He is capable only of constructing very sophisticated robots. The fact is, God's crowning act as Skillful Creator is to have made a being who can act freely and creatively. That is quite a feat—a being with a mind of its own. Even our gestures of defiance against the Almighty are evidence of His infinite skill.

He is the kind of God who insists on keeping people morally free. That idea underlies the entire scope of biblical history. Think of the Hebrews' erratic wanderings in the wilderness and God's attempts to get them back on track, think of Israel's maddening cycles of apostasy and repentance in the book of Judges while the Almighty alternately threatened and forgave, think of the passionate pleading of all His prophets, think of Paul's fierce determination to go wherever the good news had not been heard. All this becomes an absurdity if people don't make real choices that affect their destiny.

But El Shaddai *does* long and plead and wait. And human dignity is preserved in the palm of a hand held back, in a voice which whispers. The extent to which God's vast powers are restrained indicates how greatly He values our freedom.

6

THE SABOTEUR

Our two distinct pictures of God place us in a predicament. On one hand we have an Almighty Force who puts the earth into convulsions every time He drops by, a Warrior with a mighty arm whom no one can resist. On the other, an apparently powerless God who watches as evil holds sway, and pleads for justice from the sidelines.

Does God have a split personality? Is He essentially unknowable? Looking up out of the tunnel of our humanity, we have a hard time seeing how the Omnipotent One could also be a jilted lover (as in Hosea) or how the One who anxiously pleads could also be "majestic in power."

The incongruity gets to a lot of people. Many end up opting for just one picture. There are those who fix their gaze on the Almighty, period. Having seen some remarkable miracles they figure, quite reasonably, that God should be active all the time, everywhere. Many old-line Pentecostals espouse this view. God is a healer. They've seen limbs straightened, organs reconstructed, tumors disposed of—and they assert that all ailments in all people can always be healed, with the right faith. Some also expect the Almighty to make all his children rich and successful. Critics call this kind of belief triumphalism: There can't be any failures, all problems will be quickly swept aside by the Almighty's flick-of-the-wrist.

Others fix their gaze on the God of restraint. They focus on His powerlessness. For them the evil of the world is paramount. God is deeply hidden away amid the chaos and cruelty of life. He makes subtle appearances through people who love profoundly or suffer heroically. Christians on the liberal end of the theological spectrum tend to look in this direction. They relate to a deity who has adopted a permanent place behind the scenes and are almost offended at hearing of dramatic answers to prayer.

The strange thing is that both these groups can cite overwhelming evidence to support their picture of God. There is no end to stories of meaningless cruelty and tragic suffering. And there is no end to stories of God's miraculous intervention. Both the fiery-eyed proclaimer of God's power and the weepy-eyed witness of His restraint have truth on their side.

But they don't have two pictures. And that's important. Related to God's power, the Bible gives us two very distinct pictures. It's necessary to look at both of them, however paradoxical they may appear at first. Only when we open wide our eyes and accept the starkness of the contrast between these two images do they begin to come together in a single portrait of infinite depth and perfect wholeness.

It won't do to look for a happy medium. God is not half powerful and half impotent. He is not kind of strong. For example, Jesus was not half man and half God. The New Testament broadly hints and Christian orthodoxy proclaims that He was man altogether and God altogether. The incarnation miraculously combined one-hundred percent divinity with one-hundred percent humanity.

That is the model on which to base our view of God's power. For us on this planet, He is one-hundred percent omnipotent and one-hundred percent restrained. He is altogether active and altogether absent.

This is my Father's world. And this is Satan's ground. Nothing illuminates our planet more than God's intervention in human life. And yet there is no darkness deeper than His severing Himself from sinful lives.

Day and night. Thunder and whisper. Raw power and gentle touch. Mighty Warrior and pleading lover. Infinite skill and endless waiting. These are words that wrestle against each other in a struggle to picture the mystery of God's power.

I can't think of a neat theory that dovetails these concepts. For human minds there is probably no seamless synthesis. Here we may take a cue from the nature of light. Quantum physics tells us we can observe light either as waves or as particles, but not as both at the same time. In a single experiment, we can measure and quantify light only as one or the other, never both.

The two scientific models—light as waves and light as particles—don't jive on a theoretical level. Light simply behaves as both. Obviously it is something far more complex than either a series of waves or a stream of particles. Yet those two models accurately picture the nature of light.

We have the same limitation as observers of God's power. We have the capacity, generally, to analyze only one picture at a time. On a theoretical level we can't put our two pictures together. We can't quantify them and come up with a tidy sum.

But on a practical level things are a bit different. Light, for example, goes on working quite well, active in all sorts of ways from photography to micro-surgery, even though we are stuck with a paradoxical description. We can see how light functions, as a wave and as a particle, in daily life.

Similarly, God's power is more readily understood on a practical level. We can see something of the way God's might and restraint work together—and discover hints of when God is likely to act and when He isn't.

Jerusalem. A.D. 44.

NOT LONG AFTER Simon Peter discovered his calling as a powerful preacher of the good news, he found himself in prison. King Herod Agrippa had jailed the apostle as a way of shutting up the man who couldn't stop speaking about what he'd seen and heard. Herod knew that persecuting Jesus' followers was a cost-effective way of earning the support of his Jewish constituency. His execution of the apostle James had been applauded. Now he decided to present Peter to Jerusalem's crowds to be disposed of in a manner pleasing to them—as soon as they'd finished getting some religion at the Feast of Unleavened Bread.

Herod ordered Peter closely guarded deep within his fortress. The apostle was chained to a dungeon wall between two soldiers. Guards were posted outside his cell door. Other guards kept watch at points along the way to the massive iron gate leading out of the prison compound. That's what you call taking precautions.

Meanwhile Peter's fellow believers gathered in John Mark's house and prayed fervently that their beloved leader might be spared.

That night an angel appeared suddenly in the midst of Herod's maximum security. He awakened Peter and told him to get up. The apostle's chains fell right off his hands. The angel had to tell the dumbfounded prisoner to put on his sandals and cloak; then he led him out past prison guards, doors, and the massive iron gate. Out in the street the angel slipped away and Peter finally realized he wasn't dreaming. He really had escaped. The apostle hurried off to tell his friends their prayers were answered.

God had stretched out His hand in the midst of persecution. He didn't rescue everybody imprisoned for their faith. He didn't save many people from martyrdom. But He did make a point about His power to a corrupt Herod and the Jewish people. In the midst of oppressive evil He made His mark. El Shaddai left His initials on the innermost walls of Herod's fortress. In the morning, after Peter's escape, Herod stared aghast at an empty cell covered with God's graffiti: I am the One who saves. He had acted as Victorious Warrior, snatching His man right out from under the noses of His enemies. He was the irresistible Force, carving out a path through steel bars as He had through the Red Sea and through death itself.

IN A WORLD CONTROLLED for the most part by Satan, the Almighty often manifests His power as saboteur. He strikes at strategic moments in ways that will have the most impact on the most people. As saboteur, God is not quantitatively omnipotent; that is, the number of His acts of power are restrained. But He is still very much qualitatively omnipotent. The quality of His acts bespeaks an unlimited power. Nothing less could have propelled a benumbed apostle past barred gates and hardened soldiers who knew they would pay for escapees with their lives.

God the saboteur seizes opportunities to subvert evil. And we have a part in creating such opportunities. The account of Peter's escape in Acts includes a description of the church united in prayer on his behalf. Prayer, it is implied, made a difference. Elsewhere the New Testament is quite explicit: Prayer gets things done.

Apparently we who must live amid Satan's alternative system have a kind of leverage. God will not arbitrarily reach in and rearrange things His way on a planet in rebellion. But we, as free moral agents involved in the drama, can ask for His intervention. We have the right to call on the saboteur. Our prayers create room for Him to act.

Our every wish, of course, does not become God's command. He is not restricted to acting in precisely the way we prescribe. But taken as a whole, our prayers free Him to do much more than He would otherwise.

I see it in my life and in the lives round me. Every time something happens that moves me beyond generic prayer (thanks for the trees, bless us all) to genuine petition (please help Tim understand how relevant the Bible is), I see God act. Every time some prayer group gets serious about specific requests—things happen. I get the definite impression God has been eagerly awaiting an opportunity to burst out and do more sabotage in the enemy's camp.

Peter, I believe, had a firm hold on El Shaddai's restrained yet unbounded power. One incidental fact in the story of his escape strikes me as quite astonishing. Luke tells us that, on this certain night, Peter was bound with chains between two soldiers, *sleeping*.

Dungeons of course are not the Holiday Inn. It's not easy snoozing off on a bit of straw, chained to the stone floor. But this physical discomfort is nothing compared to a man's mental anxiety under such circumstances. Peter knew that the next day Herod would bring him out to be sentenced, probably to death. It's hard to imagine anyone snoring away the hours before his execution.

And yet Peter was sleeping so soundly the angel had to whack him on the side to wake him up. Obviously the apostle was not nervously fidgeting over his no-win situation. He rested in the assurance that God had a good way out. Peter had accepted an early death in Jesus' name as a good enough option. The man certainly wasn't expecting to be rescued.

Peter stands as a man at peace with El Shaddai's omnipotent restraint. He knew how to live well in the day-and-night of God's power. Doomed in a dungeon, bound between two soldiers, he slept.

This apostle had known plenty of danger and hardship during his ministry, and eventually he would meet the martyr's death that he sidestepped in Herod's prison. But the man never, never felt simply trapped or lost. People who have seen El Shaddai bare His arm never feel backed into a corner. God always has a way out. He can work good out of their adverse circumstances. He has creative options ready in the wings.

This is how God's unlimited power appears to us in the midst of sinful limitations. God has a way out. It enables us to enthusiastically answer "No!" to the Almighty's rhetorical question: "I am the LORD, the God of all mankind—is anything too hard for me?" It is why Jesus could say, in the midst of a hostile environment, "With God all things are possible." With Him around, even death is not a dead end.

So WE NOTICE in our daily life two different faces: God's omnipotence and His restraint. As we've seen they do work together. And what's more, if we look even closer, these two paradoxical qualities blend into one countenance. Although we must keep each quality undiminished by the other (God's omnipotence cannot be lessened nor His restraint compromised), there is a way in which the two combine to form something unique, something greater than the sum of the parts. Jesus' one-hundred percent divinity and one-hundred percent humanity were synthesized into a whole person. Something similar can happen with the two major facets of God's power.

Again, we are not going to create some synthesis on a theoretical level. The abstract concepts don't fit together smoothly (I don't know how much it would mean even if they did). But in "real life"—on a practical level—we do get a glimpse of the two as one.

Osaka, Japan. 1976.

SONYA CAME into my kitchen one day while I was attempting to make granola. Soggy, gray lumps lay all over the table. The girl wilted into a chair and told me she felt like a failure as a missionary, couldn't get anything across in Bible classes, didn't even seem to know Christ herself.

Sonya was the new kid in Japan, full of a wide-eyed innocence I thought had been eradicated from the earth. I had noticed her the first day of school, trembling in the hallway and taking a deep breath before entering the English class she taught. Now her vulnerability extended openly across her face. Anyone else sitting there so pale and doe-eyed, staring down at Little Orphan Annie hands, would have to be faking it. But I knew Sonya's frailty went to the bone.

We talked for a long time. Sonya ended up agreeing to try a method of devotional Bible study that had helped me a lot. I assured her that God wanted very much to meet with her and do great things through her. She promised to start writing down what she learned each day.

I began praying that God would make His Word function in her hands, sparking new insights, creating new abilities. After a few days Sonya shared something exciting she'd seen in Jesus' forgiveness of the woman taken in adultery. I thought her cheeks rosier than usual. Her eyes flickered a bit. Sonya kept learning—and sharing.

At the time, all of us English and Bible teachers were laboring with one student, Junko, who seemed hung up on hypocrites in the church. We had all encouraged her to stop looking at people and focus on Christ, but weren't getting through. Then Sonya had a talk. She told Junko to stop looking at people and focus on Christ. Bam! Junko saw the light: "Yes, that's what I need to do!" Helpless little Sonya carried the day.

The girl was taking off. Her devotional life blossomed. She began wielding the Word in Bible classes to great effect. She adopted specific goals for her students and began seeing the disinterested take a second look, and the interested deepen their commitment. She began claiming promises with confidence.

Then Sonya's emotionally disturbed sister came over for a visit. Their relationship had been difficult due to traumas in the home—the principle reason for Sonya's vulnerability. But now Sonya became the healer. Sharing with her sister what she'd been learning, Sonya had a discernible impact on the girl during her short stay. Little Orphan Annie had struck it rich.

NOW WHEN I THINK of God's great power, I think of Sonya. I see His wonderful answer for the pushovers of the world. It isn't to hype up egos. It isn't to get tough —don't be manipulated, manipulate. No. He gives the meek the power to bless others. El Shaddai empowers the weak.

Divine restraint creates human freedom. Divine intervention manifests God's power. Normally we'd expect a conflict between liberty and sovereign might—one person's freedom usually decreases in direct proportion to another's power. But God has a way of maximizing His power and maximizing human freedom at the same time. He empowers the weak.

Sonya, in the beginning, was not very free at all. Her insecurity bound her up in a world with few options. But then the God of great possibilities burst on the scene and created Sonya the powerful. Now she was free to develop her potential.

The essence of freedom is the ability to do. A lot of people hold their "freedom" in a vacuum. They have lots of space but little ability to do anything with it. But then God's power flashes forth. He enables. The weak find themselves empowered. Freedom rings. And so does God's might.

Scripture is full of examples of God empowering the weak. He seems to go out of His way to make a point of it. A disorganized band of Hebrew slaves were enabled to defy the Egyptian Empire and humble its might into the dust—and into the bottom of the Red Sea. Before routing a huge Midianite army, God reduced Gideon's freedom fighters to a meager three hundred, armed only with trumpets and torches. As a means of putting the Philistines to flight, the Almighty snubbed Saul's crack troops in favor of one smooth stone from an earnest youth named David. Later when a vast allied army invaded Judah, good King Jehoshaphat defeated it with a procession of priests singing praises at the head of his forces. The Lord used one lone prophet to break a siege by an Aramean army that had surrounded the city of Dothan. Elisha ended up leading a long parade of blinded enemy soldiers into his capital city.

In the New Testament, God's empowering of the weak is made even more explicit. Paul tells us he asked God to relieve him of a certain weakness he called his "thorn in the flesh." But instead, "He said to me, 'My grace is sufficient for you, for my power is made perfect in weakness.' "

God uses weakness as a means to power and freedom. He places His "treasure in earthen vessels" on purpose. In fact this method of synthesizing divine power and human freedom is so useful He fairly flaunts it: "But God chose the foolish things of the world to shame the wise; God chose the weak things of the world to shame the strong. He chose the lowly things of this world and the despised things—and the things that are not—to nullify the things that are."

We can see this theme echoed in elements of God's creation. The Almighty inserts the greatest organizational ingenuity into one of the tiniest of creatures, the ant. He hides the strongest force in the universe between the layers of the invisibly small atom.

God's habit of empowering the weak is a big part

of his work as Saboteur—an important part of his strategy in fighting evil in the world. Suffering can appear so vast at times as to drown all hope. Yet on occasion we get a glimpse of what can happen through one man battling against demonic odds.

India. 1947.

WALKING ON the Great Trunk Highway, long columns of refugees passed each other in opposite directions, while others filled the railways by the trainload. Moslems were moving north to the newly formed nation of Pakistan. Hindus trekked south into India. By creating a Moslem Pakistan and a Hindu India, authorities hoped to end centuries of bloodshed between the two religious groups.

Tragically, the mass migrations triggered bloodbaths. Hindus and Moslems still nursing age-old hatreds waylaid trains and massacred men, women and children. Sometimes trains would arrive at a depot, the doors open, and nothing but blood flow out onto the platform. A large boundary force tried in vain to stop the killings. Western reporters hardened by World War II battles wrote that they had never witnessed such savagery.

Hundreds of thousands of people were butchered in this holocaust. Only one city remained safe—Calcutta. In Calcutta huge crowds of Moslems and Hindus paraded together through the streets chanting slogans of unity and friendship. Observers called it a miracle, the wonder of India. The entire Punjab convulsed with uncontrolled violence, but Calcutta remained at peace.

It was not because the Hindus and Moslems there had a history of harmony. Calcutta, called by many the world's most violent city, had previously been the scene of some of the worst fighting between Moslems and Hindus. Calcutta's tranquility in the fall of 1947 was due solely to one man and his evening prayer meetings.

Mahatma Gandhi was a tiny, frail old man pitted against the forces of hatred brewing amid Calcutta's restless millions. And he was winning. Gandhi had persuaded Hindus and Moslems to enter into a nonviolent contract. Each evening he encouraged crowds to turn the other cheek and led them in prayers for peace.

Louis Mountbatten wrote Gandhi: "In the Punjab we have 55,000 soldiers and large-scale rioting on our hands. In Bengal, our force consists of one man and there is no rioting." Gandhi told his followers, "Let us all thank God for His abundant mercy."

But after weeks of miraculous peace, violence broke out in the slums of Calcutta. Trainloads of refugees arriving with tales of horror from the Punjab had ignited passions. A rumor spread that a Hindu boy had been beaten to death by Moslems. Hindu extremists launched attacks against Moslem slums. Gandhi realized Calcutta was about to join the holocaust.

So he drafted a public proclamation. The Mahatma would submit his 77-year-old body to a fast until death. His disciples tried to dissuade him. How could a fast touch bloodthirsty fanatics? But Gandhi was adamant: "Either there will be peace in Calcutta or I will be dead." Fasting, for Gandhi, was first of all a spiritual exercise, a form of prayer. This might be his last petition, but he wanted to die praying.

Gandhi's body crumbled rapidly. By the second day the chant of people calling for peace mingled with the noise of gunfire and rioting. By the morning of the third day Gandhi lay very near death; his pulse was weak and erratic, his voice a murmur. Now processions of Moslems and Hindus marched together into slums to restore order. A group of Hindu extremists came penitently before Gandhi, confessed their crimes, asked for his forgiveness, and begged him to end his fast. Other fanatics brought bloodied weapons and laid them at

Gandhi's feet. The Mahatma made them pledge themselves as protectors of their enemies. Hindu, Sikh and Moslem leaders issued a joint declaration which promised: "We shall never allow communal strife in the city again and shall strive unto death to prevent it."

Calcutta was saved from the holocaust. Its miraculous peace would last. Gandhi's fast had been answered. He ended it with a few sips of orange juice and a call to make Calcutta "the key to peace in India."

God empowers the weak. He chooses the weak and despised things of the world to shame the strong. One old man accomplished in the world's most dangerous city what 55,000 heavily armed professional soldiers could not do in the Punjab.

I SEE BOTH the whisper and the thunder of El Shaddai in Gandhi's unique ministry in Calcutta. God struggles for peace through a still, small voice, and yet that call quiets inflamed mobs and disarms butchers. God's mighty arm is held back as human beings defiantly choose Satan's murderous ways, and yet His gentle hand guides rioters back to their senses. Chants of peace are pried from the clenched jaws of Calcutta's vengeful fanatics. El Shaddai's unlimited power and His righteous restraint met together in the slums of that city.

He maximized human freedom by enabling people trapped in hatred to gain control of themselves. And in that liberating act He also displayed the breadth of His power.

At such times when freedom and power are joined, we catch sight of El Shaddai's ultimate triumph. We feel that what we glimpse is something of ultimate value; this is what should endure when all else is swept away.

Germany. 1890s.

FRIEDRICH NIETZSCHE could read aloud from his Bible with such solemnity as a boy that others were brought to tears. But at eighteen he rejected the faith of his deeply religious mother. Troops of cavalry passing through town on the way to war captured his imagination. Life shouldn't be merely a struggle for existence, he concluded; it must be "A Will to War, a Will to Power, a Will to Overpower!"

Nietzsche tried to compensate for a tender, overly sensitive nature by idealizing the values of honor, bravery, manhood, pride, and power. He began to despise Christianity as a religion of pity and weakness. The budding philosopher wanted a more "masculine" religion and so created his own deity: "superman." This new kind of man was to thrive as a powerful elite, a master race living "beyond good and evil." In his more exalted moments Nietzsche predicted that, in the future, history would be divided into "Before Nietzsche" and "After Nietzsche."

Things didn't quite work out that way. The philosopher's mind began to break down. His health deteriorated; he began losing his sight. Paranoiac delusions of grandeur and persecution haunted him. Finally friends had to commit Nietzsche to an insane asylum.

At this darkest hour the philosopher's mother entered his life again. She'd heard about her son's desperate straits and came to the asylum to claim him. For decades she had patiently born the strain of his apostasy. Her boy had rejected everything she held dear. His voice, which once read Scripture so movingly, now ranted incoherent bursts of Dionysian poetry. But she received him into her arms and devoted the rest of her life to the care of this broken, helpless superman.

AGAIN, GOD CHOSE the weak. The things that are not nullified the things that are. A nameless, unnoticed old woman rocked to silence in her arms a vast body of sophisticated philosophy. All the posturings of power dissolved in her lap. Only her spiritual strength counted in the end.

That is the wonder of God's power—restrained but ultimately triumphant. It does not force itself even on the madness of the world. It is much ignored and maligned, but it stands ready to maximize our freedom. In the end, the arms of El Shaddai will overshadow all else in their unlimited and eloquent power.

PART III

Holy, Holy, Holy

SUBMITTING TO HIS HOLY WILL,
I FEAR GOD; I HAVE
NO OTHER FEAR.

Jean Baptiste Racine

7

CONSUMING
FIRE

SERVING AS A GUARD for General Eisenhower left Merlin
Carothers, demolitions expert, plenty of free time to
enjoy the post-combat calm after World War II. His idea
of a good time generally was to drink himself to obliv-
ion and then engage in wild pranks that his buddies
would tell him about the next day.

But Carothers did get serious about one thing:
expanding his Army pay. He tried gambling but that
proved too unreliable. Then he cracked into the black
market. Cigarettes could be had from other soldiers for
ten dollars a carton. Carothers would purchase a suitcase full, stick a loaded .45 in his pocket for protection,
and stroll through the seedy black-market area of
Frankfurt. Germans there plopped down a hundred
dollars for a single carton.

Soon he accumulated an impressive pile of military
money, known as "scrip." But Carothers had no way of
getting it back to the United States. The military's tight
controls ensured that each soldier could not send home
more than his Army pay.

The enterprising Carothers, however, soon found a
way around this. He set himself up as the clerk of his
own private company, procured fake finance cards, and
had money orders made out for the "company" without

a hitch. His business expanded even further when he discovered that soldiers would exchange a thousand dollars in scrip for a hundred-dollar money order.

After his lucrative tour of duty ended, Carothers found himself back in the U.S. visiting his grandparents. This godly couple invited him to a church service. Unable to find alternative plans, the ex-GI went along so as not to hurt their feelings. Nothing could have prepared him for what happened at the meeting.

Carothers was politely following along in a hymnbook when he heard a deep voice speaking distinctly in his ear: "Tonight you must make a decision for me. If you don't, it will be too late." He whirled around. No one was there.

The God who had been completely out of the picture suddenly seemed very real. Merlin Carothers made his decision. He began devouring the Bible, driven by the conviction that the Lord of Abraham, Isaac and Jacob was still alive.

As Carothers continued his discovery of the God of Scripture, a vague uneasiness began gnawing at the back of his mind. What was wrong? He asked God to show him. Then it hit him: All that money. All the money he'd made in the Army wasn't his. He had to give it back.

Remarkably, Carothers didn't argue back. He didn't try to use the formidable array of excuses available: It was just a business opportunity. A lot of other GIs had profited. He'd been through the disorienting hell of war.

For this former good-time Joe, conviction sank to the bone. Carothers couldn't wait to get rid of the money. He called the Post Office, hoping they might take the pile of money orders still in his possession. But they weren't interested. The money orders themselves weren't stolen.

Not to be deterred, Carothers walked into his bathroom and began flushing hundred-dollar money orders down the toilet. He recalled, "With each flush I felt a mounting flood of joy."

Then Carothers remembered the money orders he'd already cashed. He called the U.S. Treasury Department. They wanted to know if he had any evidence of how he'd illegally acquired the money. The evidence had just gone down the drain. But eventually Carothers managed to impoverish himself by sending thousands of dollars he owed the government to the Treasury's Conscience Fund.

No great loss according to Carothers: "I would gladly give away everything I owned for the new life and joy I felt within."

Clearly the guy who had thought nothing of ripping off war-ravaged German citizens had met Something that sparked his conscience, or more accurately, set it on fire. Within God's heat a little larceny suddenly seemed unbearable, honesty a thing to be acquired at any cost.

THE SAME FLAMES that raised Merlin Carothers's consciousness so high rage brightly in Scripture. Bible writers picture God as a consuming fire who flashes out at sin, sometimes literally. His flames of conviction arise because He is uncompromisingly just. He is hard as flint, and when evil rubs against Him the sparks fly. The psalmists liken His righteousness to mighty mountains and His justice to great ocean depths—unreachable. (In our case it's usually the temptations that seem mountainous.)

He refuses to have His holy name profaned. We are told His eyes are too pure to look on evil. We may habitually hanker after our perverse kicks, but for God it is always righteousness that brings delight. In short, God is good—with a vengeance. For Him, being upright is not a pleasant option; it is a consuming passion.

When people get close to this God, moral neutrality vanishes. After his encounters with a righteous Lord, the English mystic Anton Wilhelm Boehme proclaimed: "If all trees were clerks, and all their branches pens, and all the hills books, and all the water ink, yet all would not sufficiently declare the evil that sin hath done." Following one of her revelations, Teresa of Avila exclaimed, "Oh the madness of committing sin in the immediate presence of a Majesty so great, and to whose holiness all our sin is so hateful!"

Consider what happened to Amos. He was just a sheepherder from Tekoa, minding his own business in the isolated hills south of Jerusalem during the prosperous and corrupt reign of King Jeroboam II. But then God's visions came to him and all of life caught fire.

The book of the prophet Amos opens with a series of conflagrations, judgments about to rain down on cities seething with injustice. Jerusalem is among the targets. Amos's blazing eyes see human beings sold for the price of a pair of sandals, the exploited deprived of a hearing in court, and the rich bowing down to idols on garments they have cheated from the destitute. He is outraged that officials accept bribes, impose a heavy rent on the poor, and crush the needy. Amos cries out: "You've turned justice into wormwood!"

The indulgent wealthy living in ivory houses Amos calls "cows of Bashan." The prophet informs shocked Israelites that God despises their hypocritically solemn assemblies and offerings. Their worship is only a grating noise to the righteous Jehovah.

Amos warns that God will "break forth like a fire," and contends for the one method of dousing His fiery judgment: "Let justice roll down like waters, and righteousness like an ever-flowing stream."

GOD DOES NOT suffer injustice lightly. The sheepherder from Tekoa fired up the conscience of a nation nodding off to disaster. You can feel God's passion for righteousness breathing hot through him.

This concern saturates the divine speeches that biblical prophets quote for us. Everywhere we read what are radical calls to goodness. Their force is often blunted by familiarity. Stirring appeals can become diluted aphorisms. God's obsession is mediated by definitions, categories, qualifications.

But once in a while someone hears His call as if for the first time. The words get through, and the force of God's original passion for righteousness ignites them.

Assisi, Italy. Feast of St. Matthias, 1209.

A PIOUS YOUTH named Francis was enjoying Mass in quiet, secluded Portincula Chapel. The priest read the appointed text, Matthew 10:7-19. Francis listened to the instruction Christ had given His disciples before sending them out to proclaim the kingdom: "Freely you have received, freely give. Do not take along any gold or silver or copper in your belts; take no bag for the journey, or extra tunic, or sandals or a staff . . ."

Suddenly the young man saw his calling, plain as day. The words of Christ struck home. Right there the young man gave away his shoes and got rid of his staff and girdle. He kept only one undyed woolen garment, typical peasant garb, and tied a cord around his waist for a belt.

More importantly, Francis had caught the spirit behind those strange words. He caught the fire. The deep impulse of total giving propelled him into the life that astounded Christendom. He led like-minded brothers around Europe, preaching peace and virtue, ministering to outcasts and the diseased, facing death in Syria to convert the Saracens, loving beggars, robbers, birds and flowers, possessing nothing, giving everything, identifying completely and to the end with the poor and wretched.

And all this from a former man-about-town who loved to spend, dress, and eat extravagantly.

"Freely you have received . . ." Lives ricocheting off words like those give us a glimpse of a God good without limit. He packs a powerful punch into every righteous appeal He makes. An explosive goodness stands behind those phrases, ready to propel the open-hearted beyond anything they could have imagined on their own.

One of the marks of God's justice is His capacity to impart it even to the spiritually deceased. His fire burns so bright that it penetrates souls hard as cold stone.

Los Angeles. 1969.

IN THE EARLY SIXTIES Tex Watson traveled to southern California in search of total freedom. He began hanging around an abandoned movie ranch with members of Charles Manson's "family." Tex proved to be a good pupil there, absorbing great quantities of pot, acid and Manson philosophy. Manson helped free his disciples from "ego" and the mores of society. He proclaimed that they must be free like wild animals to live, die, and kill.

What followed was the Tate-La Bianca bloodbath in the summer of 1969. The nation was shocked at the calculated madness with which seven people were butchered. Tex was convicted as one of the murderers. Psychiatrists had diagnosed him as "insane, totally incapable of standing trial." While in the Los Angeles County Jail he would throw himself screaming against the bars. At times his behavior was so destructive he had to be bound in hospital beds.

I remember reading about what kind of people those "family" members had become. I could not recognize anything remotely human in their casual cruelty. Their lives seemed to me a persuasive argument for the death penalty.

But several years later I read a reporter's account of his visit to Tex Watson in prison. The reporter found him in the chapel leading a Bible study. Tex, it turned out, had started to read Scripture and was persuaded to begin a relationship with Christ. The reporter noted how sensitively Tex dealt with questions and comments from the men in the study group. And as he talked with the inmate he recognized a man of moral tenderness as well. As Tex put it, "One of the greatest and yet most painful gifts I've been given by God is to realize what really took place those two nights."

Tex hadn't felt a tinge of guilt or regret following the murders. But after his encounter with God he went through agony and grief. "My own horrors," he realized, "were part of a larger horror. I began to see, too, that even for a guilt as gross as mine, a penalty had already been paid. . . . I began to see the power of God's love to overcome death and destruction, His power to heal it, not just abstractly but immediately and specifically—for me."

Tex Watson cheerfully ministers to others deep within the steel confines of a maximum-security facility. His spiritual warmth is a striking contrast to the venal numbness that had encased him before. Somehow the fire got through.

FOR THOSE AWAKENED from a spectacularly sinful life, God's justice is a spark that sets off an obvious conflagration. Righteousness sweeps into arid lives like a wind-whipped brush fire. The flames throw evil into stark outline. Divine ideals glow in contrast.

But there are also many other less obvious fires set by this dedicated Arsonist. He strikes a spark not only for the flagrant sinner but for the decent citizen as well.

In the conservative, religious world in which I grew up the greatest sins on the young person's horizon were things like yelling at your brother, goofing off in church, or sneaking off with an extra piece of chocolate cake. I had no big red-lettered transgressions to repent of. I never had the opportunity to suddenly stop shooting dope, stealing, or fornicating because I never got started.

But looking back I see God's justice has been very much alive and well in my life. I've felt the heat.

At seven I lied to my parents. It must have been the first time. They were angry and I felt like I was dangling over a deep black abyss. It wasn't their punishment I feared. Lying on my bed alone in my room didn't hurt and I knew their love for me hadn't lessened. But how awful that sin appeared to me. Premeditated transgression. It was something like breaking the sound barrier. The shock waves went right through me and I grieved.

In the third grade Pepe and I thought Juanita was pretty hot stuff. We expressed our admiration by tormenting the poor girl. One day during a break in class Juanita teased us back. She shook her curls haughtily and gave us a big shove. I pushed her too, right into the big wastebasket in the corner of the room. She fell back and smacked her head against the wall.

The teacher ran over. There was a little blood. They rushed Juanita over to the infirmary where a couple of stitches were required. I felt like I'd just taken human life.

As I walked slowly home all of creation pointed accusingly at me, the murderer. My parents were angry of course. But the evil itself loomed larger. I had hurt another human being. That burden seemed more than I could bear.

Adela, our housekeeper, fixed my favorite enchiladas that night. Everything tasted awful. Poking morosely at the food I wondered, How can I ever atone for what I've done? How can I ever erase the sound of that crack against the wall?

We smile later about how innocent and naive we were as children, about how we exaggerated those minor transgressions. But maybe kids aren't so naive as we mature adults assume. Maybe they see more, not less. Fresher from being created in God's image, not yet dulled by a thousand moral compromises, they know. More truly than their elders, I sometimes think, they know the fire.

At any rate God's justice accompanied me through the years. It stood watch around me and then seeped inside. I was reading His Word, praying, believing Him. I remember stopping and looking back. How self-centered I'd been a few years before. I saw selfish decisions so clearly. I knew God's justice had awakened me further.

That kept happening. God's righteousness always stretched out ahead of me, and drew me along in its wake. I never ran out of it. I never exhausted it. Almost all kids growing up at some point reach the end of their parents' store of conscientiousness. Mom and Dad can always be counted on to be right when you're a little kid. I'm thankful that my parents were very consistent, but most kids approaching the teen years run into some little compromise, some collapse between the should and the will. Parents aren't always just.

The shock hits hard. Kids feel suddenly bare against the world. They scramble for something to hang on to. The Rebel Without a Cause begs his father to stand for something.

But my Heavenly Father *did* stand—for uncompromising righteousness. I always found more of it to admire, more of it to seek. It never stopped. As I matured, His goodness deepened and broadened ahead of me. The righteous Lord wasn't just infinitely good in a child's eyes. During my college days God still led the way. I remember how hard certain verses about purity hit me when I was struggling with lust—after Spring

Break on a campus full of comely coeds taking in the sun. You try to grope for something resembling a clean mind so that every single female passing by doesn't become a piece of meat to "check out."

You check out, instead, a few verses of Scripture, and the sparks fly. You read from Job, of all people, a vow:

> If my step has turned from the way
> or my heart followed my eyes
> . . . let my crops be uprooted.

Instantly you see your sleazy heart following your bulging eyes. The vow sinks home.

And you see far more than abstinence. Paul's characteristic greeting—"Brothers loved by God, we know that he has chosen you . . ."—flames into a conviction about people's value. You're swept up in a new way of looking at human beings (girls) as objects of God's high hopes and tender regard.

Into adulthood I still felt the heat—and was warmed by it. God's righteousness like the mighty mountains. His justice like the great deep. Yes, I've found them inexhaustible.

Some people don't take kindly to this mountain looming over them. God's justice stretching out ahead seems oppressive. How can they ever satisfy His endless demands?

Fortunately I was taught enough about divine love to see it differently. God's justice was, for me, an enormous room in which I could grow freely. His goodness created a space for me to be. His uncompromising righteousness had carved out lovely furniture. I could rest admiringly in His accomplishments. I could absorb them. I could put my hands out toward the huge fire blazing in the corner. It would never go out.

God's justice stretching out without limit can be warmly nurturing. But then there's the other side of

His fire-without-end. God can be an implacable oppo-
nent. When confronted with stubborn evil the flames of
His wrath rage against it unquenchably. Sometimes
they devour, always they raise up a deeply felt protest.

Jezreel, Israel. c. 875 B.C.

AHAB HAD EXPENSIVE TASTES, and as king of Israel he
could indulge them architecturally. He built several
cities to his liking and a sumptuous ivory palace for
himself at Jezreel. But as he walked about his royal residence, the king kept noticing a nicely landscaped vineyard next door and concluded it would be the perfect
spot for a vegetable garden.

Ahab summoned his neighbor, Naboth, and
offered to buy the vineyard or find him a better one.
However the man declined to give up the "inheritance
of my fathers." Ahab stomped back home, threw himself on his bed, turned his face to the wall, and refused
to eat.

Jezebel the queen heard that her husband was
pouting again, and came to see what was vexing him.
Ahab whined about the stubbornness of Naboth.
Jezebel asked her weak-willed husband rather pointedly, "Aren't you king in Israel?" She quickly assured him
it was no problem; she would get him the vineyard herself.

Jezebel believed in getting things done. And evidently the Phoenician idols she'd brought with her to
Israel inspired few moral scruples. The queen wrote to
a couple of nobles in debt to her and told them to hire
witnesses to accuse Naboth of blasphemy and then take
him out and stone him.

Her orders were carried out. Jezebel informed her
hubby that all business obstacles had been removed.
Ahab took possession of Naboth's vineyard.

This was the kind of royal couple that presided

over Israel as vultures for twenty-two years. Ahab started out bad, steeped in the idolatry of his father Omri, and got worse. Under Jezebel's prodding he built a grove for the goddess Ashtoreth where worship services included sexual orgies. He apparently sacrificed two of his own children to other bloodthirsty deities while founding a city.

God had been sending prophets for some time to warn Israel off its disastrous course. But Ahab's corrupt regime called for a special divine protest. God decided to go on strike. He sent the prophet Elijah into Ahab's palace with a message: "No more dew or rain for Israel, until I give the word."

After that Elijah had to go into hiding—because no rain fell and the crops dried up. People went hungry. Ahab tried desperately to find this prophet who had brought such a disaster on Israel. But he did not repent. God stayed tough. The drought lasted three years.

It was a costly strike. And it wasn't broken until Elijah arranged that climactic showdown on the top of Mount Carmel where the prophets of Baal were defeated. The downpour that came afterward washed away the blood of slain idolatrous priests and rejuvenated the land of Israel.

GOD IS PREPARED to go to great lengths to shake people out of the grip of evil. The barren, desolate fields of Israel bore silent witness to how seriously God took sin. He's not just a pure Lord in an ivory tower grieving over wickedness. The passion that burns in Jehovah moves Him to act. He is Judge, executing sentence. The writers of Scripture warn that He cannot be bribed or deceived. He is unimpressed by titles, positions, achievements. He smiles only on a goodness that goes to the bone.

God does protest. He does break out. Fire does fall. Sodom and Gomorrah lying in a fertile valley never realized what their decadence looked like to God, until fire and brimstone fell from heaven and blackened the two cities. The man of Noah's day didn't think his moral lapses anything extraordinary. He didn't understand that "every intent of the thoughts of his heart was only evil continually." But then a flood came to drown out the din of wickedness.

No doubt about it, there is terror on the wrong side of the fire. In the end the wicked will beg rocks to fall on them and blot out the petrifying sight of God coming as Judge.

When we hear of some child molester killing his third victim, or see newsfilm of bloated bodies sprawled on some southern Asian killing field, we get angry. Evil hurts. It makes us feel violated, outraged. But our indignation is only a shadow of the pain God feels. For the Being whose life is one righteous flame, every moral failing brings anguish. For the One obsessed with goodness, sin cuts deep.

He cannot stop hurting. Evil is a horror He will always flame against. It will always elicit His revulsion. And He cannot stop calling for righteousness. That's who He is. His just demands rise higher than we can ever reach.

God is a consuming fire. We are left naked and anxious with the ancient question, "Who can stand in his presence?"

8

TENDER
HEART

On the road to Babylon. 678 B.C.

MANASSEH HAD NOT PLANNED to end his long reign over
Judah this way—prodded forward on a dusty road by
the spears of mocking Assyrian soldiers. He stumbled
along encumbered by bronze chains and looked back
for what surely would be the last time at his beloved
Jerusalem. No crown. No servants. No royal robes. A
lone prisoner enduring the ultimate humiliation. The
king was led away by a thong put through his nose, an
animal dragged to the slaughter.

Manasseh had come to power at the tender age of
twelve following the death of his father, Hezekiah.
King Hezekiah had been a reforming ruler, trying to
turn back the tide of idolatry. He'd broken up idolatrous shrines, restored the temple services, and reinsti-
tuted the Passover as a national celebration.

But his son Manasseh did not follow in Dad's foot-
steps. Instead he took up with the "Ahaz party" who
favored getting cozy with the prevailing gods of
Ammon, Moab, and Edom. As Manasseh consolidated
his hold on the throne he began casting about for more
gods to line up behind him and became quite a connois-
seur of heathen superstitions. The king rebuilt the
groves and high places of Baal and Astarte worship
which his father had zealously destroyed. His campaign caught on big among the people and soon incense

105

and offerings to Egyptian and Babylonian deities were rising from roofs throughout Judah. Business for wizards and their enchantments boomed.

When prophets protested, the king quickly had them silenced. Josephus tells us that executions took place every day, and according to rabbinic tradition it was Manasseh who had God's eloquent spokesman Isaiah "sawn asunder."

The road to apostasy steepened. Manasseh placed an image of the fertility goddess Astarte, inspirer of licentious worship, in the very temple of the God of Heaven. Most tragic of all, he raised up the hideous statue of Molech, a deity who required devotees to offer their children as burnt sacrifices.

Judah hit bottom. In this morally degenerate condition the Hebrews went limp when an Assyrian army charioted by on one of their bloody exercises. Jerusalem gave up its king. Manasseh started the long walk to Babylon.

Rotting in an Assyrian dungeon tends to promote introspection, and Manasseh did a lot of thinking there as the months dragged on. No longer the haughty monarch who defied heaven, he "humbled himself greatly before the God of his fathers." No more good times. Manasseh looked up out of his hole and begged for help.

God, the consuming fire, looked down from His holy height on this wretch who had defiled everything sacred, who had led Judah into more evil than was practiced even by their "godless" neighbors, who was responsible for the cries of broken, prostituted young women and slaughtered children—and He "was moved by his entreaty."

God *listened*. We would have expected lightning (and might even have relished it) followed by a booming voice announcing in reply that a dungeon was precisely where such a slime belonged. But listening? God moved by this joker's plea?

Yes, God was moved, moved to the rescue. He not only accepted Manasseh's repentance, but also found a way to slip the man out of Assyrian control, back to good old Jerusalem, and even back up on his good old throne!

Manasseh had day one again. For him, the horrors of the past had been blotted out, just like that.

February 10, 1959. Santiago, Chile.

ON THIS DATE the largest ring of auto thieves in the history of Chile hit a brick wall. Samuel Angel Espinoza, the group's charismatic leader, was apprehended and held for trial. Police had been tracking the man for some time. He'd left quite a wake of felonies behind him.

Samuel had first drawn a criminal conviction at the age of eleven. Just before boarding the bus on his way to detention, the boy darted for the bank of a river, dove in, and swam out from under the law. For the next nine years he worked on perfecting his skills as a thief and managed to gather quite a following of criminals who admired his expertise. At twenty he made it atop the auto theft business. Samuel specialized in hot cars used in robberies as getaway vehicles. In one forty-five-day stretch Samuel's ring "reinvested" sixty-seven automobiles.

Now awaiting trial, Samuel fell seriously ill with a paralyzing ailment. A Christian layman visited the young man in jail and told him about an influential friend he knew who could help. Samuel was interested. After several visits he discovered the "friend" was Jesus Christ.

Samuel was still interested. He learned to pray and began studying the Bible with enthusiasm. He began to place his faith in God. Doctors had told Samuel it would take from seven to ten years for him to recover, but within three months the paralysis had disappeared.

Finally, Samuel's case came to trial. He was hoping by some miracle he might be allowed to serve God on the outside, but on November 8, 1962 he was sentenced to twenty-five years in prison.

He spent a sleepless night pondering his future. He would be an old man of fifty when he got out. In the dark of his cell Samuel went through his own humbling time of introspection. He relived all the excitement and danger that had filled his life till then—but this time from a very different perspective. Samuel no longer felt like the cocky leader of a hot gang. The evil he'd done was tearing him apart.

The young man spent a long time praying, seeking the God who seemed far away from his Santiago jail. Again God was moved. Samuel experienced a profound sense of forgiveness and acceptance by the Lord. The past had been taken care of.

The next morning Samuel felt like a new man. The guards were amazed at the cheerfulness of this prisoner facing twenty-five years. A couple of visitors were happily surprised to see a look of peace on his face. Samuel was ready to serve God—anywhere, under any conditions.

That same evening at nine he received a summons for questioning. An odd hour. Why more inquiries the day after his sentencing?

Samuel spent an hour waiting around and answering a few questions from prison officials, questions that seemed quite irrelevant to his case. Then he was told to gather his meager belongings. He was free to leave.

A stunned Samuel stepped through the main gate of the penitentiary and out into a pouring rain. He walked down the street in a daze, letting the water pelt him, breathing free air. Suddenly his sordid past was gone, washed away. The countless robberies blotted out, just like that.

His release remains unexplained.

IN THE BIBLE God eloquently advertises his ability to forgive. It is something you might think an incurably just God would keep more quiet about. But Jehovah shouts: Sins that are crimson I make as white as snow. I cast iniquities into the depths of the sea. I blot them out; I refuse to remember them.

God's forgiveness draws a remarkably wide circle around humanity. His welcome is wide. And it produces strange bedfellows.

LEROY E. PASSED THROUGH boyhood under an abusive father in the poverty of red-clay Arkansas, and then tried to stake out his manhood in a Los Angeles ghetto through rape and drug dealing. Fed up with oppression, like others who became Black Panthers, he decided to hate back. His violent escapades against white racism landed him in jail. After release, he got into a shootout with Oakland police and fled the country. But in exile in southern France the Black Panther found his way to Christ.

One evening out on a balcony beneath the star-studded Mediterranean sky he saw a parade of notorious revolutionaries pass above him and quickly drop out of view "like fallen heroes." Then Christ's image appeared in dazzling light; Leroy crumbled and wept. He grabbed a Bible his wife had brought along and began reading Psalm 23. The merciful God came through loud and clear.

That night he experienced the most peaceful sleep of his life. When he awoke, "I could see in my mind the way, all the way back home, just as clear as I've ever seen anything."

The past blotted out. He was forgiven and accepted by God the consuming fire.

THOMAS TARRANTS had dedicated his life to fascist ideals. He led Mississippi's White Knights of the Ku Klux Klan,

America's most violent right-wing terrorist organization. In the mid-sixties Thomas and his racist buddies waged war on Jews and blacks, especially those speaking out for integration. They bombed synagogues and the homes of NAACP officials.

Captured after a bloody gun battle, Thomas was tried, sentenced and eventually placed in maximum security. Believe it or not, Thomas grew introspective while rotting away in Parchman State Penitentiary. He began reading the Bible he had previously used to justify his racism. This time the words of the New Testament about forgiveness, love and brotherhood sank in. Thomas renounced his right-wing activities as "diametrically opposed" to true Christianity, and embraced Christ in faith.

Forgiven, accepted. The past blotted out.

TALK ABOUT southern hospitality. There they stand. Thomas Tarrants and Leroy E. welcomed home, sipping lemonade on the great broad porch of God's forgiveness, fanning themselves with gentle talk about love and fellowship. And we wonder just how far God's acceptance goes, with these two characters nailing down perimeters so far apart.

Human beings have a hard time stretching to such possibilities. God's mercy puts a kink in our time-honored reservations about certain types. To some the past of the white terrorist seems irredeemable, his present sincerity always suspect. To others a Black Panther requires an awful lot of penance before he's pronounced fit for church. Even then they're never quite sure.

But God just keeps holding the door open on his great broad porch. Making his forgiveness real to all comers. Willfully blotting out the most outrageous pasts.

God pardons completely. But His mercy stretches even beyond that. More than a willingness to forget the past, it works aggressively in the present. It has a long reach, as well as a broad lap. Take a look at this divine advertisement brought to us by the prophet Isaiah:

> I revealed myself to those who did not ask for me;
> I was found by those who did not seek me.
> To a nation that did not call on my name,
> I said, "Here am I, here am I."

Osaka, Japan. 1979.

I HAD DECIDED to try an experiment. Actually most everything is an experiment when you're trying to communicate cross-culturally. But this was a test for myself too. I was feeling very brave that spring evening and challenged those attending the opening of our evangelistic sessions to see for themselves if God really was up there and active. My listeners were thoroughly secular. The photogenic Buddhist and Shinto festivals that highlighted the year held for them about as much religious meaning as a Fourth of July parade. Our word "God" did not resonate. It drew a blank.

So how to make Him real to these students, housewives, and young businessmen? The fact that God is known through his actions had been weighing on me. He had acted for recalcitrant Israel in dramatic ways. He had acted for skeptical Greeks and legalistic Jews in the New Testament. Why wouldn't He act for my secular contemporaries who were at least looking in His direction, even if they didn't see much?

So I proclaimed that this week of meetings would be one big experiment. We gathered every evening in small groups. Each leader encouraged the group members to identify a specific problem or need in their lives, then challenged them to discover through prayer what God would do about it. Next, the leader helped each willing member find a relevant promise in Scripture for the identified need. These promises were not selected as magic incantations but as a means for the leader to guide participants into the kind of prayers God had expressed an interest in answering.

Finally the leader carefully explained our belief that we can approach God through Jesus Christ, and showed everyone how to pray in His Name.

I promised a report on the results of our experiment at the end of the week. And so we were off. It was participatory evangelism. These people who'd come to check out God did not have to sit and listen to a lecture. They participated in small group activities that showed them what the Christian life was like: making discoveries in the Bible, learning to encourage each other, and, each evening, conducting their prayer experiment.

At the end of the week I went around to the group leaders and asked them about each of their participants. What I discovered surprised even me, riding high on my bold (or presumptuous) assumptions. Every single person who followed through on the week-long experiment had received a definite answer to his or her prayer.

I recorded the requests and answers. One young man had been sick and was worried about getting behind in his job. He prayed about this and later found that a girl he'd previously misjudged as selfish had done his work for him. One girl prayed about her parents who were treating her rather coldly because she occasionally came home late from the Christian meetings. She was surprised at the door one night by her mother asking very warmly, "Are you hungry?" Another lady expressed to God her deep longing to see her mother's grave in America someday. She received a letter from her daughter unexpectedly inviting her to come to the U.S. for a visit.

A businessman, I learned, had been wanting a red tie and prayed for that. Now if I'd been the group leader I would have suggested something more appropriate. Here we were trying to reveal God Almighty and this guy wants a red tie. However I was not there to administer my wisdom, so the man conducted his little experiment and was pleasantly taken back one day when a salesman came right into his office and sold him a silky red necktie.

None of these "answers" was overwhelming. None would have forced a committed atheist to make room for the supernatural. But what a gracious touch these responses proved for each person asking! The petitioners perceived subtle nudges— "Here I am, over here." Notes written back with a hint of affection.

People groping in the dark after a mystifying stranger from heaven did hit on something. God allowed Himself to be found.

These were not people who had "humbled themselves before the God of their fathers." They knew no such Lord. They could not claim to move the divine heart through repentance. They hardly knew what sin was. But God acted. And walking from room to room where the groups had assembled, accumulating my list of answers on the page, I felt like I was holding in my hands a piece of God's long reach, His sweeping mercy.

GOD IS EMINENTLY accessible. A tender heart, an easy touch. But there's something still more scandalous about the way God expresses His mercifulness. He doesn't just beckon the indifferent; He also, at times, blesses the willfully wicked. His compassion spills over into the darkest hearts. He "devises ways so that a banished person may not remain estranged from him."

The Atlantic. March 10, 1748.

JOHN NEWTON awakened suddenly to find his cabin rapidly filling with water. A violent sea had crashed into the British freighter *Greyhound* and torn away the upper timbers on one side. Above deck a cry went up that the ship was sinking fast.

Newton rushed up and joined other sailors desperately working the pumps, but the sea continued to gain on them, filling the ship. Some began to bail frantically with buckets and pails. Others grabbed clothes and bedding to try plugging several bad leaks. Newton continued working the pumps through the early morning hours until noon, tying himself to the deck with a rope in order not to be washed away with the passing waves which actually rolled over his head. Every time Newton felt the ship settle into a trough he expected it to sink for good into the deep.

At one point he reported to the captain about the pumps and said, almost without thinking, "If this will not do, the Lord have mercy on us."

Instantly his own words struck him uncannily. What right did he have to ask for mercy? It occurred to him that if the Christian religion had any truth at all, he could not be forgiven.

Newton had been a studious child who liked to sing hymns on his pious mother's knee. But as a teenager he strayed from religious faith about as far as one can. He became a rebellious sailor; he fought with anyone who crossed him and indulged in every appetite. As he put it, "For some years I never was an hour in any company without attempting to corrupt them."

Pressed into the British Navy, he deserted. Arrested by a military patrol, he was flogged, and transferred to a slave-trading ship. There he became "exceedingly vile."

Newton, now a militant atheist, regularly selected females from among the starving, suffocating slaves wedged in the hold and raped them.

When the ship landed in Sierra Leone he left it to

work for a slave dealer. But he then became virtually a slave himself on the man's plantation.

Newton's father asked slave ship captains to keep a lookout for his son on their voyages. In February 1747 the *Greyhound* put in at Sierra Leone and, through what would later seem providential circumstances, its crew found the young man.

For John Newton, furiously working pumps in the midst of a storm, did not expect rescue. Why should the One he had continually and willfully cursed show mercy? An early death seemed an imminently just end to his miserable life.

But somehow the *Greyhound* stayed afloat and limped all the way into Liverpool. "Taking in all circumstances," Newton recalled, "it was astonishing . . . that any of us survived to relate the story." His astonishment turned into a glimmer of faith. He thought of the way he'd been rescued in Sierra Leone; he saw the waves inundating the *Greyhound* in vain; and "I began to know there is a God that hears and answers prayer . . . though I can see no reason why the Lord singled me out for mercy."

Much later, as a beloved minister in England, Newton would memorialize God's intervention in the life of a sworn enemy with the words,

> Amazing grace! (How sweet the sound!)
> That saved a wretch like me . . .

What are we to make of this mercy? What right does a thug who deliberately turned his back on Him have to come before a just Lord and ask for favor? None, of course. And yet God strikes him with telling providences.

Gracious and compassionate. Slow to anger. Ready to forgive. Eager to welcome home. There are no obstacles, it would seem, around God's tender heart. He flaunts His grace with a shout: "I delight to show mercy."

9

HOLY ENCOURAGER

So THERE we have it. The God who is inflamed with a passion for justice also forgives the most outrageous offender at the drop of a petition. The Lord whose righteous demands loom high above us reaches out graciously toward the indifferent. The One whose wrath against sin consumes like a fire interrupts the lives of the spectacularly guilty with spectacular providences.

We have two clear pictures. The raging fire and the tender heart. The uncompromising Judge and the One whose welcome is infinitely wide.

We can't easily tone down either one. God doesn't present Himself as slightly upset or mildly merciful. From the pages of Scripture both His wrath and His compassion rush upon us much larger than life. His reaction to human evil is a conflagration of anger. And that fire of justice never flickers, never dies down. Sin remains an intolerable horror to God. At the same time He is ceaselessly devising ways to lavish His mercy on sinners. He remains an incredibly easy touch for prodigals of every persuasion.

How are we to regard these two divine qualities, headed it would seem at the speed of light in opposite directions? From a human point of view, something has to give. Which will win out? The immovable object of God's justice, or the irresistible force of His mercy?

Cambridge, England. 1890.

NINETEEN-YEAR-OLD Charles F. Andrews had been going through an intense inner conflict. Coming from a strictly religious family he realized that "an evil form of impurity" was dragging him down spiritually.

One night while kneeling in prayer at his bedside, "the extreme evil of what I was doing came quite unexpectedly upon me." That consuming fire again, making a house call. Charles agonized for hours in the dark, weighed down with the demands of justice. "Then, out of my utter need and helplessness, came a marvelous sense of pardon and release. . . . His grace and love flooded my whole being."

Charles felt that at that very moment a new life began inside him. He found release from "the bondage of sin which had bound me fast." And it seemed to young Charles that he was "living in a different world of light and love and peace. It illuminated the glory of Nature, and made me love every one I met."

After a Peter, Paul & Mary concert. 1968.

WHEN A YOUNG FAN approached Noel Paul Stookey after a show and asked if they could talk, the popular folk singer agreed, thinking he might be of some help to the boy. He wasn't prepared for the stranger's abrupt "I want to talk to you about the Lord." For some reason Paul's pulse quickened. He listened quietly as the boy talked about his conversion.

The two left together for the folk singer's hotel room. Paul tried to be a good host, but his guest just asked if they could pray. He thanked God for helping him get through the backstage guards and then said, "Now I think Paul wants to talk to you."

Paul opened his mouth. All that could come out was, "I'm sorry." He started weeping, suddenly remorseful for his indifference toward God and for using things to isolate himself from other people.

A fire began to burn. As he prayed, Paul's contrition deepened. He confessed other wrongs. He saw himself as a hollow man living up to an image—riding the obligatory limousines, existing on exotic foods and champagne, smoking expensive cigars he hated.

At that moment when God's justice blew him over, Paul fell into mercy: "I was washed, cleansed—I couldn't believe it. It was like I had this incredibly cantilevered balance. Or that I was two interwoven mobiles. Suddenly when I had admitted that I was sorry for the life I had led without God, everything collapsed and I was perfectly balanced. I had been given day one again."

Charles F. Andrews and Noel Paul Stookey felt divine justice and mercy strike almost simultaneously. God wielded them as a one-two punch. The collision of immovable object and irresistible force in their hearts released transforming energy. Both qualities poured out at full strength proved to be a powerful mix which resulted in conversion.

God somehow has the ability to express radical justice and mercy simultaneously (as we see so archetypically in the cross). His passion and compassion actually reinforce each other.

They are never really separate. We don't know precisely how these qualities interact in the divine being, but we do get a few telling glimpses of mercy and justice meshing and creating more than the sum of each part. Sometimes when we look at God's justice at its fiercest we see mercy glowing bright.

Canaan. c. 1900 B.C.

TAKE THAT PROMINENT example of the consuming fire: Sodom and Gomorrah. The fire and brimstone raining down on those two cities deadlocked in sin present a very disturbing final solution. The cup of wrath spilled over and people disappeared for good.

But let's go back a few days before the fire and look in on Abraham camped out by the oaks of Mamre overlooking Sodom and Gomorrah. He spots three strangers walking up in the heat of the day and like a good desert nomad rushes out to offer them refreshment and rest in his tents. The three men accept and sit down to a meal of bread cakes, milk, curds, and roasted calf.

At some point during this visit, Abraham becomes aware that the three strangers are actually heavenly visitors. And one, apparently, is the Lord Himself.

Jehovah had decided to let Abraham in on His plans for Sodom and Gomorrah. Their "exceedingly grave" sins have risen like an outcry against heaven. God tells Abraham He's come down to check things out personally before issuing a final verdict. The two angels accompanying the Lord walk off toward the two cities.

Abraham—perhaps thinking of his relatives down the hill, perhaps thinking of the thousands of other human beings living there—suggests an alternative plan: "Suppose there were, say, fifty righteous people in Sodom. Surely You wouldn't want to destroy the righteous with the wicked. Wouldn't you want to spare the city?"

The Lord quickly agrees: "Sure. If I can find fifty good people in Sodom I'll spare the whole place for their sakes."

Notice what is being said. The deal isn't that if there are fifty decent folk in the city then they will be removed to safety before the fire and brimstone come down on the rest who richly deserve it. No, the agreement means that if fifty good people can be scrounged out of the thousands in Sodom then there is a ray of hope for the city. Those fifty righteous souls will have earned a reprieve for the multitudes who go on abusing and abasing their fellow human beings.

Abraham is a little taken back at how readily His Lord accepted the proposition. An easy touch, if you please. So he quickly, yet humbly ("I am but dust and ashes"), bargains down a bit: "Suppose there are forty-five righteous in Sodom?" The Lord doesn't blink an eye. "I will not destroy it if I find forty-five."

At the end of this remarkable dialogue, Abraham has bargained all the way down to ten people. And His Lord promises to spare the whole wretched city for the sake of ten righteous citizens—if they can be found.

What's the point of this odd little transaction between God the consuming fire and a presumptuous little nomad? Did God really need to come down from heaven to see if his intelligence regarding Sodom and Gomorrah was accurate? Was it only because of Abraham's persistence that God decided to widen His mercy a few degrees?

I doubt it. It seems to me that God went through this scenario in order to display His fairness and mercy in dramatic terms. He is not a remote judge who flicks the F & B switch on obstreperous community A2300Z. He does not zap the unrepentant from an indifferent height. He comes down to show He's involved; He's done everything He can to prevent disaster. He wants to make sure we understand that this "strange work" is a last resort.

To help us see His mercy and justice both at full strength He gives them separate voices. He encourages Abraham to play the part of mercy pleading with justice. (God would do this again after the Exodus when He called down for wayward Israel's destruction and allowed Moses to plead eloquently for a reprieve.) The whole dialogue between the Lord and Abraham stretches our grasp of how far God is willing to go before shutting the door on the wicked.

But there is still more mercy to come in this story that seems so fearful at first glance. The two angels who went down to check out Sodom and Gomorrah were unable to find ten righteous people in it. Night had fallen. Crowds of sexual predators roaming the streets wanted to check out the two heavenly visitors and they had to take refuge in the home of Lot, Abraham's nephew.

The angels informed Lot and his family that it was time to leave. The fire could no longer be postponed. Evil had evidently reached a critical mass in these two cities, compressed into such a malevolent force that it overwhelmed every good impulse. Perhaps the Sodomites had achieved the immoral equivalent of mass hysteria.

Lot had two married daughters. He tried to talk his sons-in-law into leaving. But they held the opinion that fire and brimstone were a big joke. The next morning the angels urged Lot to take his wife and his two daughters and flee quickly lest he be swept away in the punishment of the city. Lot hesitated.

Those predators had been trying to break his door down. His two guests had been threatened with rape. He'd been assured that the place was about to blow up. And Lot hesitated! Something terribly seductive must have been at work there.

At this point God's compassion shines especially bright in the doomed city: "When he (Lot) hesitated, the men grasped his hand and the hands of his wife and of his two daughters and led them safely out of the city, for the Lord was merciful to them." What an understatement!

Tragically even this forceful action wasn't enough to save Lot's wife. Her heart remained back in the gutter of Sodom. She looked back, as the angels had pleaded with them not to do, and perished in the heat of the holocaust.

EVEN IN GOD'S FIERCEST justice we see the long reach of His mercy. They intertwine. It's equally true that in God's most extravagant acts of mercy we see justice at work as well.

Remember Manasseh the idolatrous king of Judah who was forgiven, freed from an Assyrian dungeon and restored to the throne? After this overdose of mercy he became a great reformer, a just ruler. He removed those offensive idols he'd set up and brought Judah back to the worship of a holy God.

Remember Samuel the car thief who experienced divine forgiveness and saw a twenty-five-year prison sentence melt away before his eyes? His life began to reflect a righteous God so well that other people were won to faith because of his witness, including a youth behind bars.

And John Newton the immoral blasphemer. After his inexplicable encounter with mercy and his subsequent conversion, he began to see the terrible injustice of slavery. It was his passionate testimony, more than any other, before the Privy Council that helped move a reluctant Parliament to outlaw the slave trade.

Extravagant mercy somersaults into a wealth of justice. Acceptance twists evil into good. Forgiveness blossoms into righteous acts. That's the wonder of the consuming fire with a tender heart. That's the way God works.

Samuel, for example, did not became such a dedicated individual because God ladled out a sip of mercy for the poor sinner. No, it came down by the bucketful. It was only because Samuel encountered God's great and wide and limitless compassion that he began chasing after his Lord's great and wide and limitless justice.

God is the perfect environment for human growth. He creates the security and the stimulus that are required.

THE MERCY AND JUSTICE we've seen alchemizing together at full strength produce a heady brew that might best be called holiness. God is not just good, He is holy. That's a part of His chemistry.

Unfortunately most people see holiness as the absence of something. For centuries it has been defined in the negative. Medieval ascetics in search of the holy God flocked to the desert. These "holy men" cut themselves off from life in general and human contact in particular. The assumption appears to have been that when you remove everything tangible or pleasurable, what remains is holiness or God.

That assumption, in a modified form, persists. What's holiness? The absence of all evil, we say. Not engaging in this, not indulging in that. Remaining untouched by a wicked world. Most of us believe, perhaps subconsciously, that the more you take away, the more sterile and eventless a life, the greater the potential for holiness.

But God's holiness is not the absence of anything. He is not a remainder after everything else is removed. God's holiness is an incredibly dense core of justice and mercy held in a kind of radioactive tension, ever ready to explode on the world and transform life down to its roots, penetrating every nook and cranny. God is not a sterile empty set in the sky. He is bursting with passion and compassion—holiness.

It's a bit hard for us to see this because our human models are usually so limited. We find straight arrows walking around, people who are zealous for goodness. But they are precisely the ones least likely to understand the weak or show compassion on those who fail morally.

And we have the accepting types, nonjudgmental, easy touches. But they are least likely to give a rip about righteousness.

Once in a great while we run across someone with

a little of both. People of moral character who relate easily to those without it. Women and men who cherish a burning desire for justice and still sympathize with the morally watered down.

These rare individuals have the most powerful influence on their contemporaries. They stimulate the most upward mobility in the hearts of their companions—because of who they are. When they speak their words burn; passion and compassion intertwine.

I remember well watching a film made about Corrie ten Boom a few years before her death. The ten Boom family hid Jews in their home during World War II. As a result Corrie spent years in a concentration camp. She took the worst the Nazis could dish out and came out with a shining faith and a deep love for people. This woman had stood for justice in Holland when all hell was breaking loose, yet she retained a wonderful sense of understanding and forgiveness for those who had failed during that terrible time.

As I watched the film I heard Corrie say the most ordinary things about Jesus being with us and acting as our Victor. They were familiar words I had nodded off to countless times in church. But when she spoke everything was different. Old phrases pierced to the marrow. Clichés resonated in the depth and breadth of this unassuming matron's heroism. I almost wept. Upward mobility.

That's the way God is. That's why He moves and inspires so many of us. No one sees more deeply into our moral failings and no one believes in us so ardently. When He whispers words of mercy we are warmed by a soul burning for righteousness. When He shouts in fiery judgment we know that His tender heart is breaking. He is the great encourager. The One who pulls us out of the pit, lifts up our heads, and fulfills all our desires for goodness.

Naha, Okinawa. Winter, 1979.

THE HOSPITAL SAT on a hill overlooking a sprawling city. Its streetlights sparkled below me in the night. I walked back into the small guest room by the chapel and lay down. It had been a long day of shooting—the nursery, surgery ward, worship services, interviews with doctors. The public relations film was finally coming together.

As I lay on my bed thinking, it hit me. The magazine shop. Down the hill, beside a narrow street—I remembered seeing it. A rack jutted out on the sidewalk filled with the smirking covers that flag people down.

They grabbed me in the little room by the chapel. Alone in a strange town, tired, disconnected from the Word, my defenses were down. I decided I really needed to go out jogging. It would be just the thing to help me unwind.

I slipped into my tennis shoes and started down the hill in the dark toward the flickering lights. I ran down the main boulevard, past a sullen row of steel grates, past vacant taxis and neon invitations, and somehow found that narrow side street. I ran toward the magazine shop, glanced in, and kept going.

I was fighting it, unwilling to be easy prey. The night air felt cool and invigorating. I sucked in all I could and ran faster—around the block. There it was again. Smirking covers. I ran by again, my eyes dragging back through my head.

And so I kept circling in the black stillness, caught in limbo between giving up and fighting altogether. Perhaps I was thinking of Jericho. If I could just run around the shop enough times, maybe it would simply collapse.

It didn't. Finally I stopped and palmed down on the counter my contribution to porn. Okay, you win. I made my way gloomily, but in very good time, back up the hill and settled down to "read" those clichés of the flesh.

Afterward of course I was quite disgusted with myself. Seizing the magazine in no uncertain terms, I stomped out the door, down the hall, through the exit, down the cement stairs, over to the dock, and threw it unceremoniously into a huge garbage bin. After such a humiliating defeat I was desperate for decisiveness.

Back in my room I made earnest, if well-rehearsed, confession, pleaded for forgiveness, and repeated promises to the Lord. Sleep did not come easy.

Very early and barely bright the next morning it hit me again. The very first conscious thoughts that arrested my attention were of the garbage bin. The beckoning garbage bin. I struggled to pray, I protested halfheartedly. But now I knew I was easy prey.

Jumping into my jeans I calmly rushed out the door, down the hall, to the exit. But the door to the outside hit against something. Nudging it open I peeked out and almost passed out. There at the top of the cement stairs were my Bolex 16mm camera, tripod, and lip-sync tape recorder. Thousands and thousands of dollars worth of equipment sitting there waiting for any thief with half a brain to snatch up. I looked around. No one in sight.

First I felt a surge of thankfulness. Somehow these essentials for my work were still in my possession. Praise the Lord. Then I felt terribly curious. How did they get there? I certainly didn't put them out by the dock. They weren't there late last night when I went out to the bin. Surely none of the hospital staff would have put them outside.

I was completely befuddled as I carried the equipment back to the safety of my room. And in my bewilderment God nudged me, as if to say: "Here's your equipment buddy, a gift from Yours Truly. Do you still want to betray Me?"

At the time it did indeed seem that my camera and tape recorder had materialized out of thin air and were

God's gracious gift. At the very least He had placed them as a stumbling block in my way. I was moved that He would extend His mercy so particularly and precisely to one who had turned his back.

But I was not moved enough. My thanksgiving dissolved before the mighty pull of the garbage bin. I had already dropped into the rut and couldn't get out. I rushed out the door, down the hall, through the exit, down the cement stairs, and over to the garbage bin. To my amazement I found it stuffed with mounds of shredded paper.

When I had decisively cast in the magazine late the previous night, the bin was almost empty. Now, very early in the morning, before anyone was stirring—these mounds of paper. I hadn't heard any truck pull up and dump them in. Who would have done it in the middle of the night? Someone obviously did, but it seemed awfully peculiar.

However, still caught up in my singular quest I started digging through the shredded paper—a hog with its nose to the trough. I flailed about in the mounds of trash until my predicament finally burned through to me. This time, at last, I moved when God nudged: "Hey, is this what you want, digging through the garbage as if your life depended on it?"

I rushed back to my room, fell on my bed, and poured out my misery to God in repentance, as best I could. Finally I saw God's merciful call to justice altogether. His concern for me seemed more unfathomable than all that had just happened. He was willing to go to such lengths to reclaim for righteousness someone actively despising His grace. He was there, at the top of the cement stairs, in the garbage bin, encouraging me out of my rut.

In the end, His holy fire rescued even easy prey.

PART
IV

Here
Beyond

THE FOREFATHERS TAUGHT US THAT
THAKUR JIU [GENUINE GOD] IS DISTINCT.
HE IS NOT TO BE SEEN WITH FLESHLY EYES,
BUT HE SEES ALL . . . HE NOURISHES ALL,
GREAT AND SMALL.

*Kolean, sage of the
Santal people of India*

10

MOST HIGH

RABI MAHARAJ'S MOTHER and aunt had invited neighbors
and relatives to a *puja* worship service in their home.
As the guests filed in, many bowed respectfully toward
Rabi. The fourteen-year-old yogi read admiration in
their eyes. These people believed he soon would bring
fame to their town as a guru with many followers.

Rabi's deceased father, a holy man who'd spent his
whole life meditating, had been worshiped for many
years. Now Rabi believed that he also had achieved
unity with Brahman, pure consciousness. In his trances
he had experienced heavenly music, psychedelic colors,
and spirit visitations. The boy saw himself as an
embodiment of the Lord of the Universe.

Doubts came on occasion to be sure. Meditation
brought peace but didn't help him get along with his
quarrelsome aunt. Rabi felt a conflict between the petti-
ness he felt inside and the lofty image he projected toward others. Still, it felt good to be the object of
reverence.

Baba Jankhi Maharaj, the acknowledged leader of
the East Indians in Trinidad, had been invited to perform the elaborate *puja* ceremony. Rabi proudly assist-
ed him in offering gifts and incense to Hindu icons.
This was a great honor.

After the service the boy stood by the altar finger-

131

ing the fragrant garland of flowers around his neck, and greeted the guests. A neighbor came up—a poor widow who earned a pitiful wage for long hours of hard labor —and laid several coins one after another at Rabi's feet.

Rabi felt a twinge of guilt for accepting this offering. But he realized he had much to give in exchange. The widow bowed low to receive her yogi's touch—the *shakti* pat-on-the-head which devotees coveted as a supernatural blessing.

As the incense rose about him Rabi reached out to touch the woman's forehead, but a voice "of unmistakable omnipotent authority" startled him with the words: "You are not God, Rabi!" The boy's arm froze in midair. The forceful voice repeated, *"You . . . are . . . not . . . God!"*

This fourteen-year-old Lord of the Universe crumbled. "The words smote me like the slash of a cutlass felling the tall green cane," he recalled. He began trembling, certain that the true God, Creator of all, had spoken to him. At that moment he felt like he should fall down at the feet of the Most High and beg for forgiveness. But all those guests were looking on, and the widow was kneeling there, staring at his frozen, outstretched arm.

Rabi ran to his room, locked the door, tore off his garland of flowers, and flung himself on the bed, sobbing.

Bethel, Israel.   c. 930 B.C.

KING JEROBOAM WAS ONLY trying to consolidate power in his northern kingdom of Israel. He feared that people making regular pilgrimages south to Judah and Jerusalem's temple might start feeling some loyalty toward his rival there, King Rehoboam. Very sensibly, he established alternative places of worship closer to home, in Dan and Bethel.

Without Jerusalem's glorious temple, however, he needed a main attraction, something to draw the crowds in. Taking a cue from the Caananite bull cults in the neighborhood, the king settled on two golden calves, one for each center of worship. Jeroboam didn't mean to imply that Jehovah was a calf. Even this hard-nosed politician knew better. The idol merely served as a seat for God, suggesting that He rode on the beast or was enthroned above it.

But of course the deity worshiped didn't remain above the calf; He came to be identified with it and then with the seductive fertility cults of Canaan. This new religion went over quite well. Jeroboam started making more up as he went along, establishing feast days, priests, and high places.

One day the king went to Bethel to offer incense on an altar to the golden calf. As fragrance ascended from the sacred fire, a Judean prophet walked right in and interrupted the proceedings. He rudely announced that the very priests officiating there would be killed on this altar. He further predicted that the abominable altar would split apart as a sign of disasters to come.

Jeroboam took an instant dislike to this irreverent stranger and pointed guards toward the man, commanding, "Seize him!" But the arm he stretched out withered in front of everyone's eyes. It froze. The king couldn't move the ghastly thing.

As if that weren't enough, the stone altar began shaking violently. It split wide open, collapsed, and spilled its ashes on the ground. God had made his point. The king got religion (the right one) for a few moments, and humbly begged the prophet to pray that his withered arm might be restored. He did and it was. (Even when God is at His most implacable, He can't resist a touch of mercy.)

JEROBOAM THOUGHT HE MIGHT get away with a little symbol. A place where the pious of the land might focus their attention. A nice, healthy calf. But the answer was No, period. It always was No. Idols provoke Jehovah. On no subject does He speak so loudly and long as on idolatry.

When He thundered down His Ten Commandments, He sounded most adamant in the second: Make no idol, no image of anything in heaven, on earth, or in the sea. Do not bow down to any such thing or worship it. I am a jealous God who punishes sin.

Centuries later Isaiah reminded Israel that God had not changed His mind: "Molten images are wind and emptiness." Jeremiah asked how people could possibly worship wood cut from the forest, decorated with silver and gold, and nailed up so it won't totter. Why fear something that stands there immobile and silent as a "scarecrow in a cucumber field?" Habakkuk wondered aloud how lifeless stone idols could give guidance. They can't even wake up.

Everywhere in the Old Testament Jehovah is firmly opposed to idol-worship, a time-honored, widely shared religious tradition. It was in fact practically the only way to worship at the time.

Moses coming down from Sinai, fresh from an awesome close encounter with Jehovah, saw Israel partying to a golden bull-calf, one of the Egyptian favorites. In a fury he ordered the image melted down, ground to powder and scattered over a stream. Then he made the sons of Israel drink their latest god. No transcendence there.

This continued throughout Israel's history. Every reforming king worth his salt, from Asa to Josiah, felt compelled to start by smashing idols and high places.

Jehovah refuses to be nailed down. In that area He won't give an inch. He will not be identified with any object. He will not be confined to any symbol. He will not be manipulated.

Some people are a little bit like that. Free spirits. No single pigeonhole is big enough for their restless lives. Observers can't quite put a finger on them, no category sums them up, there's always something more that leaks out.

Free spirits hate confinement of course. Their wide-ranging interests push them in several directions at once. Never content with just one job, one town, one hobby.

These kinds of people provide a hint of the God who will not be idolized (although they are fuzzy black-and-white snapshots of a much more colorful character.)

God the Most High is the ultimate Free Spirit. He is always more than what we can reasonably conclude or wildly imagine. There is always more of Him leaking out of our symbols.

God transcends. He is far above it all. Independent. Uncontainable. Isaiah made that clear in his tour de force against idolatry: chapter 40. The prophet asked: How can man, who is blown away like grass, make anything that represents the One who measures the oceans in the hollow of His hand? How can the nations, drops in a bucket, compare God to rotting wood overlaid by a goldsmith?

As an alternative to idols, Isaiah proposes that people look up:

> Lift up your eyes and look to the heavens:
>   Who created these?
> He who brings out the starry host one by one,
>   and calls them each by name.
> Because of his great power and mighty strength,
>   not one of them is missing.

The hills surrounding Bethlehem.   c. 1000 B.C.

THE SHEEP HAD SETTLED down in their favorite hollows or were grazing in tight bunches. A clear wind from the

Great Sea blew over the winter green hills. The sun threw its light over a string of clouds hovering over the western horizon. Gold. Magenta. Vermilion. Sunset splashed across the dark blue sky and David the shepherd stared in awe. Then the cool blue of dusk submerged the colors. Finally night settled over the hills in earnest. Later he would remember it this way:

> The heavens declare the glory of God;
> the skies proclaim the work of his hands.

New England. July 22, 1878.

WALT WHITMAN, the poet, had gone out in the country for a visit and encountered what he believed comes only once or twice in a lifetime: a perfect night. A little after eight o'clock, three black clouds rose suddenly in the dusk light, swept with broad windy swirls across the sky, and threatened a violent storm. But they vanished as quickly as they'd come up, and from nine to eleven the whole atmosphere shone with an exceptional clearness and glory.

"A large part of the sky," Whitman wrote, "seemed just laid in great splashes of phosphorus. You could look deeper in, farther through, than usual; the orbs thick as heads of wheat in a field." For a few moments this sky spoke eloquently to Whitman. He felt himself under the sky of the Bible, of Arabia, of the prophets, and of the oldest poems.

This "superhuman symphony" gave Whitman a "flashing glance of Deity," and moved him to write:

> As if for the first time, indeed, creation noiselessly
> sank into and through me its placid and untellable
> lesson, beyond—O, so infinitely beyond—anything
> from art, books, sermons, or from science, old or new.
> The spirit's hour—religion's hour—the visible sug-

gestion of God in space and time—now once definitely indicated, if never told again.

In the book "From Immigrant to Inventor." 1890s.

MICHAEL PUPIN, world-class scientist, pioneer in x-ray photography, wrote at the close of his autobiography:

> Fifty years ago, when as a member of a herdsman's squad of boys I watched the stars on the black background of a summer midnight sky, I felt that their light was a language proclaiming the glory of God.

After years of deciphering starlight scientifically, their basic message for Pupin hadn't changed:

> The light of the stars is a part of the life-giving breath of God. I never look now upon the starlit vault of the heaven without feeling this divine breath and its quickening action upon my soul.

SHEPHERD, POET, AND SCIENTIST see the same picture in the stars, the suggestion of a glorious God who transcends all human limitations, all manmade symbols. When theologians use terms like infinite, transcendent and absolute to describe God, the words carry a rather hollow echo. We can't hold up any samples of the infinite, transcendent or absolute. But we can look up at the stars. They help illuminate this mysterious part of God's nature. The stars have been speaking for a long time. Modern science has only amplified their voice.

The Universe. All the time.

TRY TAKING a mathematical stroll out into the deep black of space. You start by blasting away from the 25,000-mile circumference of the earth. That kind of size is in itself hard to grasp. But then you approach the sun, a blazing fireball one million miles across. If the sun were the size of an orange, the earth would be a grain of sand.

Traveling out from the solar system, farther into space, you see that the sun which so dominates our heavens is only a mid-sized star. Others are so large they could hold 500 million suns the size of ours.

Moving through the vast hazy field of stars that is our Milky Way, we have to talk in terms of light years (distance traveled in a year at a 186,000-miles-per-second clip) between the pin-pricks of light. They seem packed together, but the average distance between stars in our galaxy is four or five light years. And there are two hundred billion of them swirling through the Milky Way's incomprehensible spaces.

Then we have to try to think about the billions of other galaxies sprawled across the observable universe.

These immensities chill our brain. Yet even more remarkable is the fact that all these heavenly bodies travel in precise, predictable paths. They don't just tumble through space undirected, crashing into each other. Even galaxies sweep their load of stars in graceful spirals. There is a majestic order to the movements in the heavens.

Our own planet, for example, moves in several separate, synchronized ways. It spins on its axis at precisely one thousand miles per hour, producing a nice mix of night and day to modulate our climate. The earth also orbits the sun at eighteen and a half miles per second, its journey of millions of miles never varying more than a fraction of a second.

Then we've got our solar system in motion, revolving in an orbit around the Milky Way. We move, precisely in step with countless other star groups, around the center of our galaxy at 180 miles per second. And the entire Milky Way is also rushing through space at terrific speed, its billions of stars pulled along in the same journey.

Somehow all this motion is synchronized. All the orbits within orbits proceed on track, on time.

THIS IS THE MOST HIGH in action. The God who directs galaxies surely must transcend all human abilities. With His indescribably immense reach He acts in dimensions infinitely beyond ours. God is not just a man pumped up to largest size. There are qualitative leaps between our footprints in the sand of Earth and His confident steps amid the vast choreography of the stars.

After craning our necks at the heavens should we just write off this "transcendent" stuff as incomprehensible and go on with something more our size? Perhaps this chapter would have been more honest as a series of blank pages.

But let me explain one aspect of the infinite God that I find extremely comforting.

A small church in the midwestern U.S. The Lord's Day.

THE SMALL ELECTRIC ORGAN whines out a hymn full of staid quarter notes. A few cracking voices struggle to keep the melody suspended in the stuffy air. I follow along in the heavy black hymnbook with its carefully preserved lyrics, artifacts from the nineteenth century.

The sermon that follows is something I need to hear, but it comes in old cadences that lull to sleep. It's familiar oratory one gets only in the pew, complete with those hoary illustrations about safe harbors and dangerous billows.

I wonder, for the hundredth time, why the God that I willingly worship is celebrated in this way. Why must I approach Him through an alien culture?

A LOT OF PEOPLE see God only through the windows of a church, and that can suggest a very narrow picture. Is He really someone who slows the pulse and bores to tears? Are nineteenth-century hymns the only music He's comfortable with? Is being slightly behind the times His fondest ideal?

The answer, from the heavens, is a resounding NO. God cannot be contained in the few faded strands of culture that conservative church people usually cherish. He can't be summed up by any religious subculture.

The stompin' and shoutin' churches can't hold Him in. The cathedrals resplendent with liturgy can't sum Him up. The progressive churches pulsating with Jesus rock can't encompass Him. God wouldn't fit into all the churches put together.

That was very apparent back in Solomon's day when people had more time to look up at the stars. As the Hebrews were proudly dedicating what they thought was THE great dwelling place for Jehovah upon the earth, wise Solomon declared: "The heavens, even the highest heavens, cannot contain you. How much less this temple I have built!"

God is transcendent—always *more than*. He cannot be culturally dished out and He cannot be intellectually boxed in. Philosophers have carried out long struggles with the idea of God, hoping for a definitive mental encounter. They came up with categories like Absolute Spirit, Substance, Thought, Ground of Being, Ultimate Reality. These perspectives sometimes helped, but there was always plenty of God left over for the next thinker to try to encompass.

Even those saintly people who've dedicated their whole lives to a soul encounter with the Most High don't claim to have pinned Him down. They see More Than.

A Roman named Plotinus had mystical experiences around A.D. 200 in which his soul seemed to merge into the One "wellspring of Life . . . fount of good, root of the Soul." All he could describe was "a going forth from self, a simplifying, a renunciation."

Church father Gregory of Nyssa concluded that a true knowledge of God "is the seeing that consists in not seeing, because that which is sought transcends all knowledge, being separated on all sides by incomprehensibility."

Saint John of the Cross talked at great length about mystical knowledge to an admiring Christendom in the 1500s. But when it came to the subject of God Himself he was less articulate. He did experience a "sweet-tasting wisdom" that entered his inmost soul. But God appeared to be something that transcended the senses: "We get neither form nor impression, nor can we give any account or furnish any likeness."

Mexico. 1950s.

MY MOM always liked to see the sights. So when I was growing up in Mexico the family took our little Hillman on long meandering drives through places like Cuernavaca, Oaxaca, Orizaba, and Coatzacoalcos. We went almost every holiday. At the age of eight my only hope was that we'd hit a beach at some point. I have long since lost or discarded sombreros, serapes, and other tourist paraphernalia. And I have forgotten being at most of the places Mom keeps in her photo albums. But two things do remain embedded in my mind: the poverty and the cathedrals.

Poverty can be very photogenic. Those huge loads balanced on the heads of barefoot women as they walk to market. The white burro pulling a cart loaded with yellow bananas, green mangos, and two runny-nosed toddlers. But it is poverty nevertheless.

I never knew how stuffed I was with possessions till I peered into those dirt-floored adobe rooms occupied by a fire pit, chair, pair of chickens, shelf—and nothing else. The naked children who peered back at me sometimes went to bed hungry.

We skimmed the surface of a deep ocean of the poor, camera clicking. But that ocean had its glorious islands—the cathedrals. Even the smaller villages often could boast of a great church. Mom always wanted to look inside. She would put a dark scarf over her head, dip her fingers in the holy water according to custom, and walk through the massive front door. I was usually apprehensive.

Beneath the high arching ceiling I half expected some grand inquisitor to descend on me. Like every good Protestant boy I had listened attentively to stories of the reformation's martyrs. Now I was in the antichrist's lair. The stone structure smelled like a tomb. The Latin which I could not decipher on those stained-glass windows way up there seemed to conceal dark secrets.

Yet at the same time I saw beauty all around me. I craned my neck toward glorious, heroic scenes. Real gold and silver glistened in the candlelight. Such costly beauty. How had these peasants done it? My parents always wondered about that.

People subsisting on a few tortillas a day had erected a temple of gold and silver. Their whole lives were muted by grinding poverty, but here they shouted glory. In their sacrifice they pointed toward the God who transcends all things.

THOSE CHURCHES in places like Jalapa, Tabasco, and Campeche have become, for me, an inspired portrait of the God who is More Than. In a way it's an ironic picture. It could be argued that the poor in those towns were exploited. The church could be criticized for how it used the treasures entrusted to it. And a case could be made for these cathedrals as centers of idolatry. I did see food placed before statues of the saints, and old women praying desperately into stone faces. Pagan customs die hard among the Indians.

They probably could have used a few choice words from the prophet who zapped Jeroboam's idolatrous altar. And yet these same people lived out a testimony to the God-above-all more profound than any theological volume on the Infinite.

God sometimes brings us full circle. He wrests a graphic picture of His transcendence from places tainted with idolatry. He appears Most High where we expect Him to be dragged low.

He always remains the free spirit, uncontainable, full of surprises. We cannot box Him in. We can only stand and celebrate the One exalted far above all gods, Most High over all the earth, dwelling in the height of heaven, rich in glory, inhabiting a light which no man can approach.

And that is the wonder. God exists infinitely beyond us, always more than we can grasp, and yet He remains so desirable. His bigness haunts. God the Wholly Other beckons and people respond, stretching toward the mystery. Francis of Assisi spends a night on his knees fervently repeating "My God, my God!" and nothing else. The Trappist of the Sahara, Charles de Foucald, feels compelled to "breathe myself out before God in total exhalation of self." Mexican Indians bring silver and gold.

11

CLOSE COMPANION

IT HIT ME all of a sudden one balmy Saturday afternoon by the pond near our house. I was in college and yet to hit on a legitimate career. Out for a walk around our pond and its ugly, unkept environs I decided for some reason to sit down amid the tall grass and wait. And in the quiet I began to see.

Seven shades of green and gray. Textures. The skin of a beetle. A piece of bark. Nothing in that rather bleak episode of Illinois autumn shouted beauty. The colors were long gone. But everything around me did say "good"—with confidence. The dying scrub buzzed with what seemed exotic insects. The scum on the pond's surface brought forth a wondrous array of animal life. Every nondescript weed suddenly took on an intriguing character. I longed to know names and precise properties. What species did those long slender leaves and those gray-brown fuzz balls belong to?

This was good, worthy of a human life's devotion. I had one of those primitive automatic cameras with me, the kind that casts a disinterested focus on the world in general. I peered through its tiny window and earnestly sized the contour of a stem, the flight of a dragonfly, not yet feeling ready to shoot a frame. I just waited. I felt honored to be silent and still, to do nothing but wait amid this miniature splendor in the grass

145

and capture for the senses whatever might be given me.

And so my destiny was sealed. Someday I'd get a real camera. I'd become a nature photographer. I'd go deep into the warp and woof of creation and come out with glimpses of—God.

My destiny lasted about two-and-a-half weeks. Being a nature photographer had its weak points. But I did eventually get a decent camera and photography did become a part of my work. And that sense of waiting did not go away.

Early in my labors as a photographer I treated every snap of the shutter like a cosmic event—especially when aiming at nature. My poverty and the price of film had something to do with it. And I did not have sense enough to shoot up a great scene from every angle and f-stop.

Instead I worked religiously for the one perfect shot. I remember in particular a series on flowers I did during my macro-lens phase. Extreme closeups held me fast at the time. Taking vengeance on that old automatic, I could now focus on a fly's navel.

Well, here was this flower, yellow-petaled and perfectly symmetrical. How could I shoot it without making a cliché? I got close of course. Into the pistil, around the pistil. Would this translucent gold ever reproduce on film? How about a side view, the curve of the petals. How about including the tip of another flower?

I worked an hour for a couple of pictures. They're nice. But looking back I see that the reverence was what counted. Kneeling down and hovering over those splashes of yellow in the mud by my apartment, I still waited in earnest for glimpses. And those flowers too shouted, "Good!"

PEOPLE HAVE BEEN WAITING in nature for God since time began. And, according to wide testimony, He shows up.

British chaplain Thomas Traherne saw "Eternity" in the broad daylight of an ordinary day when green trees "transported and ravished me" and the dust and stones of the street seemed "precious as gold."

The poet e. e. cummings was once moved to psalm:

i thank You God for most this amazing
day:for the leaping greenly spirits of trees
and for a blue true dream of sky;and for everything
which is natural which is infinite which is yes

Francis of Assisi praised the God he felt come close in Brother Sun, Sister Moon, Brother Wind, Sister Water, and Mother Earth. He felt a kinship with God through all these.

George Fox, founder of the Quakers, saw "creation . . . opened to me" and felt "wrapped up, as in rapture, in the Lord's power."

The choreographed stars of the universe sign down to us a strong suggestion of an infinite God who transcends all we can imagine. But here below we seem to find God Himself in the flowers. Immanent, close at hand, accessible.

Nature up close appears to be more than an exhibit of God's brandname handywork. The leaves and wind and sunshine embody Him. Gurgling brook and chirping robin suggest to many that He is not remote but very much with us.

The Bible affirms that Jehovah is very near to all who call on Him. He comes into the closet with those praying. He's at our right hand to support us. Human beings can walk in the light of the divine countenance and behold His beauty in the temple. Paul assured the intellectuals of Athens that "He is not far from each one of us. For in him we live and move and have our being."

That's getting pretty close. The infinite God is Close Companion. He's not out there somewhere; He's here. God is immanent in the world. And His closeness is not just some benign substance spread around, Essence of God sprayed on the world to spiritualize things up a bit. No, when God comes close, He comes close altogether.

Canaan. The desert between Kadesh and Bered. c. 1925 B.C.

HAGAR DIDN'T KNOW where she was going. The road she was on led to Shur, but that lay many miles to the south. All this Egyptian maidservant could think of was getting away. Blinded by bitter tears, she'd walked into a wasteland, away from the tents of Abram.

It all started with Sarai, Abram's wife, trying to help God out of a jam. The Lord had promised Abram descendants as numerous as the stars. He was to become the father of a great nation. But Sarai had been unable to produce a single heir. Now she was old, long past childbearing. How was the divine plan going to work now?

Sarai thought of Hagar, her young Egyptian maidservant. If Abram had a son through her, wouldn't that be a fulfillment of the promise? Sarai offered Hagar to her husband and the girl became pregnant.

Now things got hot around camp. The barren wife and the pregnant mistress exchanged unpleasantries. Sarai knew she'd brought this mess on herself and, unable to bear that thought, unloaded on Abram in fits of jealousy. She told him she couldn't take it anymore. Abram then made cruel peace by telling his wife she could do whatever with Hagar. Sarai mistreated her maidservant so badly that the girl was forced to flee.

Pregnant, alone, no place to go. God's chosen couple had blamed the victim. In the sandy wasteland she'd become a zero. A slave with no one to work for. A mother with no family. An Egyptian in wild Canaan.

Finally exhaustion broke through the emotions

driving her on. Hagar stopped by a spring to rest. In this moment of total despair and isolation, someone called her by name: "Hagar, servant of Sarai."

Who knew her out here in this wasteland? And who cared? As it turned out an angel of the Lord did. He asked where she was going. She replied, "I'm running away . . ."

God, through this angel, gave Hagar the same kind of promise He'd laid on her master: "I'll make your descendants too numerous to count." Her baby would be a boy, to be named Ishmael, meaning "God Hears."

And so Hagar found the strength to survive. She returned to Sarai and Abram, had her son, and became the mother of the Arab nations, strengthened by the knowledge that God was not just up there in the stars over Abram, but also down in the desert by her side. She now called Him "The God who sees me." She knew. He'd come close. He'd called her by name.

England. The moors near Bamburgh. 1920s.

ONE SUMMER NIGHT a Scottish youth, active in church work, decided to take a shortcut across the moors on his way to Bamburgh where he had a job. This Northumberland countryside was noted for its limestone. One deep, deserted quarry lay near Glororum Road. But the lad thought he could avoid it.

Though the night was a starless inky-black, he set out through the rock and heather. He could sometimes hear the faroff bleating of sheep, the wind rustling through; occasionally a moor fowl he disturbed fluttered up noisily. Otherwise he was very much alone in the night.

Suddenly he heard a voice call out with great urgency, "Peter!"

The youth, a bit unnerved, stopped and called back into the dark, "Yes, who is it? What do you want?"

No response. Just a bit of wind over the deserted moorland.

The lad concluded he'd been mistaken and walked on a few more steps. He heard the voice again, more urgent than before: "Peter!"

He stopped in his tracks, bent forward to peer through the dense black, and stumbled to his knees. Reaching out a hand to the ground before him, he clutched thin air. The quarry! Sure enough, as Peter carefully felt around in a semicircle he discovered he had stopped on the edge of the abandoned limestone quarry—one step before a fatal plunge into the deep.

Out there in the desolate moor someone knew him and someone cared. Peter Marshall never forgot that. Dedicating his life to the One who'd called him by name, he became one of America's greatest ministers.

THIS IS WHAT IT MEANS to be immanent. God is no abstract presence. He calls people by name. God is with us. He's involved. Page through the Bible and you'll see the remarkable range of His involvement. God appears in the midst of a fiery furnace, expressing solidarity with three Hebrews who refused to bow down to Nebuchadnezzar's idol. He shows up in a den of lions, shutting the mouths of those starved beasts so His faithful servant Daniel can emerge unscathed. He follows Jonah when that reluctant prophet gets the original idea of running away from His presence—and ships off to some port at the end of the then-known world. But the middle of the sea isn't far enough. God is there. Jonah is thrown into the sea and into the belly of a great fish. Even that isn't far enough. Guess who appears on the scene and prevents His man from being digested?

God is not immanent in a passive sense. Hyperactive would better describe it. He is with us altogether. He comes close, physically close.

The Bible routinely describes Jehovah as a Being

who raises His arm, stretches out His hand, gazes down on the earth, treads on the high places, turns His face toward those in trouble. These statements imply that the Infinite One has a body. But scholars assure us that such phrases are merely metaphors for the real thing: divine activity of a spiritual nature. They have a point of course. God doesn't need to gesture wildly with His arms in order to make things happen.

But is He physical? Is the physically active God pictured by Bible writers only a symbol—an anthropomorphism, as they say?

Adam and Eve produced a child in their "image and likeness." God produced human beings in His "image and likeness." We can infer things like spirit and personality from the word "image." But what about "likeness?" God is said to be "immortal, invisible, the only God." But is He invisible only from a human perspective limited by sin? Aren't we urged to look forward to a "face to face" encounter in heaven?

It's reasonable to conclude that the God of the galaxies is not limited by a physical body. But does that mean He never expresses Himself in one?

For some people it seems demeaning to think of God in a body. The old notion that flesh is inherently evil and spirit inherently good comes into play. If that is true then God must be all spirit.

Thinkers and Bible scholars have projected for us a Deity completely "above" the physical. But then thinkers and Bible scholars don't tend to be very physical people. We might expect them to idealize abstractions. There are others, however, who would rather tend a garden or play baseball than read philosophy. Are they on a lower level of existence, further from God's "image and likeness?"

Billy Sunday found God while chasing a fly ball in right field with runners on second and third. The championship was on the line. One more out would win it for Billy and the Chicago White Sox. Bennett, the Detroit catcher, had just smashed the ball right on the nose and Billy knew it was going over his head. He turned and ran flat out toward the crowd at the edge of the field.

As he ran, Billy said the second prayer of his life. The night before he'd said his first as he "staggered out of sin and into the arms of the Savior." Now the outfielder called out, "God, if you ever helped mortal man, help me to get that ball."

He jumped over a bench and stopped. "I thought I was close enough to catch it," he recalled. "I looked back and I saw it going over my head and I jumped and shoved out my left hand and the ball hit it and stuck." Billy's momentum carried him on and he sprawled beneath a team of horses—but jumped up with the ball in his hand. God had become physically real to this physically gifted young man. Billy Sunday made Him very real to thousands of others during his career as an evangelist.

God has shown Himself a physical reality to others as well. There's the occasional prophet or holy man who sees a brilliant form in his visions. But for many more people, God becomes flesh in a different sense.

One eight-year-old, asked about his feelings for the Almighty, said, "I feel closest to God, like after I'm rounding second base after I hit a double." I can understand that. I happen to feel most physically alive when I'm playing flag football. And I can't help believing that my Creator is capable of being alive in the same way, physically alive. After all, He's the One who enables us to exult in bodies wondrously crafted, pushed to the limit. He's the One who produced the smorgasbord of textures and colors we enjoy in nature. He is a sensory God, a physical God.

He is certainly more than a body. But neither is He less than one—a brilliant paraplegic in the sky who does amazing things with His mind. God is with us in our physical world, altogether with us. A close companion who gets His hands dirty.

Himeji, Japan. 1976.

HARUO LEANS FORWARD, pressing his point home. "You wonder how I can believe in all this intangible religious stuff? Well, what if I told you there are private detectives and samurai battles, Hawaii beaches and lovers' dialogues floating around in our room right now? You would find that hard to believe too, wouldn't you?"

Seigi nods.

Haruo reaches over and turns on the television. "But it's true. I can't sense the dots of color that float into this TV set, but I can tell by the results I see that something invisible is acting on the television.

"It's the same with God. He can be known by His actions. At first, I found the talk about angels and God's Spirit living in people pretty odd too. But I've seen the results in people's lives."

Cut. That was great.

Haruo and Seigi were doing a good job of acting out the parts of a new Christian and his skeptical friend. They had become accustomed to the heat of 2500 watts and the purring of my Super-8 camera. Kazko, the Bible teacher who translated my script, was coaching the two young men well.

The film was my attempt to show that God is active and knowable. I was also hoping it would help solidify the faith of Haruo and Seigi, both new believers.

I had come some distance from the pond where I first peered through a camera in earnest. But "Seedling" was no Hollywood production. I had to make do with a small budget, miscellaneous equipment, and lots of could-you-spare-a-few-minutes.

This was to be our last night of filming. The camera had to be back in another city the following day, so we were trying to squeeze in the final retakes.

If only once I could set up a scene without being in a hurry. Makeshift movie making, it seems, always must be done on the fly with antsy volunteers. In college I had a phenomenally patient roommate who let me spend hours composing shots of him walking down the sidewalk. But now when it really counts—the pressure never lets up.

One of Seigi's lines wasn't recorded properly last week. We set up to shoot him in a closeup. He sits behind a low table looking over the script. The lights are adjusted to lose his shadow on the wall. Camera and mike are ready. We roll. Seigi does his isolated line pretty naturally, but the camera sputters and skips. Groan. I check all the wires, battery light, batteries, switch and lock. Everything seems okay. I shake the film cartridge.

Lights. Second take. Seigi is into his line but the camera still rattles unevenly. Please not now. Just a few little pickup shots and the film is done. Disgusted and desperate I take out the old batteries, which are working fine, and insert a new set into the camera grip.

Lights. Take three. The camera stutters again. "Okay," I tell Seigi, "Let me roll about ten feet of film in case something is jammed in the cartridge." For some reason I put the old batteries back in.

Lights again please. Take four. I squeeze the switch with great intensity and shoot a minute of film, willing it to clear. No go. The camera sputters on, doggedly erratic.

My head goes hot and blank. I stare at my little black blankety-blank camera, completely flustered. There are no more switches or cables to fiddle with.

Then Kazko makes a suggestion, "Let's pray about it."

So the four of us kneel together, tell the Lord about our genuine need and put our trust in His abilities.

We finish praying and look at each other for a minute. I stare at the recalcitrant camera. There's nothing more anyone can do.

Take five. Action. The camera makes such a melodious purr in my ear that I can hardly hear Seigi's line. The chronic sputtering is gone. We're all shouting together, slapping each other on the back.

We shot without a hitch the rest of the evening and completed the film. I was anxious to see our last roll. As soon as the footage came back from the lab I projected Seigi's one-line pickup. The picture frame jumped and skipped during the first four takes; the sound wandered out of sync. On the fifth take picture and sound were perfect.

I rushed off to tell Haruo, Seigi and Kazko. We celebrated a completed project, and also our glimpses of immanence. Haruo and Seigi had heard plenty about the God of Heaven. But they said they'd never experienced Him brush by so close. He seemed to be projected up there waving at us, on the fifth take. God close up, with His hands dirty, fiddling with camera parts.

GOD APPEARS specifically, physically, not in benign generalities. He calls us by name and also gets involved in the nitty-gritty of life. And His here-ness goes one better. The Bible swears up and down that the infinite God dwells in human hearts. A casual reader might conclude that this seems to be stretching a point. God the close companion, His Spirit hovering about us. Perhaps. But God moving into our souls with His imposing array of attributes? Surely that would cramp His style.

Yet Scripture pushes the point. The New Testament in particular waxes eloquent about God abiding within, filling us, making us one with Him.

Immanent to the ultimate degree. And we have witnesses to that effect. Some mystical pursuers of the Infinite do talk mystifyingly of seeing only the incomprehensible or some great abyss. Others offer more tangible evidence. Some who seek God with all their hearts find Him there.

The peasant saint Brother Lawrence discovered that "we may make an oratory of our heart, wherein to retire from time to time, to converse with Him in meekness, humility, and love."

The mystical writer Lady Julian of Norwich felt that "God is closer to us than our own soul."

Dwight L. Moody in his early days as an evangelist wanted God that close. He was praying earnestly for God's Spirit to fill him. And He did. It happened one day while he was walking down a street in New York City. God arrived altogether. His love overwhelmed Moody. The experience was so intense, he recalled, that "I had to ask Him to stay His hand." The man couldn't contain all that was poured into him.

Singer Ethel Waters, as a teenager, knelt at the "mourner's bench" during the last night of revival meetings in her town and prayed hard. She felt a great need of something in that little church and yet didn't know exactly what it was. So she asked: "What am I seeking here? What do I want of You? Help me!"

Then she found "the peace I had been seeking all my life. Love flooded my heart and I knew I had found God and that now and for always I would have an ally, a friend close by to strengthen me and cheer me on." Church members told Ethel afterward that she appeared as one transfixed and that the light in her face electrified the whole church.

Intimations of immanence at any rate. Something more than human rushing in.

God, of course, doesn't dwell inside us in the most literal sense. He doesn't constrict His existence to the inner life of human beings. But the remarkable fact is this: He is there altogether, as if we alone shared His intimate companionship, as if we alone received the full force of His divinity within. The measure of His unique closeness is that He makes individuals feel that way. It's our name that is called. It's our broken camera that gets fixed. It's our heart that is filled to overflowing.

12

SURPASSINGLY PRESENT

GOD IN THE HEAVENS and God in our hearts. Cosmic Reality and Companion. Spiritual and physical. Unfathomable and face-to-face. Science and sentiment. God's transcendance and immanence seem unfathomably far apart, but they have on occasion fused together quite dramatically, according to certain awed witnesses on our planet.

Irian Jaya, Indonesia. Christmas Day, c. 1970.

FIFTY GUESTS from Mauro village approached warily in their narrow dugouts on the shimmering Kidari river. The Haenam village men waited on the banks. Some watched with sorrow in their eyes; among the dugouts pulled ashore they spotted warriors who had killed members of their families. But these people from Maruo had been invited for a very special celebration.

This was to be the first large-scale intervillage feast the Sawi tribe had known in living memory. Five fat pigs roasted over large cooking fires. Other Sawis from encampments along the Kidari began arriving. But the guests stayed cool, hovering in their own little village groups, watchful and apprehensive.

Then a dugout from Kayagar appeared on the water bearing a patient dying of pneumonia. It was a man named Hurip, gasping for breath. Several of the

159

Haenam hosts ran to summon Don Richardson, the American missionary who had organized the feast. Don hurried to the riverbank. Just as he reached out to checked Hurip's pulse he heard a sharp, bitter voice behind him call, "You won't give medicine to that man, will you?"

It was Amio, trembling with emotion. He had just recognized this Hurip as the man who'd killed and cannibalized his baby brother years before. Amio had been waiting all this time for revenge. With a word he could summon dozens of friends with weapons. He gazed fiery-eyed at the Kayagar warriors who now gripped their spear-paddles tightly.

Richardson prayed for wisdom. How could these people come to the point of actually forgiving their enemies? Would it ever be possible? Then he reached out, in Sawi fashion, and gripped Amio by the earlobes. "Tarop Tim titindakeden!" he said slowly and carefully. "I plead the Peace Child!"

"The peace child my father gave to Hurip is dead!" Amio shot back. "Hurip himself killed him!"

Richardson responded, "But the Peace Child God gave still lives! And because He lives, you may not take vengeance against Hurip. Forgive him, Amio, for Jesus' sake!"

Richardson read an agonized conflict in Amio's young face, overwhelmingly intense. Every fiber of his being cried out for vengeance—it was the one Sawi truth drilled into him from childhood.

Among the Sawis, training for war began very early. A child who got his way by throwing violent temper-tantrums was admired for being "strong-willed." Sawi boys were goaded to take revenge every time they were insulted or hurt. They were nurtured with stories that upheld violence and treachery as traditional obligations. And their elders gave them an unceasing example of violent retaliation against any threat.

Besides chronic fighting between villages there were run-of-the-mill family quarrels: a husband punishing his wife by shooting an arrow through her arm, or beating her with a flaming fagot. Wives whose eyes strayed were forced to sit staring into a corner for days on end and beaten every time they looked away.

In Sawi culture the highest ideal consisted of something called "fattening for the kill." A man cultivated a friendship with someone from another village. He gave gifts, invited the friend to feasts. It might take years, but slowly his confidence would be won. Just when the friend could relax in trust, he was killed and eaten. For the Sawi, the more involved and skillful the betrayal the better.

When Don Richardson first communicated the story of the Most High God who came to be born in Bethlehem and live as "God with us," he received a shock. The Sawi elders perked up only when he came to the part about Judas, the trusted associate who betrayed Christ. Here was a hero they could admire— one who so skillfully fattened Jesus for the kill.

Richardson thought he'd reached bottom. There seemed no way to break through the Sawi cycle of violence. But in this darkest hour the light broke through. Richardson found out about one Sawi custom which embodied the gospel perfectly—the exchange of a Peace Child. The only way for feuding groups to stop fighting was for a family from each village to give up a child to the care of their enemies. A father had to make the supreme sacrifice—giving up a son to establish peace. That definitely rang a bell for Richardson.

He presented Jesus as the ultimate Peace Child for the world and everything clicked. The Sawi absorbed the gospel like good news crafted just for them. It was as if their entire history and culture had prepared them for this climactic confrontation with the Messiah.

But now on the shore of the Kidari the test had

come. It was evident in Amio's face. Had God the Peace Child really penetrated? Could He lift up to forgiveness a people ingrained with the impulse and obligation to strike back?

In Amio's soul, generations of Sawi warriors cried out for the kill. But on this day he rose above the ancestral voices. The Peace Child pulled him up. His tortured expression changed. Richardson watched him "looking down in gentleness upon his dying enemy Hurip." The warrior squared his shoulders and said firmly, "Let me carry Hurip alone!"

The Kayagar warriors watched in awe as Amio carried the man toward the clinic where Richardson's wife waited. Now many Sawi believers began mingling with other still-reluctant guests. One by one they yielded to friendly persuasion and stepped inside the Haenam church. Three or four looked back fearfully toward their canoes—it was a long way to run. But then they began to relax, amazed at the joy radiating from the faces of men and women around them transformed by God the Peace Child. On this memorable Christmas Day many guests were welcomed into a fellowship strong enough to conquer any threat of "fattening for the kill."

The world of the Sawi was transformed. Adults fixed into patterns of violence and revenge learned to forgive enemies. Men who'd abused their wives as slaves began to respect them as companions. Richardson saw women who habitually fell into screaming tirades take on a new, warmer personality. Children were no longer primed for war.

God was present in hundreds of Sawi hearts. Very much there. But what a presence! What leverage. It lifted them above generations of bloodletting, years of training for revenge. The transcendent God, the Most High, pulled them out of an age-old rut to live on a higher plane. And this leverage is not restricted to reforming the stone age. The surpassingly present God stands over every generation and every culture.

New York City. 1876.

EACH EVENING for ten weeks thousands of New Yorkers from all walks of life converged on the Hippodrome, drawn by an energizing presence. The large choir led out in gospel choruses. Ira Sankey sounded inspired on the organ keyboard. Evangelist Dwight L. Moody, full of life and spirit, delivered his simple creed with earnest passion. The life that had been poured into him on the New York City street some time before was now spilling out.

Churchgoers with their faith on hold caught a spark. The campaign disarmed sophisticated New Yorkers accustomed to looking down on the mass distribution of God. One observer noted, "Nothing has ever reached our great masses of non-churchgoing people as these meetings have."

God seemed powerfully present. People poured down to the "inquiry room" and committed their lives to Him. It was easy for the religious to observe an electric presence pulling at every soul in the Hippodrome. It was easy for skeptics to talk about mass hysteria. But the telling point of course was the results. That's when the transcendent God showed Himself, close at hand.

At first the *New York Times* had choked on Moody and his methods. But at the close of the campaign it had to concede that "the work accomplished this winter by Mr. Moody in this city for private and public morals will live. The drunken have become sober, the vicious virtuous, the worldly and self-seeking unselfish, the ignoble noble, the impure pure, the youth have started with more generous aims, the old have been stirred from grossness. A new hope has lifted up hundreds of human beings, a new consolation has come to the sorrowful, and a better principle has entered the sordid life of the day, through the labors of these plain men."

Results like that impress me. God made very present to a multitude. I don't know of any other wholesale changes for good in human life that can match these times when earnest prayer and witness bring the transcendent God very close.

God's presence is unique precisely because He transcends, is More Than, is the Most High. That gives Him leverage. The Wholly Other enlarges human hearts beyond their customary boundaries. The Most High lifts us beyond our human limitations. He is a "very present Helper," someone who is always there and who has more to give than we possess. God's surpassing presence makes a difference.

When we see Him so very near and so very active among thousands of different people at one time—say, in the Hippodrome—another word comes to mind: *omnipresence.* Unfortunately that weighty concept can seem neither here nor there.

A girl coming home from Sunday School once asked, "Mommy, where is God?"

"God is everywhere," the mother replied.

"But I don't want God to be everywhere," the child said. "I want God to be somewhere, and I want him to be somebody."

How can an omnipresent being be somebody? From our limited viewpoint we usually can only imagine this divine Everywhere to be something administrative or organizational. We have models like the British Empire in its heyday on which the sun never set. We picture outposts flying the Union Jack, trying to keep order in African rain forests or the vast Indian subcontinent.

And so we wonder: In a Universe where the corner drugstore is light years away, isn't God spreading Himself a bit thin? You'd think a speck of dust like the Earth might get some token presence. A benign recording that repeats: "I am watching over you, have no fear, live in peace. For more information, consult sacred handbook."

I can't get a mechanical picture of omnipresence. It doesn't work in my dimensions. But God does seem to function in that way quite well without my endorsement. He assures us that His presence never thins, He is altogether there, everywhere, One who *"fills* the heavens and the earth."

Land of the Chaldeans — and Bethlehem. Start of the first century.

THEY WERE ASTROLOGERS, maybe astronomers, members of an ancient sect which sought a higher knowledge in the heavens. Perhaps they'd become acquainted with Old Testament prophecies. At any rate one night they saw a particularly bright star overhead that spoke to them. The Messiah, the King of the Jews, was about to be born. They felt compelled to go and worship Him. So the magi, or wise men, loaded their camels and set out on the long journey to Jerusalem.

About that time Joseph was trying to figure out what to do with Mary. How to explain a pregnant bride-to-be to the good folk of Nazareth? He couldn't understand how his sweet, beloved Mary could do such a thing. Reluctantly he decided to break the engagement, but to do so quietly.

However an angel appeared to him in a dream and revealed that the incredible had happened, Mary had conceived a child by the Holy Spirit. The Savior of Israel rested in her womb.

So Joseph accepted his rather awkward role in the divine drama and, when the Roman census rolled around, took his pregnant wife to Bethlehem, his birthplace, so they could register as a family. It wasn't an easy trip. Mary bouncing on the donkey. Joseph afraid she'd go into labor any minute. They arrived safely but could find lodging only in a stable at one of the crowded inns.

Meanwhile the magi arrived in Jerusalem. They began asking where the new King of the Jews could be located. King Herod did not appreciate such inquiries. He nervously consulted the priests. They nervously consulted their Scriptures and found that the prophet Micah had indicated a shepherd and ruler would come forth from Bethlehem.

As soon as the magi heard this they set out for the town. On their way, that same unusual star appeared overhead leading the way to Bethlehem. When they saw this dramatic confirmation that they were on the right track, the men almost leaped off their camels: "They rejoiced exceedingly, with great joy."

That star sailing up there in the infinities of space, transcending the earth by light years, led the magi to the right suburb, the right inn, the right stable—and "stood over where the Child was."

Mary and Joseph watched in wide-eyed wonder as these visitors from the East laid gold, frankincense and myrrh beside the feeding trough where Jesus lay and bowed down to worship the gurgling infant. The travelers had intersected perfectly. God simultaneously present in Nazareth and "the East" guided the two parties to their memorable rendezvous.

Siberia and Europe. 1961.

ONE DAY a Christian believer in Siberia had a most unusual dream. He was told to go to Moscow where he would find a Bible for the church he attended. The man resisted the idea at first, knowing that Moscow's churches had precious few Bibles of their own. But the dream had seemed so vivid and authoritative. And he kept thinking of his 150 fellow church members without a single copy of Scripture among them. So the man set out on a journey two thousand miles across the tundra.

About that time another believer, known as Brother Andrew, and his companion Hans drove their VW from Holland down through Poland, crossed the border into Russia at Brest, and traveled on seven hundred miles to Moscow. Soon after arriving in the city the two men decided to check out the midweek service at a certain Baptist church. They hoped to make contacts there so they could unload some hot merchandise. Andrew and Hans had managed to maneuver past border check points and prying guards with a load of Russian Bibles tucked away in their car.

But distributing the Bibles was as risky as slipping them through the Iron Curtain. It's not like you could advertise. And one never knew who might be a KGB informant in a church, or even if the pastor was under pressure to report everything.

So when Andrew and Hans walked into the Thursday night meeting carrying a sample Russian Bible, they had a plan. After the service the two lingered in the vestibule checking out the twelve hundred worshipers milling past. Each man prayed separately that God would direct him to someone they could safely entrust with their smuggled Scriptures.

Soon Andrew spotted a thin, balding man in his forties standing against the wall. He felt a familiar "moment of recognition." The directive to talk to the man seemed very clear, but Andrew waited for Hans to inch over towards him. Before Andrew could speak, his companion said, "I've spotted our man!" In that vestibule crowded with hundreds of people Hans nodded toward the worshiper Andrew had chosen.

With hearts thumping they walked up to the stranger and attempted to introduce themselves and explain where they'd come from. He only stared at them, perplexed, until he caught the word "Dutch." It turned out he spoke German. So the three began a vigorous conversation in that language.

Andrew and Hans listened incredulously as the man told his story. This was the believer who'd come all the way from Siberia to find a Bible for his church, hoping against hope that God would somehow come through on the dream. Hans had the privilege of delivering the good news: "You were told to come eastward for two thousand miles to get a Bible, and we were told to go westward two thousand miles carrying Bibles to churches in Russia. And here we are tonight, recognizing each other the instant we meet."

When Hans handed the Siberian the Russian Bible they'd brought he was speechless. He stared at the book, then at the two westerners, then back at the book. Finally it all sank in and he burst out with a stream of thank you's and bear hugs. Andrew managed to calm him and whispered that there were more Bibles; he could have a dozen to take back home the next morning.

GOD'S REACH does stretch from horizon to horizon and yet His presence never thins. He is all there in the dreams of a Siberian Christian and in a star burning in the hearts of the magi. At the same time He's the close companion of Andrew and Hans navigating check points and of Joseph and Mary headed precariously toward Bethlehem.

Omnipresence is not just a great quantity of God filling space. It's a quality as well. The Psalms speak of God as "very present" to help us in time of trouble. He is present in a way qualitatively different from our own "being there."

I have a problem of not being present on many occasions. Someone is talking to me and my eyes are on him, my ears take in his words, but my consciousness has bowed out. This forces me to try to pick up conversations in midstream as if I had been present all along. My boss, for one, does not find this amusing.

Most of us find, upon recollection, that our most pleasurable moments occurred when we were most present—our senses tuned to the precise colors, textures, intonations, and gestures around us. The more bored we become, the less present we are. The complacent and cynical tend to become increasingly absent.

I do remember times when I was very present. I was in Japan, making films and falling in love with Kazko Nozaki. She'd made an immediate hit on me because I recognized two things: She wanted very much to teach Bible classes and she was very fetching. That combination intrigued me to no end.

I recall specifically an afternoon at a pizza place, one of the first times we had opportunity to be alone together. We'd just run from a subway exit in the rain. Sitting across from her I read the colors in her flushed face. I voyaged into her dark eyes. The pizza was hot. But time froze while I took in her brown trench coat, windblown hair, smooth hands.

I was very present. Unfortunately we human beings are not able to sustain that kind of intensity. We can't keep on gazing at the beloved forever; we have to blink. Our emotions can't remain at a peak; we have to rest.

Being sated is a common experience. Once I rushed through Disneyland with a wide-eyed younger cousin. We only had a few hours to take in pirates underground, whirling tea cups, Circlevision, junk food, crowds . . . Toward the end I was squinting at these delights through a headache. When I subscribed only to *National Geographic* and *Reader's Digest* I ate them up, once a month. Now I have to go through several magazines a week and my mind goes into an energy-saving mode as I flip the pages. There's just too much. I can't be present for it all.

But God is never sated. His capacity to absorb is infinite. He remains very present, surpassingly present.

He sustains an intensely caring gaze on all His beloved children. We hear assurances like "I notice every sparrow that falls in flight. The very hairs of your head are numbered."

When the One who transcends, who is More Than, focuses His presence so intensely in one human being, the result is expansion.

Beverly Hills, California. 1977.

AL KASHA TOLD his friends he had to be alone in order to create. What they didn't know was that he had to be alone in order to survive. Crowds terrified him. Out in a restaurant or at a supermarket he'd start to hyperventilate, his heart would palpitate, his hands perspire. The panic attacks would send him rushing home. Al had become agoraphobic, afraid to go out anywhere, a prisoner in his own home.

It all started after he made it big as a songwriter: thirteen gold albums, two academy awards. "I had created a life based on doing and having and achieving to the point where I had a nervous breakdown," Al recalled. Then fear closed in and began systematically constricting his life.

One morning when Al was "at the lowest ebb of my life" he flipped on the TV and caught a minister quoting the verse, "Perfect love casts out all fear." Those words struck deep. He listened intently as the minister talked about God's kind of acceptance.

Al Kasha began weeping and crying out to God. He saw a white light and heard a voice say, "I love you and you are My son."

That message took about twenty-four hours to sink in. But when it did Al left his house to see his wife, then separated from him, and daughter. "I got in the car," he said, "and I did not have the shakes and I was not perspiring. God had healed me."

Al continued venturing out in wider and wider circles and found that God's love had indeed cast out all his fear. Eventually he began traveling around the country, speaking to groups about how to overcome phobias.

THE VERY PRESENT GOD was able to reach inside Al Kasha's very particular fears and then help him break through to a wider world. It's as if Al's painfully compressed life expanded in God's omnipresence.

God stretches boxed-in lives because He communicates His own unrestricted presence. God pushes people outward; they get out of the tangle of their own problems and into helping others. The very present God touches us accurately and specifically. We are freed to venture out beyond our usual ruts under His reassuring gaze.

God's reach goes very wide and also very deep. I discovered that one day while writing a letter home to my brother from Japan, not long after I had fallen for the aforementioned Kazko Nozaki over pizza. Just as things had really started to warm up, Kazko was assigned to work at an English School in Himeji, an hour by bullet train from where I worked in Osaka. Parting resulted in the customary sweet sorrow and our bond had grown more conspicuous.

I'd finally found a girl spiritually alive. The Word acted in her life. God resonated. I could see it in her animated face as we talked about Him.

Not wanting to let go of a good thing, I telephoned the Himeji English School a lot. To this day Kazko's voice on the phone brings back the longing I felt then. We were separate yet intensely together. I wanted my whole life intertwined with hers.

Then Jerry had written, telling me about Wittgenstein. My philosopher brother had discovered this Austrian who seemed to untie a lot of very old philosophical knots, or at least explain exactly why they were nonsensical. Because Jerry was into Wittgenstein I got into Wittgenstein. I had gone to the English bookstore, picked up a book on the man and his thought, and made a brave effort to follow his convoluted trail of concepts.

Then I wrote Jerry at his graduate school in Davis, California. And in writing the letter I felt totally identified with my brother, caught up in his intellectual struggles, identified with his longings. Faith, for him, was not an easy alternative.

There was of course a blood bond between us, a family history: wrestling in the yard, sessions of marathon Monopoly, help with homework. Our pasts intertwined. I felt very present with Jerry, especially in that foreign country. Distance from my roots had made me more aware of them.

As I wrote I felt myself stretching, mellowing. I realized at that moment I was totally present with two people very far apart. And they were so different: the hard abstraction of Jerry's philosophical pursuit in Davis, California; the soft excitement of Kazko's spiritual quest in Himeji, Japan. I felt completely given to both of them. The sense of occupying two separate worlds simultaneously threw everything around me into slow motion for a few minutes. I felt very alive.

That became for me a little taste of divine omnipresence. For in the end, we are really speaking of God's deep and wide heart. He is big-hearted. It's not some ideal that fills up the heavens and our innermost selves. It's not some cosmic force. It's a big heart. God possesses an infinite capacity to give of Himself.

Perhaps this is most visible in the joy the intensely present God imparts to those who draw near. That big heart beating close to us beats joyfully. There are no boundaries, no dark pockets, no reservations in God's heart. His delight reverberates clean and unbounded. As David, that shepherd psalming under the wide Canaan sky, put it: "In Thy presence is fulness of joy."

This joy of the Most High enables people to transcend; they experience much more than their surroundings should allow.

Kiev, U.S.S.R. 1930s.

MALCOLM MUGGERIDGE, British journalist, watched as his dream of a socialist kingdom of heaven on earth dissolved before his eyes. Gray, starving figures aimlessly padded the gray streets of Russia's cities at the height of the collectivization famine. True believers still sent out press releases describing bursting granaries and rosy-cheeked dairymaids in the Ukraine. But Malcolm could no longer speak.

So he went to listen instead, at an Easter service in Kiev's Orthodox Church. The place was packed. Standing in the congregation that slowly wedged its way toward the altar, Malcolm felt himself pressed against a stone pillar, scarcely able to move. But that's not what took his breath away.

He stared in awe at the "many gray, hungry faces, all luminous like an El Greco painting; and all singing." Malcolm listened as the compressed, reverent crowd lifted up hymns in praise of the ever-present Helper who alone could bring comfort, and he felt God near, near enough to touch. He was not just something spoken by the bearded priests up front, who chanted and swung their censers. He showed Himself specifically through one of the worshipers—"one of the gray faces, the grayest and most luminous of all."

Dallas. 1972.

WHILE EIGHTY THOUSAND TEENAGERS and college students yelling Jesus cheers in the Cotton Bowl certainly had an impact on me during Explo '72, it was two faces in particular that I remember to this day. I was walking toward my seat in the stadium through one of the upper-level entryways when I spotted an elderly couple standing there, pressed against the concrete wall, their faces lifted up, enraptured.

In one brief moment as I passed they painted an unforgettable portrait in my mind. The couple clung together and whispered, their joy electric between them. I wondered why they didn't go in and take a seat. Then I noticed both were blind. Unwilling to occupy a place in the crowded stadium a sighted person might want, they stood where they could hear those praises echoing big and bold. And they seemed to bless, without a word, every person who brushed past.

I have never seen faces say more. They were bright and tender, not at all the blank stares one might expect. Their rejoicing seemed so different from the easy happiness of the rest of us, jumping up toward heaven with youthful energy. Their praise had been carved out of isolation, but they were there exulting with us, transcending the dark.

Bowersville, Ohio. c. 1910.

WHEN NORMAN VINCENT PEALE was a boy he saw Dave —the town drunk, wife beater, vile mouth, and all-around holy terror—come forward in his father's church after a strongly evangelistic sermon. The man felt that God had come close to him and he was moved. "I was awed by the look on his face," Peale wrote, "a look of wonder and inexpressible joy. It is printed on my memory to this day."

Most of the upstanding folk in Bowersville were sure Dave's "conversion" wouldn't last. They couldn't fathom a renegade changing in a minute. But Peale tells us that it in fact lasted a lifetime: "He became literally a saint, a new man in Christ, and for half a century he blessed the lives of everyone who knew him."

THERE'S SOMETHING to that "inexpressible joy." It flashes forth when Someone big enough to maneuver the heavens into place over a manger focuses His transcendent being into the confines of a human heart.

PART V

Sovereign
Servant

GOD DOESN'T HAVE ANYBODY TO
PRAY TO SO HE'S GOT TO MIND
EVERYBODY ELSE'S BUSINESS.

from *Children's Letters to God*

13

KING OF KINGS

ROBERT MEELER BENT DOWN under a blazing sun to pick a mess of peas for supper and heard a voice booming out of the blue: "I want you to go preach."

The man jerked up and glanced around, sure someone was playing a joke on him. No sign of a soul. Puzzled, he ran to a hilltop rock and gazed around on miles of open farmland. Nobody in sight. No sound except a few birds chirping.

Robert concluded the Lord had called. But he had objections. Why ask a dirt-poor, illiterate farmer to preach? He couldn't even read the Bible. And he was just a new Christian.

For five years Robert managed to keep the call at bay. He kept busy, easy enough to do on a farm, and attended church infrequently.

But one day while burning off his fields for spring plowing he got caught in the fire. Dashing through a wall of flames, Robert yelled, "Lord, save me! Save me, and I'll do what You want!"

Robert recovered from his burns and decided to keep his promise. He began attending church faithfully and managed to memorize a good deal of Scripture just by listening hard. He could not yet preach but did "testify" for his Lord.

A couple of years passed and the church deacons

talked Robert into teaching an adult Sunday school class. He was still ashamed of his lack of education, but fellow church members gave him a lot of encouragement.

Robert's wife Nell read the lesson to him before each class, though there were many words she couldn't make out herself. After two years Robert felt frustrated. He needed schooling. But how was a codger in his fifties going to learn the alphabet with the kiddies?

One day he decided to will himself to read. He grabbed his Bible and stomped into the woods. Opening the Good Book under a pine tree, this farmer glared at the black marks filling the page. He concentrated on them till his head hurt, but nothing made sense.

Robert sobbed out his despair to God: "Lord, You know my misery. You know I'm trying to serve You. I want to do what You want me to do, but I don't know how. I need to read Your Word, but I can't. Dear God, help me!"

The farmer sat there crying and pleading for help until a feeling of peace came over him. He sensed that things would be all right.

That evening Robert sat listening to Nell read from the Bible. She stumbled over a word. Without thinking, Robert leaned over to look at the page and corrected her: "That's 'impoverished.' " Nell read on and then stumbled over another word. Robert took a look and pronounced, "Inhabitants."

The third time this happened Nell did a double take. Something strange was going on. "You know this Book better than I do," she said.

And suddenly Robert realized his wife was reading verses he had not memorized.

Trembling, he took the Bible from Nell and ran his eyes over the page. Every sentence made sense. He flipped page after page, picking up the magic of meaning from that mass of black letters. "I can read, Nell," he shouted incredulously. "I can read!"

The couple got down on their knees and gave thanks. Robert stayed up late that night, feasting his eyes and mind for the first time on the Word. He would continue feasting, and eventually become the preacher for a church in Alabama.

ROBERT ENCOUNTERED the call of a Sovereign. This was not a God who merely made suggestions—He gave orders. He wanted His man, illiterate or not. He overruled all the odds against that. Calling without question. And making it possible.

It was the same God who called Moses out from his shepherding in Midian to lead Israel out of Egypt. Moses tried to put off the call, sure that God had the wrong man. How could he become Jehovah's spokesman before mighty Pharaoh? He didn't think he could ever become an authority figure. He pleaded inadequacies: "I am slow of speech and slow of tongue."

God answered, "Who has made man's mouth? Is it not I, the Lord? Now then go, and I, even I . . . will teach you what you are to say."

The Sovereign overruled shortcomings. He wanted His man, tongue-tied or not. Reticent Moses, united with this King of Heaven, did become a leader, and found the gumption to stand up to the most powerful monarch of his time.

God is a sovereign. That's an aspect of His character easily overlooked. Occupying no visible throne, working principally behind the scenes, He can appear short on authority. We expect God to be nice, of course, the nicest being in the universe. And nice people don't make waves, they aren't noisy. With our limited human models to work from, we sometimes unwittingly paint a picture of a great wimp in the skies, minding His manners, always asking permission.

But God, in Scripture, is no timid monarch; He makes waves and raises His voice on occasion. He is more than just a deity for the quietly pious. He is also a charismatic leader of the hyperactive and strong-willed. They find in Him much to admire and follow. Those who've followed Him wholeheartedly, from Paul to Martin Luther to Billy Graham, find themselves caught up in the ever-expanding plans of a Mover and Shaker.

The Sovereign Lord leads people on great quests and missions: Hudson Taylor in the forbidden interior of China, David Livingston deep in unexplored Africa, William Booth in London's slums during the industrial revolution. God is leader enough to move people into such ventures.

Scripture defines Him as "the blessed and only Sovereign, the King of kings and Lord of lords." He reigns, we tremble. He is enthroned from of old above the cherubim, the earth shakes. He rides in the heavens, the earth is His footstool. All the silver and gold are His. He is clothed with splendor and majesty; the monarch to end all monarchs. Biblical writers would have us believe that this Lord makes all other rulers petty by comparison.

Egypt.   c. 1290 B.C.

RAMESES II COULD SEE no reason in the world why he should play second fiddle to Jehovah, the God of his slaves. When Moses marched into his palace and passed on a command from the God of Israel—"Let My people go"—Rameses replied, "Who is the Lord, that I should obey him?"

Pharaohs were not accustomed to taking orders from anyone. They were regarded as gods made flesh by their people and could use up countless human lives in the building of heroic mausoleums, the pyramids, to ensure an equally honored place in the hereafter. So after listening to Moses' impertinence, the god-king exercised his absolute sovereignty. He ordered the work of the Hebrew slaves doubled; now they must gather their own straw for their already back-breaking quota of bricks. Rameses wanted these uppity foreigners to feel who was really in charge—down to their aching bones.

Pharaoh was playing hardball. The King of Kings played back. He commanded Moses to confront Rameses on the banks of the Nile. There, in front of Pharaoh's retinue, Jehovah's servant lifted his staff and struck the water. The Nile turned to blood; Jehovah made His point: Osiris, the Nile god, was worshiped as the "source of life" by the Egyptians; now every living thing in its waters was killed.

But Pharaoh hung tough. His was a will hardened by absolute power. He ordered his magicians to do a little trick. They turned water red, nothing to it. As his subjects dug desperately for fresh water, Rameses pretended nothing had happened.

Jehovah wasn't going to back down. Again He ordered, "Let my people go." Pharaoh refused. Now Jehovah struck repeatedly. Several other creatures deified in this highly polytheistic culture were turned into plagues. Frogs, gnats, swarms of insects, and locusts afflicted the Egyptians.

"Let my people go," Jehovah persisted. Pharaoh stood proud and stubborn as his kingdom crumbled. Cattle died, boils broke out, a heavy hail fell. "Let my people go."

Finally the King of Kings blotted out the mighty sun god, Ra. Egyptians groped about in a terrifying midday darkness. The night lasted for three days. Pharaoh still didn't get the point; he just kept whistling in the dark.

Rameses continued whistling a defiant tune until his army was swallowed up by a sea that had just obediently parted for his fleeing slaves.

The despot had met more than his match. He

never dreamed there was a God who could really shove him up against the wall, One whose authority over-shadowed his own. Two unshakable wills clashed. In the end, one ruled in the heavens, one lay at the bottom of the Red Sea, and the people were let go.

Nineveh, Assyria. c. 850 B.C.

JONAH, AN EXTREMELY reluctant Hebrew prophet who somehow carried a grudge against God's penchant for mercy, found himself on the streets of Nineveh. He walked about warning that the Sovereign God was going to smash the city in forty days.

Jonah believed that these Assyrians, of all people on earth, least deserved to be warned. And he had a point. After all, who could like haughty Assyria, most militaristic of states, gloating in its captives skinned alive?

Well, wouldn't you know it—Nineveh got religion. The warning from a God ruling over all really sank in. Instant revival. Citizens everywhere were springing to repentance and belief.

Then the incredible happened. The bloodthirsty monarch of this bloodthirsty empire "rose from his throne, took off his royal robes, covered himself with sackcloth and sat down in the dust." He also issued a decree calling his countrymen to fast, seek God urgent-ly, turn from evil and violence, and hope for a divine change of heart.

Hard-as-nails Nineveh had met its match. The King of Kings humbled the violent. And then of course he relented and gave the city its reprieve.

Babylon. c. 580 B.C.

NEBUCHADNEZZAR, PROUD BUILDER of the neo-Babylonian empire, was no pushover either. A brilliant military strategist, success had attended his every venture. He wined and dined in golden Babylon surrounded by the treasures of conquered kingdoms. Bronze vessels from Armenia, carved ivory furniture from Syria, and precious stones from Egypt all added to the splendor of his palace-fortress by the Euphrates. "Yes men" disguised as prophets massaged his ego with moral approval. Eager servants satisfied their monarch's every whim.

But then Jehovah tapped him on the shoulder with a haunting glimpse of the beyond. In a dream Nebuchadnezzar saw a statue of gold, silver, bronze and iron. He couldn't sleep; this had to mean something. Only a Hebrew youth named Daniel, gifted with divine insight, could tell him.

Nebuchadnezzar saw that he was part of a succession of kingdoms: Babylon, Medo-Persia, Greece and Rome, which would climax in an indestructible kingdom of the Sovereign Lord.

The despot was impressed, but not fully persuaded. He was not yet ready to acknowledge history moving by providence in someone else's direction. His own splendor loomed too large.

Out on the plain of Dura he constructed a massive, ninety-foot-high statue covered head-to-toe with gold. This was Nebuchadnezzar's revised edition of the revelation he'd received through Daniel. He planned to make what he thought was an improvement on God's plan. Why not extend the gold of Babylon clear through to the end of time?

Nebuchadnezzar gathered all the officials from his vast empire. They made quite a spectacle spread over the sands of Dura in their bright uniforms. The royal band assembled, with flute, harp, pipes and lyre. On a given signal the band was to strike up a triumphant hymn to Nebuchadnezzar, and the thousands of distinguished guests were to fall prostrate before the statue of gold.

The king wanted to make a statement about the

eternity of Babylon loud and clear, a divine plan modified by acclamation. Surely he and this Hebrew deity could work out something reasonable. Perhaps Babylon and the kingdom of heaven could form a merger.

As the band struck up its hymn there were only three sour notes: Shadrach, Meshach, and Abednego. They would not bow on cue. This conspicuous irreverence enraged the despot. Discovering that these men were friends of Daniel, he tried to reason with them. He also pointed to the blazing furnaces nearby. But the three Hebrews were unmoved, and their flabbergasted king heated up his fires and had them thrown in.

Nebuchadnezzar was sure he'd ruled out all further opposition. But Jehovah overruled him, not willing that his protesting servants be silenced so quickly. The King of Kings stood with them in the flames. They emerged unsinged from the blazing furnace.

Now Nebuchadnezzar was really impressed. He blessed the God of Shadrach, Meshach, and Abednego. He saw there was a God in heaven who alone is worthy of worship.

The King of Kings had bent an autocratic will, but still it had not broken. One last citadel in this proud man's soul remained unyielded.

One day the king was strolling on the roof of his royal residence. He looked out over his capital, resplendent with palaces, broad boulevards and elegant temples. The seven-storied ziggurat and great temple of Marduk lay directly before him. His hanging gardens were one of the seven wonders of the world.

Before this cityscape Nebuchadnezzar exulted: "Is this not the great Babylon I have built as a royal residence, by my mighty power and for the glory of my majesty?"

The king had acknowledged in principle God's sovereignty, but in practice he was still very much the absolute monarch, still the center.

As Nebuchadnezzar gloated, something inside him snapped. The king lost his sanity. The mind that had drawn up into itself suddenly collapsed. "He was driven away from people and ate grass like cattle."

Crawling out in the fields, Nebuchadnezzar finally saw the barrenness of the self-sufficient life. Jehovah finally got through all the way. Babylon's king realized his utter dependence on the King of Kings. As he himself described it: "I . . . raised my eyes toward heaven, and my sanity was restored . . . I honored and glorified him who lives forever."

THERE WERE THREE major powers in the ancient world: Egypt, Assyria and Babylon. In various ways God showed Himself the Sovereign over each of them. In an illiterate era, His actions spoke volumes to Israel's contemporaries. He made it plain that He was indeed King of Kings and Lord of Lords.

This God still rules. Heavy-handed confrontations are the exception, but He still has ways of exercising His sovereignty, usually by bending unruly events into a more benevolent shape. Like any king, He has vested interests to look after. At times God seems to command circumstances quite directly, enabling His work to go forward on the earth.

Bangladesh. 1963.

SURGEON VIGGO OLSEN walked into the surveyor's office in the town of Cox's Bazar and laid the necessary papers on his desk. He wanted badly to start construction on a hospital to meet the desperate needs of the Bangladeshi people. He'd just watched hundreds die of typhoid and cholera following a devastating typhoon, because no vaccine was available.

It was monsoon season. As rain beat on the office roof, the chief surveyor chuckled knowingly at Olsen's request. "It will be impossible for us to survey tomorrow because of the rain," he said.

"But we *must* survey tomorrow," Olsen answered, "Our whole hospital work depends upon getting this survey done immediately."

"But it is impossible to survey in such rain," the official insisted. "It has been raining like this for days, and it will probably rain for days to come."

Olsen had recently seen other obstacles to the project removed in what seemed very providential ways. He'd had many occasions to excitedly thank his Sovereign God. But he still could hardly believe himself say: "Don't worry about the rain; we are God's men doing God's work, and He will take care of the rain. We will be back at eight-thirty in the morning for the survey."

That night the surgeon and a companion prayed urgently that their heavenly King would stop the rain —all the while listening to the steady downpour outside.

They awoke to the sound of rain pelting the roof. The two men prayed "as though our lives depended on it." They then proceeded to the surveyor's office, walking under two large umbrellas and wearing heavy raincoats. The chief surveyor was there waiting with a big "I told you so" smile.

Olsen said matter-of-factly, "Gentlemen, get your chains and other tools. It's time to get started." The chief surveyor and his colleagues thought the surgeon was mad. They protested loudly. It took a lot of pressure and persuasion before a surveying crew piled into a jeep and started the thirty-two-mile journey toward Chittagong.

As they drove, the rains increased in intensity. Blinding sheets poured down, forcing the driver to slow to a crawl. The surveyors smirked at each other. After twenty-six miles of this, Olsen's lips went dry; his heart thumped hard. He prayed silently from the depths: "O Father, will You help us now? Will You uphold Your own name and do something to help us for Your project's sake and for Jesus' sake? Amen."

The inscrutable sky kept dumping it by the bucketfuls for a few more minutes and then abruptly stopped. The surveyors stopped smiling. Olsen looked up to see a small patch of blue appear in the endless gray expanse overhead. It seemed an eloquent and authoritative word from the Sovereign.

Half an hour after arriving at the hospital site, the gently sloping land had drained enough for the surveyors to demarcate twenty-five acres, and install concrete corner posts. Mission accomplished. Thank you, Lord.

THE KING INTERVENES. And His subjects find His boldness contagious. With such a Lord around, life isn't set in cement. There's always the possibility of an authoritative act coming in to disarm danger or nudge aimless events onto an orderly track. This God is capable of turning things upside down. One of His most attractive characteristics is His habit of working good out of evil, blessing out of calamity. He makes things work out for His followers—usually with a subtle touch.

Ravensbrook, Germany. 1944.

CORRIE AND BETSIE TEN BOOM, prisoners 66729 and 66730, were led into Barracks 28, past rows of worktables and into a large dormitory room filled with great square tiers stacked three high. Here they would sleep, squeezed among hundreds of other inmates at the concentration camp.

Fighting claustrophobia, Corrie and Betsie squirmed into an upper deck and found their assigned places on the reeking straw. Suddenly Corrie jerked up, striking her head on a cross-slat. Something had pinched her leg. The two sisters scrambled off the tier and dropped down in a narrow aisle. Moving to a patch of light they saw them—fleas! "The place is swarming with them!" Corrie groaned. "Betsie, how can we live in such a place?"

The insects were the last straw for Corrie. She and her sister had been starved and humiliated. They'd endured filth, cold and back-breaking labor. They'd witnessed unforgettable cruelties. And now to be infested with fleas . . . Corrie wondered how she could go on.

Betsie had an answer. She'd read it in the Bible that morning—in First Thessalonians, where Paul urged believers to "give thanks in all circumstances; for this is the will of God . . ."

Betsie suggested they thank God for every single thing about their new barracks. Corrie stared around at the dark, foul-smelling room and couldn't generate much gratitude. Betsie thought of two things to thank God for. They'd been assigned to this place together and they'd managed to hang on to their Bible. Corrie murmured assent.

Clutching the Bible, Betsie prayed, "Thank You for all the women, here in this room, who will meet You in these pages. Thank You for the very crowding here. Since we're packed so close, thank You that many more will hear!" Corrie grudgingly murmured assent.

Betsie continued serenely: "Thank You for the fleas and for . . ."

This was too much for Corrie. "Betsie," she interrupted, "there's no way even God can make me grateful for a flea."

But Betsie insisted, " 'Give thanks in *all* circumstances.' It doesn't say 'in pleasant circumstances.' Fleas are part of this place where God has put us."

There in the narrow aisle Corrie bit her lip and thanked God for fleas.

Corrie and Betsie did find many women in Barracks 28 eager to hear from those pages. Each evening after receiving a cup of turnip soup they'd make their way to the rear of the dormitory where a bare light bulb cast a yellow circle on the wall, and they would read from the Bible. Soon a large group of women were gathering to listen.

The worship service broadened. Meetings might include a recital of the Magnificat in Latin by Roman Catholics, a whispered hymn sung by Lutherans, a liturgical chant by Eastern Orthodox women. At the close of each clandestine gathering the ten Booms always read from the Scriptures. They translated their Dutch verses into German, and then eager listeners packed together on the tiers would pass the precious words back in French, Polish, Russian, Czech. To some it seemed a small preview of Heaven.

Night after night the meetings grew larger and yet no guard ever came near. So many wanted to join that the sisters started a second service after roll call. Guards patrolled everywhere at the camp; half-a-dozen always paced about in the center room of the barracks, yet for some reason none ever entered this dormitory. The women couldn't understand it.

One day Betsie discovered exactly why they could enjoy their island of religious freedom. There was a mixup about sock sizes in her knitting group. They'd asked the supervisor to come and settle it. But she refused to step through the door into the room. None of the guards would either. They said, "That place is crawling with fleas!"

WE MAY NOT SEE proof of it very often, but God is a Sovereign Lord. He can be discreet, gently nudging good from evil. Or he can command unequivocally, shoving blessing through the clenched jaws of a curse. The bottom line is that He's in charge. Only *His* commands will stand in the end. Life isn't quite as random as we think, even on this rebellious planet where God confines Himself to the tactical strikes of the saboteur. Through the chaos and meaninglessness, patterns emerge—usually seen best in individual lives. I, for one, have found it exhilarating to detect that Sovereign in charge.

Osaka, Japan. 1975. Journal entries.

Friday, March 14

Should I stay another year in Japan? I have to make a decision. Bible classes and friends are great, but can I take another year of English drills at the language school? Having read *God's Smuggler*-type adventures, I'm inspired to try for direct guidance from God. I'm a bit tired of the old God-opening-doors approach which often boils down to whatever happens, happens. So I try special prayer. For an hour I quieted body and mind, listening.

March 29

The main drawback to staying another term has been the "insignificant" tedium of English classes. But I've come to see them in a different light. Shouldn't I be willing to accomplish the "unimportant" for people if my "real vocation" of Christian service is to have any meaning? Why should I be ready to act as a servant only in giving the glorious Good News and disdain serving these people's need to speak English?

After another period of meditating on the Word and listening quietly today, God's guidance crystallized. No audible voice broke through but the issue came clear. I have dreams of writing and making music—the big time in the States. Well why not start here as a servant? Be happy to lead choruses in Bible classes here, God may have bigger plans later. The prevailing idea in my head, anyway, was: do the work at hand, be a servant here. So I've decided to stay.

It doesn't seem like there will be any change in my work next term, I'll still be teaching English and Bible. But I felt like thanking God for the new phase of ministry He'll create. Looking back I see that every time God led me clearly through a decision about where to go, he opened up a new level of witness. I wanted to go to a Christian college, not the wasteland of Western Illinois University, but He pointed me rather decisively to the latter. And there, to my surprise, I discovered a great new world of discipleship with Campus Crusade.

So, feeling like we're on a roll, I thanked God ahead of time for what He's going to do.

August 18

Bruce Bauer found out about my Mass Media studies in college and has a proposal. He'd like me to make films for his evangelistic meetings. Plop, right on my lap. Wow, making films has been the big someday dream for so long. And now here in Japan when I least expected it. . . .

This is the new phase of ministry I thanked God for by faith (presumption?) a few months ago. It's come out of nowhere. Right after Bruce left and my head was spinning I felt like someone who finally sights a sub-atomic particle he knew was there before only by mathematical calculation. Pretty heady stuff.

How clearly God leads. First removing my chronic groan about teaching English by convicting me that I must be a servant first. Then through quiet meditation He gave me further reasons for staying. And finally the decision was confirmed by the fact that I am still the only contact "Chestie" and Rika have with Christianity.

Bonanza. This kind of well-made-novel existence impels one to exclaim, "Listen Lord, if there's anything at all on your mind, PLEASE let me know."

14

BURDEN BEARER

Little Grassy Lake, Illinois. 1973.

HERDING EIGHT FEISTY adolescents through the routine of morning inspection, craft classes, kitchen duty, and campfire took all the energy and patience I could muster. Sometimes it took more. It was a constant struggle to preserve a semblance of order in my explosive little troop that summer at Little Grassy Lake Camp.

I worked as a cabin counselor. Nothing in my college classes had prepared me for the challenge of mothering squirmy urchins. But our goals were clear. We were supposed to make the living Christ real to these boys, many of whom had grown up with only a vaguely forbidding religious presence in their homes.

Each morning before breakfast all the campers filed out of their cabins toward the parade ground for a short worship. The camp director, standing tall in his immaculate uniform, usually gave a short talk on some Christian virtue. Then we divided by cabins into prayer groups.

Most of the kids in my circle bowed their heads, shuffled their feet, and mumbled a few words of greeting at the Lord above. They weren't that well acquainted, but, having been persuaded that reverence was the better part of valor, figured it was the decent thing to do.

All except Alan. During prayer he stood up straight, arms folded, communicating his disapproval of the whole affair. Every morning it was the same. Something about petitioning the Lord bothered Alan. As the rest bowed their heads, he always glanced around impatiently and tried to look as bored as possible.

I wanted to find out what could have made the boy dislike religion so early in life, but Alan was aloof. A strong-and-silent type at the age of ten. On occasion I could get him to talk about his trail rides on the camp minibikes, but he showed enthusiasm for little else.

One day during free period our group was out practicing for a softball game. The boys were lined up in the outfield catching flies. I smacked one over Alan's head into some bushes behind right field. He couldn't come up with the ball so I ran out to help him look. We searched through the undergrowth for several minutes but couldn't spot it.

Then I realized this might be a golden opportunity. "Hey Alan," I suggested, "let's pray and see if God can help us find the ball." He responded with a languid "Okay."

Alan bowed his head ever-so-slightly this time, and I said a short prayer. We turned for another look through the bushes and quickly came up with the lost ball. I tried to get Alan excited: "Hey, that was great! God really helped us find it." The boy was glad we could go on with our practice but I wasn't sure whether our "luck" in retrieving the softball had really registered. The incident seemed quickly forgotten.

The next day at lunch I found myself with a few moments of peace and quiet after my kids had raced off to their swimming classes. It was nice to be able to eat without simultaneously acting as referee, janitor and crisis prevention expert.

As I lingered over my spaghetti Alan came rushing up to the table, his face animated with an uncharacteristic excitement. "Guess what," he burst out, "I got my swimming honor. We took our test today. I prayed that God would help me and I did good. He really helped me. The teacher said I did good." Alan proudly showed me his signed certificate.

I pounded the boy on the back and congratulated him on his successful collaboration with the Lord—trying not to show my surprise. I hadn't expected Alan to take up the challenge of prayer so quickly. I really hadn't expected it at all. Now his eyes sparkled with a great discovery.

I spent the last two days of camp in the infirmary, down with the flu, wondering what was happening with the kids. Just before boarding the bus home they came in to say goodby. Alan was beaming. The previous night at a special campfire he had responded to the camp chaplain's invitation to receive Christ. "And I'm going to be baptized too as soon as I get home," he announced proudly.

After the buses rumbled off and left the camp strangely quiet I thought a lot about Alan and his joyful Yes to God. He had so completely filtered out all our recommendations of the Lord's greatness. But when God appeared as a servant, Alan came to life. Lying there in the infirmary I was very thankful for a God handy amid the minor details of life—a softball in the bushes, thrashing limbs in a swimming pool.

GOD HUMBLED HIMSELF to woo a stubborn kid. He'd been quite unobtrusive. No one noticed any miracles. But He presented Himself to the defiant as a servant, helpful in what must seem from a sovereign distance to be trivialities.

Most kings would expect their subjects to yield allegiance in a dignified fashion, won over by majesty and glory. It would be most fitting if people came to bow before the Sovereign of Heaven because of lofty spiritual truths or high ideals. But that rarely takes place. Usually we come running in scared by some disaster, or crawl in after having exhausted every other possibility. Still, God takes us any way we come. Pride never gets in His way. Approaching the Almighty for petty, selfish reasons, we find a gracious welcome. God is willing to woo on the bended knee of a servant.

It's remarkable how long He's willing to stay on that knee, even before the obnoxious.

Wilderness of Zin.　c. 1270 B.C.

SECOND MONTH, fifteenth day from the exodus. There it was again. The same old chorus rising in the desert from a long stream of Hebrews, aptly named the children of Israel. They were whining their way to the promised land. Jehovah, the fiery authority of Mount Sinai, had to listen as the stumbling procession wailed: "We used to sit around pots of meat and eat all we wanted. Why did we come out here to starve to death?"

Instead of thundering against their chronic grumbling, God patiently replied, "I'll rain down bread from heaven for you." The next morning a layer of dew lay over the rocky wilderness. When the dew burnt off, it left a "fine flake-like thing" on the ground which looked a bit like frost. The stuff tasted good. Israel had their bread from heaven: manna.

Manna began to appear morning after morning everywhere the children of Israel camped. They were assured of sustenance even in the desolate wilderness; all the people had to do was go out and gather a basketful of heavenly bread after sunrise.

But the miracle of daily bread got monotonous. The Israelites grew tired of manna. Again their characteristic grumbling ascended: "If only we had meat! We remember cucumbers, melons, leeks, onions and garlic in Egypt. Now all we see is manna."

Jehovah replied, "You're going to eat meat for a whole month until it comes out your nostrils." Then a sea wind drove huge flocks of quail into the camp and the people gathered them in piles three feet deep. Over the next few weeks they gorged themselves sick.

THAT'S THE WAY it went for forty years in the wilderness. The childish chosen ones griping about every discomfort. God the patient provider seeing to their needs. In the end Moses could tell the Israelites, "He has watched over your journey through this vast desert. These forty years the Lord your God has been with you, and you have not lacked anything."

When we see God faithfully care for the obnoxious like this, it's difficult to conceive of Him as a potentate on the throne. He's at our feet, the longsuffering servant.

Most anywhere. Year after year.

I BLEW IT AGAIN. All those promises to the Lord just dissolved under pressure. No backbone, no guts. I stared gloomily out the window at two autumn-bare trees and my motley row of laundry on the line. The other guys in our apartment were getting ready for work; I needed to find a hole to crawl into.

After they left I started praying out my misery to God. I said I was very sorry. I asked for forgiveness. But every plea was something I had uttered countless times before. The same words, the same thoughts. I felt like such a fake. Year after year I came with the same worn-out whining, the same monotonous litany of failure.

God should have had enough by now. At best He should have been yawning. But I did not find His back turned; He was not indifferent at all. Continuing in my hackneyed prayer I felt some encouragement. Old promises came back to me dressed a bit differently. I found a new foothold in familiar verses.

Reviving a bit, I turned to the life of Christ and started reading. He was praying in Gethsemane in preparation for the big showdown. I noticed again how loaded His every word was with meaning, and how He expressed concern for His disciples in the midst of His greatest ordeal.

I felt the call of that perfect life again. My will picked itself off the floor and stood at attention. I was warmed by hope. God had lifted me up, one more time.

LIKE A LOT of people who look back on their lives and trace an embarrassingly lengthy pattern of sin, I am impressed by God's patience. He stuck by me all those years, through my thick and thin of repentance. I did feel badly when I blew it, but I never once sensed that God was fed up. He always remained close by to bind up my wounds after I had slashed myself. He always managed to get through the scar tissue.

He was a patient servant to me—a butler standing by ready with immaculate white cloth while the householder at supper makes a mess of the formal dining room. How can God bear to keep serving us while we do our boorish worst? He's more forbearing than we can imagine.

Most servants want to graduate at some point, step up to something more meaningful than waiting on people. Acts of service are seen as means to an end. The prospect of always being at someone else's beck-and-call fills most of us with horror.

But God seems to exult in serving. He advertises Himself as One who opens His hand and satisfies the desire of every living thing. He does not assist mere mortals grudgingly; He's eager to serve, He's here to serve. People sense that eagerness when God involves them in His acts as gracious provider.

Pacific Beach, Washington. 1973.

ROBERT FOSS KNEW that something was troubling his Aunt Lana; she kept staring at the wall silently in her room. Polio had left her crippled twenty-four years before, but Robert didn't think she was brooding over that. Aunt Lana was an outward-looking woman with a firm grip on the life of the spirit.

Finally Robert asked if there was anything he could do. She told him about a picture that had come into her mind a few days before: sand, rocks and a smooth body of water. The picture kept coming back, intruding on her thoughts and prayers.

"I have a feeling that the picture comes from the Lord," Aunt Lana explained. "He's trying to tell me something. But what?"

Robert helped his aunt take the picture apart piece by piece. After a little detective work, they concluded it represented a quiet cove up north near the Quinault Indian reservation. Both were now eager to go check it out. Robert's grandmother suggested that, since they were heading up toward the reservation, they drop off some old clothes she'd been saving.

Aunt Lana rolled out in her wheelchair to her specially modified car, and Robert deposited a pile of clothes in the back seat.

They drove up the coast past storm-sculptured rocks, creek canyons and turbulent breakers. Nothing clicked until they reached Point Grenville in the Quinault reservation. Aunt Lana stopped the car and shouted, "Quick, Bob, over there! Run to the beach." Robert ran down to the sand, circled around some rocks, and beheld a scene just as Aunt Lana had described it.

"It's there!" he said breathlessly as he got back to the car. Aunt Lana hugged and kissed him. "You didn't see anything odd?" She asked. Robert hadn't. They waited; Aunt Lana prayed. But nothing else happened.

Finally they decided to go ahead and take their load of clothes to a certain Indian family. When they drove up to a small house painted canary yellow with a blue stripe around the middle, a very old grandmother stepped out. "You've come," she said happily. "I've been expecting you."

Robert and Aunt Lana looked at each other. "You were expecting us?"

Then the old woman poured out a story about trouble in the family, men out of work, a relative in jail, hunger, lack of warm clothing for her many grandchildren. One day when her need and feeling of helplessness had been greatest she went down to the beach. She walked aimlessly past the rocks where great waves splashed. "Then I came to a place where the ocean is more quiet and the wind is very kind and there I talk to God. 'Please God,' I say, 'tell someone to bring help. Not for me, God—for the little ones.' "

Robert and Aunt Lana discovered that this woman had gone to the very same cove that Aunt Lana had seen so vividly, and they learned that she had made her earnest petition on the same day and hour when the picture first came into Lana's mind.

After they had delivered their clothes, greeted a crowd of children, and waved goodby, they heard the grandmother say, "God is taking care, God is taking care."

Osaka, Japan. 1975.

SOMETIMES THE SCRIPTURES drive home a point and you want to do something about it. Early in the morning, staring out my window at the bonzai tree, I was moved to pray for something to happen. I'd just read some pointed verses on encouragement and building up one another. Tired of that amorphous goal of being nice, of sliding through days without observable ripple, I felt an urge to take God from my devotions out into the next sixteen waking hours; somewhere surely there must be a specific rendezvous with His will.

So I said, "Lord lead me to someone I can really help today." It was not your everyday nod toward goodness. I wanted to be aimed at a target.

I went through my English classes as usual. Then we had our staff meeting. Afterward a teacher named Peggy stopped me in the hallway. "I need to talk to you," she said with unsettling directness. "Can we go somewhere?"

We went to an unoccupied classroom. There she spilled the beans. Peggy felt like a fake, didn't know why she was there as a missionary. She unleashed on me a flood of insecurity and inadequacy, hinting that her family life had been raw on the edges. The English teacher dissolved into a hurting, fearful child.

She'd been perceived by the rest of us as a loud, graceless type. Not the easiest to like. Now I saw deeper.

Nothing like this had ever happened to me before. I had not been much of a listener or shoulder to cry on. Just the old male cliché: quiet, self-sufficient, content with work and an occasional game of football.

Now I was so excited about having reached that rendezvous with the person God wanted me to help that I did become all ears. I did try to understand weakness. And I managed to offer a few suggestions on how to acquire a stable spiritual life.

With time, other earfuls would follow from other rendezvous (like the one with Sonya). Because in that providential meeting God's eagerness to serve became contagious. I sensed it deeply. He was someone just standing around with the answers or waving the flag of righteousness over people's heads. He was anxious to help. He was humbly, patiently there for His children's needs.

GOD MOVES PEOPLE into servanthood. Out of wheel-chairs, out of male disabilities, we are propelled along by His enthusiasm for service. God's inclination to give Himself away comes from having so much to give.

The Bible presents Him as a Servant who prepares a banquet table for us in the presence of our enemies and fills our cup till it overflows. He stores up good-ness to bestow; we feast on the abundance of His house.

This God makes promises almost compulsively. He longs for us to test His generosity. Bring in the tithes and offerings, He says, and "I will open for you the windows of heaven, and pour out for you a blessing until there is no more need."

San Jose, California. 1980.

MY OLD FILM PARTNER Mark was going back to Japan with his wife Akemi. They were going to be indepen-dently self-supporting—no church structure to keep them going. But they had that telltale fire in the eyes.

While we were up visiting them at his parents' home, my wife, Kazko, felt we should do something. I'd just started a real job. How about giving them one hundred dollars to get started? She was confident that's just what we should do.

I gulped, not quite overwhelmed yet with the spirit of generosity. I'm usually a little slow in that area. A hundred bucks is a good chunk that leaves a hole behind. But I couldn't turn away from Kazko's glowing look, so we made our initial donation.

The next day, maybe two days later, the manager called from the apartment complex where we'd just rented. Could we use some furniture? Could we!? We had little besides suitcases to put in the apartment.

After driving back down south we discovered that the manager had a nice couch, end table, coffee table, lamps, double bed, dresser with mirror, two side dress-ers, and a single bed—all for a hundred dollars. The whole apartment almost furnished just like that. Later we learned that the furniture had been available for some time. But for some reason the manager called us.

OURS WAS A CLEAN GIFT, no strings attached. Fortunately we didn't know enough at the time to fall into the give-to-get trap. Through this experience and other encounters with the Provider, we sensed God's eagerness to amplify generosity. It's almost as if He gets carried away. There's a cliché loose called "You can't outgive God." It's a cliché because it proved true so often. God responds to the echo of that essential part of Himself, the Servant.

All this giving, this humility and graciousness, this patience add up to one thing: a Servant who is capable of carrying us. Whatever our troubles, burdens, or bents, He can sustain the load.

Tegel, Germany. January 10, 1945.

IN A LETTER to his wife, statesman and jurist Helmuth James, Count von Moltke, expressed amazement at the "high spirits" in which God had sustained him. He was about to be executed by the Nazis, yet he found himself pondering his last twenty-four hours not in terror but with a sense of blessedness.

Even at the trial when the president of the "People's Court" roared at him and he knew there could be only one verdict, James had felt secure. He wrote: "It was just as it is written in Isaiah 43:2—'When thou passest through the waters, I will be with thee; and through the rivers, they shall not overflow thee.' "

James believed that God had been close, guiding him "firmly and clearly" during the last two days. "I am so full of thanks," the condemned man wrote, "that there is actually no room for anything else."

He felt grateful for the last visit with his wife which assured him she was standing fast, and for the opportunity to put all his affairs in order. He realized that public censure had enabled him to let loose of all pride and rely more wholeheartedly on God's mercy and forgiveness. He'd been able to put the anguish of parting and fear of death behind him and now was "endowed with faith, hope, and love, all this in a plenitude truly lavish."

James recalled with satisfaction the decisive pronouncement at the trial: "Count Moltke, Christianity and we National Socialists have one thing in common, and one thing only: we claim the whole man."

So many different events had conspired together to enable him to come to this point as a whole Christian man. "At the very moment when there was danger of my being drawn into active preparations for the coup I was taken out of it," he had written, "So that I am free and remain free of any connection with the use of violence. In addition, God had implanted in me that socialistic trait which freed me, although owner of a great estate, from any suspicion of representing vested interests." And though he was a Protestant, his friendship with Catholics was well-known.

Because of all this, James told his wife that he stood before the Nazi judge "not as a Protestant, not as a landed proprietor, not as a nobleman, not as a Prussian, not as a German—but as a Christian and nothing else."

Feeling greatly comforted, James walked off to his execution.

Camden County, Missouri. September 15, 1977.

JOY SWIFT SAT in a motel room trying to erase that terrible date, two days earlier, when she had arrived home to find ambulances and police cars surrounding her house and her four children murdered. The hours since then had been a blur of police interrogations, newspaper headlines, and searing pain.

Joy had to be alone. She sat on the floor facing the wall, closed her eyes and plummeted into her feelings. "I felt like an empty fifty-five gallon drum, cold and hollow," Joy recalled. "The real me was a tiny speck inside the drum. This tiny speck was screaming for answers, but its words only echoed back in the cold, empty space."

This young, very broken woman silently screamed for God to hear her. She told him she couldn't live without the kids. They were her whole life. She begged Him to bring them back.

Her voice felt like an echo inside the steel drum. Then the echo faded. "A hole was punched in the side of the drum, and a fluid, warm and comforting, began to fill it," Joy said. "The tiny speck basked in the security of the fluid, like a fetus in its womb." For a long time she sat there relishing the peaceful calm.

Joy was given the assurance that the kids were in God's hands. Then . . . "All of a sudden it felt as if all my children were sitting on my lap. My arms caressed the air around me as I imagined touching and holding them." In this tranquil quiet, Joy felt a voice telling her she would be with them again.

Macomb, Illinois. 1972.

WALKING THROUGH the student union one day as an anonymous sophomore at Western Illinois University, I paused for two reasons at a table loaded with books: the smiling blonde behind it, and the sign which read: Intervarsity Christian Fellowship. Trying not to ogle the Intervarsity representative too obviously I scanned the titles and picked up *The God Who Is There* by Francis Schaeffer. The girl recommended the book highly; I listened appreciatively and bought it. That proved to be the perfect ending to a great furlough.

A year earlier God had delivered me from a quirky obsession with doubt. I was able to stop compulsively defending the faith. But finding good reasons for it remained a concern. I'd always been interested in apologetics and the big questions. So for a while I kept in touch with the more respectable doubts.

Soon however I realized I needed more than freedom from an obsessive skepticism. I needed a clean break; I needed a vacation from apologetics. It was a burden that I wanted to let go of for a while.

I asked the Lord for a year's furlough, and got it with surprisingly little effort. God simply carried all the weighty philosophical problems for me. I lost touch.

Was this just a cop-out? Turn off brain, let God handle it? Not quite. At the end of that year or so, I walked by the table in the student union and discovered Francis Schaeffer. His book blew the lid off the defensive little box I had put Christian apologetics into. Here was the biblical world view competing and winning out in the world of art, philosophy, literature, and popular culture. I was swept off my feet. I had never dreamed Christianity provided such a thorough answer to all the big questions.

God had carried me along to the perfect dénouement.

GOD THE SERVANT carries all our burdens. He soothes anxious souls (like Helmuth James's), comforts broken hearts (like Joy Swift's), eases troubled minds (like mine). A multitude who've fallen into His everlasting arms have found Him to be a humble, patient, giving Servant who sustains them.

We are not always a pleasant burden to bear. God is not unfeeling; He sorrows when we act like demanding, impatient children. "I am weighted down beneath you," He says, "As a wagon is weighted down when filled with sheaves." But through it all He remains an irrepressible Servant, pledging eloquently: "Till you grow old I am He, and when white hairs come I will carry you still."

15

LOWLY LORD

EVERYBODY HAD A GOOD EXCUSE that Wednesday evening for being late to 7:30 choir practice at the Baptist Church. Ladona Vandegrift, a high school sophomore, always came early. But on this night a thorny geometry problem detained her. Royena Estes and her sister Sadie were ready to leave home on time. But their car wouldn't start.

Mrs. Schuster could be counted on to arrive ten minutes early for practice. But she was held up at her mother's house preparing for a later missionary meeting. Pastor Klempel and his wife, always punctual, didn't make it at 7:30 either. His wristwatch, usually very accurate, was five minutes slow this evening.

Joyce Black felt it was so cold that she waited till the last possible minute to leave—a few minutes too long. Harvey Ahl had been invited over to a friend's home for dinner and in the pleasant conversation lost track of time.

Even Mrs. Paul, the choir director, failed to arrive on time. She'd always come fifteen minutes early. But on this night her daughter, who played piano for the group, fell asleep. Mrs. Paul hurriedly awakened Marilyn and they rushed to finish getting ready—but drove up to the church a few minutes late. This was the first time either had ever been tardy for choir practice.

Eighteen people made up the West Side Baptist Church choir. Tonight every one of them arrived late, something that had never happened before.

No one was there at 7:30 when the basement furnace, situated directly below the choir loft, ignited a gas leak. The loft blew up; the church was demolished. Then the choir members arrived on the scene—too late.

MOST PEOPLE with the good fortune to be able to save the lives of eighteen human beings wouldn't mind getting a little credit. A headline in the local paper would be nice, an award from the mayor better.

But the King of Kings seems to carry out His deliverances on the sly, almost anonymously. No fanfare. No angels with a vivid warning, no bells. No strings attached. Just an unobtrusive rescue.

Coincidence is one answer to events like the one in Beatrice. And we should admit that this is no open-and-shut case of the miraculous. But the coincidences here are so artfully contrived that it's very easy to see a Sovereign at work, One who can precisely align a whole series of unrelated events, One who overrules at will.

But what an unassuming Sovereign this is! In His perfectly assured Majesty there is plenty of room for humility. He is the Sovereign Servant, not using His authority and control to dominate, but to help. He carries us without our knowing it.

Insecure people typically need to make noises; they hint broadly about their important positions. But God knows who He is. He is very comfortable in His role. He doesn't campaign for recognition; He earns it quietly.

The Sovereign with the airs of a servant. Bible writers saw such a picture of their Lord of Lords. Psalm 113, for example, praises a God "enthroned on high" who "humbles Himself." He "raises the poor from the dust," and lifts up the needy to sit with princes. He is on the throne altogether and in the dust with the lowly altogether. The exultant praises of Scripture tell us God is a Lord who requires everything of His servants; we lose ourselves in His majesty. At the same time, the prophets of Scripture, loudly calling for justice, assure us He's completely identified with the downtrodden and functions as their active advocate in the world.

We all know people who are dynamic leaders, the kind who get things done, type A personalities who enjoy being in control and are good at it. Unfortunately the best of them often use people insensitively and the worst become ruthless tyrants.

We also know about people who always seem to be on the serving end. Compulsively helpful, they invariably find an excuse to scurry around the kitchen or tidy things up when everyone else is stuffing their faces. They are the ones taking care of dishes or toddlers when others are glued to the TV. Unfortunately the downside of these servants is that they become doormats, people who'll do anything to please their peers. They follow well, but don't stand up for right very well.

It takes both of these kinds of people to suggest what God is like, both of them in their extremes, yet without their respective liabilities. God fits the two together seamlessly, creating something wonderful from the disparate parts. He is the Sovereign Servant, the Lowly Lord.

London. 1947.

DAVID would someday spearhead a church renewal movement in America, but at the moment he was wandering around post-war London without much organizational or financial support. Still freelancing for the Spirit, he had been directed by an authoritative Voice to go to America—specifically, to an important church conference in Grand Rapids, Michigan.

He had ten days to get there. Unable to afford

even bus fare, he shuffled through Trafalgar Square from one travel agency to another. They all said the same thing: "You can't get a berth on any ship for ninety days." At the time scores of refugees were flooding into London hoping for a place to settle, most looking for passage across the Atlantic.

As dusk settled over the city, David found himself in Piccadilly Circus. Surrounded by crowds hurrying home, he felt discouraged and homesick. Piccadilly's bright lights glared down indifferently. The wanderer prayed, "Dear Lord, have I missed your guidance today? I can't find anybody, any shipping agency, that will take me."

The familiar, gentle voice came back: "I didn't say book a berth. I said book a seat."

That meant a plane. But David didn't even have enough for boat fare. The voice assured him, "I said I'd pay the fare."

Across the square one huge neon sign stood out: "Parry, Leon and Hayhoe." David decided to give it a try. The agent there politely listened as the minister explained his plight. Yes there was a ninety-day waiting list, but he'd do his best to find a cancellation. David left a number where he was staying. The agent said, "All right. You pray, and I'll work, and we'll see."

That weekend David spoke at meetings in Manchester and received a generous offering for his ministry, but it was not nearly enough to get him to Grand Rapids. Soon after he arrived back at Blackheath, where he was staying with some friends, the phone rang. It was the travel agent.

"Did you get me a seat?" David asked.

"Yes, but you've got to leave tonight," the agent replied urgently. "You must go to Brussels tonight, then fly out of there on Sabena tomorrow morning."

After a pause the young agent went on in a softer voice, "Sir, you must have prayed with great faith because there was not really the remotest chance last Friday night that you would find a vacancy."

The agent promised to hold the ticket for an hour and a half. David would have to hurry to pick it up in time. He told his hostess reluctantly that he'd accepted a seat on a plane to America with no money to pay for it.

She was incredulous.

But God's directive had been so clear. "There's only one thing to do," David told her as he finished his cup of tea, "and that's go to the travel office."

"You're going there without money?"

"Well, something's got to happen."

Just then the doorbell rang. His hostess left the room and returned with a small manila envelope. "It's for you," she said. "Maybe the money's in there."

David didn't think it likely. Beneath his confident exterior he was getting quite anxious. But inside the envelope he found a check for 165 pounds, 17 shillings and 6 pence. A Christian friend from York had sent it. His note said, "Do you remember in Wales I told you I believed the Lord wanted you to go to America? Well, He woke me last night at eleven o'clock and told me to get up and make a check for this amount and send it to this address."

David made it to Parry, Leon and Hayhoe in seventy-five breathless minutes. The agent glanced at his watch and held up a ticket already made out to him. "You did it," he said with a smile. "I had six customers waiting for it."

·David took the ticket and stared at the figures. At that moment the Sovereign Servant seemed as real as any human being could apprehend Him to be. The minister's eyes filled with tears as he read the bottom line: 165 pounds, 17 shillings, 6 pence.

IN DAVID'S CAREER one sees a man possessed with a mission, scurrying about from one improbable rendezvous to another as a King's obedient emissary. And yet that King is simultaneously servant to the passion He inspires. He provides air fare, not just boat fare. He plans ahead of time and appears in the thrilling nick-of-time. At His most authoritative in directing a man's affairs, He acts most dramatically as a servant, fulfilling specific needs. Exact and generous. A provider with a flair for providences that leave His name as clearly legible as a sweeping signature on a check.

There are people who feel uneasy about falling into the hands of a sovereign deity. We all have our fears about being under someone's thumb, having our destiny sealed. But God doesn't rule that way. The heavenly Sovereign doesn't constrict people's lives, He blows them wide open. He enables us to be and do far more than we could without His presence as a quiet, powerful Servant.

East of the Jordan. c. 860 B.C.

AFTER ELIJAH ANNOUNCED God's strike against corrupt King Ahab and the rains stopped and the crops failed, the prophet had to flee from the wrath of the king. Ahab focused his frustration on the messenger, Elijah, whom he named the "troubler of Israel." This king didn't really understand that he'd taken on a Sovereign much bigger than himself.

Elijah was instructed to hide by a brook called Cherith. It would supply him with water through most of the drought. But God also provided two square meals a day there in the wilderness east of the Jordan, through a catering service operated by ravens.

The Sovereign Lord persuaded these eat-anything-that-moves-or-stinks creatures to carry in bread and meat to His prophet. Every morning and evening ravens flew by and dropped tasty morsels at Elijah's feet. Crows doing God's bidding. There was no doubt about who was in charge there.

And yet I like this Sovereign's touch. He didn't make a spectacle of His daily provisions. Some birds just stored up food in the right place. Common black ravens, not some exotic flock gloriously plumed for the occasion. No noise, no pyrotechnics. God displayed as unmistakably Sovereign never shakes off that Servant spirit. It goes too deep into the divine being.

Consider a couple of real spectacles.

Joshua is battling the bad-news Amorites at a place called Gibeon. Israel is winning, but not decisively enough. Joshua knows these dedicated idolaters and implacable enemies will be back to seduce the Hebrews unless their army is devastated. The Amorite soldiers are getting away. The shadows are lengthening. Joshua needs more time.

So he reigns in his horse, looks up toward heaven and makes a perfectly ridiculous request. He asks God to make the sun stand still.

But God doesn't laugh. He honors the one sincerely trying to do His will and halts the solar system, or parts thereof. Time is suspended. The Amorites fall in a long and broad daylight.

The sun standing still is a pretty heavy statement about who's in charge, who reigns over all creation. Yes, message received. Yet notice that God did not arbitrarily impose this unique happening on the field of action. He responded to a request. He waited in the wings, servant-like, to oblige the leader of His people who was stretching himself to the limit in faith.

And then there's Elijah's farewell. Another spectacle. Elijah walks along with his disciple and successor Elisha as a group of student-prophets trail behind. There's a lot to talk about. Elijah knows he's departing and Elisha longs to share in the spirit that empowered the older man's legendary career.

Suddenly a chariot of fire drawn by horses of fire

appears on the scene. The two men are separated. Elijah is drawn into the chariot and upward in the heavens by what appears to be a whirlwind. Elijah's mantle falls to the ground and Elisha stares in awe as master and fiery chariot disappear into the sky.

Here is theater. Only a small audience of about fifty student-prophets attended the performance, but it was theater indeed, blazing in the sky. Yet it wasn't the King of Kings in the starring role, hot-rodding around, showing off His way with the elements. It was limousine service for someone else. God was honoring a man who'd given his life to speak the truth while a whole nation played deadly games with Baal and Ashtoreth. God the Sovereign went out of His way to limo into heaven someone very close to His heart: a selfless servant.

Umeda to Nishinomiya, Japan. 1975.

IT HAD BEEN a long day. I wearily made my way through the jerking cars of the 9:48 express toward the front of the train as it pulled out of Umeda station. I must admit that I stopped at the precise location by the train door because I thought I caught a pretty girl's flickering eyes smiling at me. Coming to an abrupt halt a ways down the aisle I stared out the window at the flow of neon and wondered if I'd seen correctly.

Before I could persuade myself I had, a middle-aged gentleman approached and, excusing himself, asked, "Do you know anybody who is interested in religious things?"

Knowing full well that things like this happened only in missionary stories, I didn't know what to say. The only people who ever broke the polite reserve of Japanese commuter culture were insane derelicts or the pathetically drunk. Before I could recover from the shock he continued, "I'm getting older and material pursuits are seeming like a dead end to me now." The man spoke English quite well.

I smiled stupidly in wonder and managed to respond, "Well I'm employed by a church to teach English and I have some Bible classes."

As we talked, the man kept stealing all my best lines about the meaninglessness of just making money and the need to find "something more" on which to base our lives. I could only nod open-mouthed as he gave the sermon on the secular age I was supposed to deliver.

I got off the train with him at a little stop somewhere between Umeda and Kitaguchi. He gave me his phone number and I told him a little about my Bible classes. The man asked me to call him by his English nickname, "Chestie." We agreed to get together the next Saturday morning.

Chestie proved to be intensely curious. A driven man. At our meeting I tried to start him out in Ecclesiastes. Someone had told me that its passages on the vanity of life echoed Buddhist thought. Chestie tried hard to understand but quickly bogged down amid Solomon's brooding and I realized how little I had to say on the subject.

Still, we kept meeting on the 9:48, and occasionally would disembark together, walk the narrow streets by his station and drop into a tiny tea room where they served an exotic fruit mix and played horrible music.

But everything was shut out before this man's intense searching. One day after he came back from a trip to South Africa to clear up snags in his import-export business, Chestie asked, "This may seem like a strange question, but how did I get this searching, this problem?" He told me that it just sort of dropped on him one day. He had begun asking, "What am I living for? What's the purpose of life?" Suddenly he felt a compelling urge to find spiritual values.

Nothing in his typically busy life as a Japanese

businessman had prepared him for this disturbing line of thought. It was an interruption he could not explain.

Later he would ask me earnestly, "Why did I walk up to you that night in the train? I never do things like that. I don't understand it." It seemed a profound mystery to him. He would ask his wife at night, "Why did I do that?" He'd had no idea I was a missionary, no idea that some American stranger could give him any clues to the nature of his quest.

Finally, after several esoteric discussions, I got Chestie into the New Testament. "Chestie, I can talk to you all night," I told him. "But it's just a man's words. I think you should find out about the words of God."

We started with the book of John. I was eager to find out how Jesus would appear to someone meeting Him as a perfect stranger. In a few days Chestie had questions at one of our tea room hangouts beneath the rumbling tracks. What does this "Word" that comes into the world signify? Who are the Pharisees? Why is Christ the Lamb of God? It felt good to answer specific questions instead of talk into the wind of abstraction.

As Chestie studied, he was gripped by something more than curiosity. "It's very strange," he told me, eyes closed, concentrating on his thoughts as if they were someone else's, "I feel compelled to go on—continue reading you know. Nothing like this has ever happened in my life. I hear a voice in my mind asking, 'Have you read yet?' And I think, *No, I can do it later.* But this voice insists, 'You better hurry, get it done.' "

"I'm a businessman. I'm supposed to be after the money. How can I have these thoughts?"

Chestie continued stealing my best lines for some time. All I could do was hang around the action and wonder.

I HAD NEVER seen God so Sovereign. He seemed to take by the scruff of the neck a man deeply rooted in the almighty yen and drag Him up to a spiritual height where he dangles uneasily at the strange sights.

But I also saw God very much as Servant. Through scores of conversations with Chestie I came to realize how patiently God had been working with this man and his rambling, restless thoughts. I often couldn't follow them, but God obviously had been for some time. And I saw my friend moved step-by-step to a new moral sensitivity. God seemed to be always there, humbly nudging, dropping just the right suggestions. Chestie was carried along on his quest. God had moved trains and schedules and pretty girls just so this man could get a little help in hankering after "something more."

Chestie encountered a voice speaking with authority, definite, not easily ignored. It resulted in an awakening tailor-made for him. The voice became a companionable servant.

‖ PART ‖
VI

Absolutely Personal

TRUTH IS HIS BODY,
AND LIGHT IS HIS SHADOW.

Plato

16

AGELESS ROCK

THE TWO MEN STANDING before that august court should have been trembling. They faced Caiaphas the high priest and his colleague Annas, men whose authority and power no ordinary Jew could ignore—and men who had just helped do away with a man whom the two detainees believed to be the Messiah. If Jesus Himself became a victim in the hands of these officials, what hope could there be for Peter and John, His disciples?

The court began its questioning. Peter had been so bold as to heal a cripple in the name of the officially discredited Jesus—right on the temple steps. Annas must have considered this a personal affront. At any rate he and his fellow jurists were confident they could easily intimidate Peter into silence. The man's record as a follower of Jesus invited attack.

This was Peter the betrayer. On the night of Christ's arrest he'd been ready to defend his Master with a sword, but when Jesus allowed a mob to bind and lead Him away, Peter suddenly found himself unable to stand by Him in humiliation, and fled with the other disciples into the night.

A little later a servant girl's pointed questions compelled him to deny he knew the Man who meant everything to him. Peter had just boasted rather arrogantly: "Even if all the other disciples fall away I never will." But under pressure he found himself still fleeing in the dark.

Peter had always had a wide streak of instability. He acted on impulse and was often propelled in erratic directions: Peter courageously walking on the water after Jesus. Peter sinking in the waves, terrified. Jesus starts to explain why He must go to Jerusalem and die. Peter takes Him aside and tries to talk Him out of it. On the mount of transfiguration Jesus is glorified before Peter's eyes and he starts babbling on about building three tabernacles.

Peter wrestled with a maze of inner contradictions. Always the first to speak, often the most off-base. He wore macho courage and hid deep fears. He had left everything for Jesus and yet couldn't even stay awake with his Lord in Gethsemane during Jesus' greatest ordeal. He had moments of intense spiritual illumination, yet often failed to grasp Jesus' most basic teachings.

And so Annas and Caiaphas looked down from their bench at Peter and smiled at that wide streak of instability. They demanded to know by what power he'd performed his miracle, thinking Peter wouldn't dare defend the name of Jesus before the Sanhedrin, where he faced well-placed enemies, not mere curious servant girls.

They were greatly mistaken. Peter immediately launched into an articulate defense of "Jesus Christ the Nazarene." The one interrogated became prosecutor, identifying Jesus as the one "whom you crucified but whom God raised from the dead." What an awesome indictment in one simple sentence!

Peter went on to cite an Old Testament prophecy concerning a rejected stone which becomes the chief cornerstone, and argued that it had been fulfilled in Jesus, the rejected Messiah.

The Sanhedrin realized they were getting far

more than they'd bargained for and quickly called for a short recess. This wasn't the same Peter they'd hoped to intimidate or at least confuse. This "unschooled, ordinary" man astonished them with his confident courage.

Before that court Peter stood as exhibit A of the chief cornerstone, as well as its expositor. He was firmly embedded in the Rock. A few weeks before on the day of Pentecost, God had poured Himself into this disciple. Now he embodied a very present Rock, stable, focused, persevering.

The priests filed back in and seated themselves. Annas cleared his throat and, almost politely, ordered Peter not to teach any longer in Jesus' name. The disciple didn't flinch: "We cannot help speaking about what we have seen and heard."

Following his release Peter continued to grow as a leader. The early church rallied around him during a time of persecution. The man who'd always stuck his foot in his mouth now moved thousands to repentance with his preaching. He stood firm on the Cornerstone, and pulled people to it. Perhaps the most poignant example of his newfound poise and stability was that night in Herod's prison under sentence of death when the delivering angel found him sleeping soundly—on God the solid Rock.

Chesapeake Bay. 1970s.

IT DIDN'T TAKE LONG after Ruthie Turner began working as a maid in the 1814 colonial mansion on Chesapeake Bay to discover that the lady of the house had serious problems. Mrs. Treena Kerr had been going downhill for years. Recently she'd been judged totally incapable of managing her life and was to be admitted to a mental institution for an undetermined period. Only a high daily dose of Valium kept her going.

Ruthie told fellow believers at her tiny church and they began to pray for Treena. Ruthie knew everything else had failed the woman. Her husband, "Galloping Gourmet" Graham Kerr, took in over a million a year, but their personal life was a disaster. They'd just taken a dream cruise around the world in a beautiful yacht and come home more miserable than ever.

One day, after three months of praying, Ruthie found Mrs. Kerr screaming at the ceiling and got up enough courage to suggest, "Why don't you give your problems to God?"

Treena took up the challenge angrily: "All right, God, if you're so damned clever, you deal with it, because I can't."

A week later she found herself in Ruthie's church. Saxophones and drums opened the service. Worship among these black parishioners was not quite what she'd expected. Suddenly Treena knelt and began weeping: "I'm sorry, Jesus. Forgive me, Jesus." The good folk there put a white robe on Treena and baptized her. They prayed that she'd be filled with the Spirit.

The woman from the colonial mansion left feeling she'd been touched by God. Back home she started reading a Bible Ruthie had given her. It got late; Treena went to get her sleeping pills. But a little inner voice said, "You won't need anything like that anymore." So she took all her drugs and poured them down the bathroom sink.

Most people don't just quit that much Valium cold turkey, but Treena slept soundly and woke up refreshed, invigorated, and clear-eyed.

A week later Mr. Kerr returned to find his wife transformed. He thought her peace and kindness must have something to do with the season; it was Christmas time. But it lasted beyond the holidays. For the next several weeks Graham kept analyzing his wife. He'd known her since she was eleven. He had seen her slowly destroyed over the years. But now, he said, "she was totally put back together again, and really better and more loving than any time I could remember."

The woman falling apart had encountered a solid Rock. Even Treena's doctor confirmed it. "Your wife is a miracle," he told Graham with tears in his eyes. "I believe in miracles; I had never seen one, but now I have."

THE UNSTABLE grab hold of God and discover an unshakable Rock. Spiritual and emotional transients find a home. This is the Lord celebrated in the Psalms as the Rock of Ages. He is a fortress, a strong tower, a shield for those who take refuge in Him. Jehovah stood as a great mountain over Israel, their stability and strength.

He has that effect on people because He is eternal. We find such a stabilizing home in Him because He is "our dwelling place throughout all generations." He will never let us down because "his righteousness endures forever." He's always been around; He'll always be around, from everlasting to everlasting.

And part of "everlasting," as a description of God, involves the fact that He doesn't change. He's immutable. God doesn't get up on the wrong side of the bed. He doesn't hope to get through Monday. He doesn't wait for the weekend. He's not up and down. He's up.

God doesn't get bent out of shape by man's mis-behavior and go too far sometimes. As He told a pathetically immoral Judah: "I, the Lord, do not change; therefore you, O sons of Jacob, are not con-sumed."

When someone intones in a nightclub: "I did it my way . . . I've had regrets, but too few to mention," it sounds like hot air. But God indeed has no regrets about His way. He doesn't look back a few thousand years and wish He'd treated some Assyrian a bit differently.

God doesn't change. He's dependable. Faithful to a thousand generations. He's that way not just in the "spiritual" realm of things like faith and love. He expresses His eternal nature amid the daily human struggle for bread as well. The solid rock has made His faithfulness known in terms of cold hard cash.

Bristol, England. Tuesday, February 8, 1842.

ENOUGH FOOD REMAINED in George Mueller's orphan houses for that day's meals, but that was it. There was no money to buy bread or milk for the following morning. And two of the orphan houses needed coal.

Mueller believed that if God sent nothing before nine o'clock on Wednesday morning, "His name would be dishonored." Tuesday afternoon nine plum cakes arrived from a kindly sister. But the situation was still grim, as Mueller noted in his diary: "Truly, we are poorer than ever; but, through grace, my eyes look not at the empty stores and the empty purse, but to the riches of the Lord only."

Any other man responsible for the continual care and feeding of scores of children would have been climbing the walls. But Mueller believed in a God who is eternally faithful. He had, in fact, bet his entire career on the proposition that such a God could be relied upon implicitly and exclusively.

Mueller would not be disappointed. Wednesday morning just after seven he walked confidently to the orphan house on Wilson Street to find out how his Lord was going to provide food for that day. Mueller discovered that the need had already been met. A Christian businessman walking to work early that morning had suddenly wondered whether "Mueller's children" might need funds. He decided to take something by the homes that evening. But, he later said, "I could not go any further and felt constrained to go back." The man delivered three sovereigns just in time to make purchases for the orphans' breakfast.

Timely provisions like this came in to Mueller's homes countless times in his more than six decades of work. Never once did the orphans lack for food or clothing. There was always enough, sometimes just enough, but the children never knew a moment's anxiety.

Mueller's work was entirely supported by donations. During his 63-year career nearly 1,500,000 pounds was given, enough to care for some ten thousand children and to build several orphanages. It was quite an undertaking: two thousand children to be fed each day, their clothes washed and repaired, five large buildings to be kept up, matrons, overseers, nurses, and teachers to be paid. . . .

And, according to Mueller, over these six decades God never missed a step. No child ever went without a meal; no baker or milkman ever settled for an IOU.

But now we come to the real catch: George Mueller accomplished all this without ever once asking a soul for a penny and without ever making any needs known. This man had embarked on his enterprise as a grand experiment. He wanted "something that would act as a visible proof that our God and Father is the same faithful God as ever he was . . . to all who put their trust in Him."

Sleepy, complacent England seemed to Mueller to have lost real faith. Religion was observed, but to actually rely on an active God for something as real as daily sustenance—that was going a bit far. So this devout believer decided to demonstrate that the Almighty "had not in the least changed" by the fact that "the orphans under my care are provided, with all they need, only by *prayer and faith,* without anyone being asked by me or my fellow-labourers, whereby it may be seen, that God is FAITHFUL STILL, and HEARS PRAYER STILL."

This German immigrant, without connections, relatively unknown even in Bristol, made his point. God proved Himself reliable through decades of remarkable providences.

Mueller's work became doubly impressive to me after I started writing fundraising letters for a religious telecast. With national exposure and an entire denomination behind us, we still had to cry for funds each month—and cry very loudly. We were forever coming up with some new effort to "upgrade donors" or "expand our donor base." Nothing was more of a proven fact than the reverentially quoted statement: "If you don't ask, people won't give."

But Mueller not only never asked, he never hinted that his orphanages were in dire straits. Mueller published an annual report and conducted annual meetings as he was obligated to do. But when times were hard these were postponed until he could say all was well. Mueller wanted to make sure his experiment remained credible, no hidden pulleys or levers. He relied on the Rock alone.

Mueller himself pictures for us the stable, unchanging quality of that solid Rock of Ages. His calm faith never wavered. When calamity threatened he never panicked, but waited patiently for the faithful One to come through.

What makes the picture even more telling is how different George Mueller was before his conversion. He started out early in the wrong direction. Before the age of ten he began stealing from his father. When caught and punished he resolved to do it more cleverly the next time.

On the day before his confirmation, after confessing to a clergyman, he handed over only a small part of the fee his father had given him.

Mueller's dissolute lifestyle as a youth landed him in debtor's prison. He resolved to improve many times but quickly slipped back into a well-worn rut of irresponsibility. At Halle University he drank, wasted his money, pawned his belongings, borrowed extensively, and drank some more.

But then Mueller, the picture of instability, ran into the eternal Rock.

THE ROCK OF AGES isn't relative. He doesn't bend with the times or flow with the current. God is perfect just the way he is, was, and shall be. He doesn't need to update Himself.

He's absolute, one indivisible thing. An eternal statue to our endless posturing. What He says is frozen, forever true: "The grass withers and the flowers fall but the word of our God stands forever."

No modifications, amendments, qualifications. God's promises create a firm space of their own. People slip-sliding through their nights and days have found those promises a sure foothold, carved in granite.

Encountering the Rock we run into a still spot. The constant flux which makes us not walk but stagger through life stops. We discover an immovable place of rest.

God's immovable quality is contagious. The Rock seeps into people and solidifies them. We can best see that in the long trail of martyrs who throw a spotlight on the granite will of their Lord, eternal, unbending.

Rome. c. A.D. **156.**

JUST OUTSIDE THE STADIUM, Herodes, a high sheriff, suggested persuasively: "What is the harm of saying,

233

'Caesar is Lord,' and offering incense . . . and saving your life?"

But Polycarp, bishop of Smyrna, disciple of John the Apostle, wouldn't budge. Given the choice between making a little gesture with incense that compromised his allegiance to the eternal God and burning to death, Polycarp chose the latter.

They proceeded inside to the execution grounds. The proconsul there had a hard time making himself heard above the din of the crowd. But he pressed the aging Christian to deny his faith. "Swear by the fortune of Caesar," he urged. "Repent. Say, 'Away with the atheists.' " The Romans, with their plethora of gods, regarded followers of Jesus as nonbelievers.

Polycarp looked up at the bloodthirsty, chanting crowd that filled the stadium, waved his hand toward them and said, "Away with the atheists."

The proconsul persisted, "Swear and I set you free, curse Christ."

Polycarp flashed back on a lifetime of leaning on the faithful Rock and replied, "Eighty and six years have I served Him, and he did me no wrong. How can I blaspheme my King, who saved me?"

The old man removed his outer clothing and stood by the pyre. They were about to nail him to the stake but he said, "Leave me as I am; for he that enabled me to abide the fire will also enable me to abide at the stake unflinching without your safeguard of nails."

Polycarp said a prayer. The stakes were lit. And he perished, immovable.

Tsingham, Tibet. c. 1900.

ON ONE OF HIS MANY journeys through the Himalayas the Indian evangelist Sundhar Singh discovered a Tibetan preacher in a certain village whom the people treated with superstitious reverence. He could proclaim Christ in that time and place of violent religious intolerance without fear of reprisal. The preacher told Singh his story.

He'd been secretary to the lama in Tsingham once but then had come under the influence of a Christian from the Punjab, and eventually declared himself a follower of Jesus. He first confessed his faith to his own master, the Buddhist lama, who unfortunately happened to be an ignorant fanatic.

Within a few days the preacher was sentenced to death. In front of the lamasery walls men bound a wet yak-skin around him and sewed it up tight. They then left him out in the scorching sunshine, where the contracting skin would crush the apostate to death.

He did not die quickly enough. Red-hot skewers were thrust through the yak-skin into his body. Later they tore off the skin and dragged him through the streets to a refuse dump outside of town. After further abuse the preacher was dropped on a dunghill. His body showed no signs of life. The crowds left; vultures gathered.

But this mutilated victim had not died. Somehow he managed to crawl away and recover. And then, instead of fleeing for his life, he marched right back into Tsingham and began preaching about Christ. Unbending. Immovable. Standing on the Rock.

THE ROCK OF AGES enables people to stand firm against the tide, and one of the reasons they do so is something called peace. God's immovability is not just cold stubbornness taken to the limit; it's more a calm assurance of who He is. His servants do not bend because they enter into that assurance, that still spot of rest. God is the kind of being who projects peace.

When I was a kid I didn't think much of peace. It only made me think of slow religious music on some interminable afternoon following church. Spiritual tranquility stood stodgily opposed to excitement in general and hide-and-seek noise in particular. I wanted as little of it as possible in my life.

Even through adolescence I maintained my distance. Coming from a loving, peaceable family, I saw no need of the quality that had been a hidden possession for so long. When people testified about Jesus bringing peace I nodded unenthusiastically. The logical extension of resting in peace, to me, seemed death.

Now, however, my children want to play hide-and-seek noisily all the time and, being a wiser adult, I have had to modify my disdain of peace and quiet. Also, deadlines and bills and household chores piling up have at times made the ideal of tranquility downright attractive.

More importantly I've finally caught on to what God's kind of peace is all about. All those people down through history who've spoken in awe of the peace their Lord created within weren't just talking about rest. My contemporaries still testifying about the peace they've found in God aren't just referring to quiet.

They are pointing to something more: a profound sense of well-being, belonging, finding the soul's home, a contentment that lasts. And I realized that this is exactly what almost every human being on this planet is running after: happiness, peace.

Now I see that I can be thankful for peace. And I add my voice to all the others. When I've come close to the eternal God, it is good; I've felt belonging, contentment. No, God does not throw me into a catatonic daze. But yes, He creates peace. It's something that fills you up.

God is rock steady, supremely at peace. Tranquility flows out of the eternal One; it's part of Him. It's been flowing for some time. The changeless, consistent God has been bestowing this priceless quality on all kinds of people down through the ages.

Bethlehem, Judah. c. 1000 B.C.

DAVID, SON OF JESSE, grew up dodging danger. He had to struggle for many years as a fugitive before his calling to the throne became a reality. But through it all he discovered a God who gave peace. David wrote:

> The Lord is my shepherd, I shall not be in want.
> > He makes me lie down in green pastures,
> he leads me beside quiet waters,
> > he restores my soul . . .
> Even though I walk
> > through the valley of the shadow of death,
> I will fear no evil,
> > for you are with me;
> your rod and your staff,
> > they comfort me.

Jerusalem. c. 750 B.C.

IN A TIME when mighty Assyria threatened tiny Israel with annihilation, the prophet Isaiah discovered that "the Lord is the Rock eternal." He had the confidence to proclaim:

> You will keep in perfect peace
> > him whose mind is steadfast,
> > because he trusts in you.

Ephesus. c. A.D. 54.

THE APOSTLE PAUL was writing from prison to friends in Philippi anxious about his condition. But he never mentioned the cold and dark of his dungeon, or the harshness of his Roman guards. Instead his letter flowed with encouragement and joy. (The man in an intensive care unit sending out a get well card to his relatives.) He could recommend "the peace of God, which transcends all understanding."

This man lived on the road, fleeing murderous fanatics, battling heresies, carving out islands of Christian belief in a rough sea of paganism. Shipwrecked, falsely accused, mobbed, beaten, whipped, stoned, constantly in danger—he should have been a basket case. Instead he calmly handed out peace from prison: "I have learned the secret of being content in any and every situation . . . through him who gives me strength."

Constantinople. A.D. 403.

THE EMPRESS EUDOXIA wanted badly to get rid of John Chrysostom. This reforming archbishop had delivered a sermon against extravagance and vanity in women which Eudoxia took as a personal attack. So she decided to strike back and plotted with a rival of Chrysostom to have the archbishop deposed.

John Chrysostom was popular with the people of Constantinople, but no match for the power of the Holy Roman Empire. Pliable bishops were assembled, articles of impeachment drawn up. Eudoxia's husband, Emperor Arcadius, charged Chrysostom with treason and issued an order of banishment.

For three days Constantinople raged against this injustice. Many in the city would rather have laid down their lives than give up their beloved archbishop. But Chrysostom remained a steadying influence amid the passionate conflict of wills. From the pulpit he testified: "Violent storms encompass me on all sides, yet I am without fear, because I stand upon a rock. Though the sea roar and the waves rise high, they cannot overwhelm the ship of Jesus Christ. I fear not death, which is my gain; nor banishment, for the whole earth is the Lord's."

Then Chrysostom surrendered to an official—secretly so as to avoid a public outcry that might result in bloodshed—and was taken off into exile.

The Atlantic. October, 1735.

THE *SIMMONS* was a rather light vessel. The storm which struck it midway between England and the colonies blew with a determined fury, and the boat rocked its passengers into a state of panic. Even the seasoned crew feared for their lives.

One passenger, John Wesley, huddled below deck in terror. Glancing over at a group of Moravian believers, he was shocked to see them calmly singing a hymn. Earlier on the voyage, Wesley had concluded they were rather heavy-minded, dull-witted folk. But now the more wildly the ship was tossed about, the more calmly these Germans sang praises.

After the storm subsided, a deeply shaken Wesley asked a young Moravian, "Were you not afraid?"

"I thank God, no."

"But were not your women and children afraid?" Wesley wondered.

"No," he answered, "our women and children are not afraid to die."

Wesley was trying to practice the Christian life at the time, but he realized these people had discovered a peace that was still foreign to him. He wanted to find out what enabled them to proceed through a sail-ripping, skin-drenching storm without missing a beat.

The following day he struck up a conversation with Spangenberg, the Moravian pastor. The man asked Wesley, "Does the Spirit of God bear witness with your spirit that you are a child of God?"

Wesley was stumped. This was a new one. Spangenberg tried again: "Do you know Jesus Christ?"

Wesley replied, "I know He is the Saviour of the world."

"True, but do you know He has saved you?"

Obviously the Moravians had this knowledge, this still spot of assurance. They had come close to the eternal God and His peace enveloped them. It was a peace so remarkable that seeing his own lack of it propelled Wesley toward a more intense spiritual quest and eventually to a religious revolution in England.

Beaver Marsh, Oregon. Thanksgiving Day, 1961.

MERRILL WOMACH'S SMALL private plane didn't clear the trees at the end of the runway. It whipped around and plunged a hundred yards through icy branches to the ground. When Womach, gospel singer and businessman, regained consciousness he saw flames all around him. Before he could scramble out his legs, arms, chest and head were badly burned.

Womach couldn't see, but he stumbled through the deep snow toward the sounds of a nearby highway.

Fortunately two men saw the plane go down and rushed to the scene in a station wagon. They saw a man crawling toward him who looked like a monster. No eyes, nose or mouth, his head charred and swollen.

The men placed him gently in the back of the car and drove off toward a hospital. He lay there feeling the terrible pain sweep over him. But, as Womach recalled, "an incredible thing happened . . . I felt like singing."

Forcing one eye open, he looked down at his ghastly hand and began to realize how badly he'd been burned. But as they moved down Highway 97, Womach's feeling persisted: "My head was swelling and the pain grew more and more intense," he said. "Still I felt like singing. It was an old gospel song I had learned as a child. I don't know why that song came rushing out of me instead of cries of pain and pity, but it did."

As the two men in the front seat listened in disbelieving silence, these words emerged from a crack in Womach's blackened face:

> I've found the dear Savior
>   and now I'm made whole;
> I'm pardoned and have my release.
> His Spirit abiding and blessing my soul,
> Praise God, in my heart there is peace.

At Collier State Park an ambulance met the station wagon. The attendants transferred Merrill on a stretcher and raced away. Through the scream of the siren and through Womach's own loud pain, the song still emerged unchanged, lyrics intact, a tune with eternal resonance:

> Wonderful peace, wonderful peace,
> Peace that the world cannot give.
> When I think how He brought me
> From darkness to light,
> There's a wonderful, wonderful peace.

17

A Thousand Faces

HE APPEARED to Joshua as a soldier with drawn sword. Elijah hiding in the cave of a quaking mountain found Him to be a gentle whisper. To a youthful David He acted just like a good shepherd. For Israel journeying erratically through the wilderness He hovered companionably over their campsites as a pillar of fire. Moses managed glimpses of Him on Mount Sinai that proved He was an unapproachably glorious being. To the boy Samuel, He came as a voice calling fatherlike in the night. To Saul the zealous persecutor of Christians, He was a blinding light that stopped him dead in his tracks.

God certainly displays a remarkable variety of faces in the pages of the Bible. The great Immutable One seems a veritable chameleon of adaptation. We could of course just assume that different kinds of people projected different pictures of God. But if we take His overt appearances in Scripture at face value that's hard to do. People seem more to run smack into another surprising manifestation of Jehovah rather than imagine one.

The Rock who stands eternally constant through the upheavals of biblical history also lets it be known that He is the flowing water of life. He is not up and down. But He is very much moving along with Israel's ups and downs, say, during the time of the judges. This living stream flows still, washing up against all kinds of people in all kinds of ways.

Death Row in the Deep South. 1960s.

WHEN GRANDMOTHERLY MISS NELLIE stepped inside the cell of the condemned multiple murderer he jumped from his bed and began cursing and shouting. The guards had tried to talk her out of this; it usually took two or three of them to control the huge convict.

Miss Nellie stood still and prayed. The man began yelling about how no one had ever understood him.

"Jesus understands you." Miss Nellie interjected.

"Don't give me none of that Jesus crap!" he yelled and shook his fist at the ceiling. Miss Nellie kept praying.

Suddenly the convict quieted. His eyes widened. "What's that? What's that I feel? What's comin' over me?"

"The Holy Spirit," she informed him serenely.

"But I'm happy! I never felt like this in my whole life!"

Miss Nellie explained, "That's the joy of the Holy Spirit." For an hour she sat with the murderer and told him the story of Jesus and His sacrificial love. Periodically a guard would peer in to stare amazed at the prisoner shouting for joy.

Next week Nellie came back to visit. He was waiting at his cell door, arms lifted high, calling out to her, "He ain't left me yet. He ain't left me yet." Before this man walked to the electric chair he managed to convert every inmate on his corridor.

God flooded in. An undeniable emotion out of the blue. A visceral presence. And the murderer met Him—gut-to-gut.

Magdalen College, Oxford. 1922.

C. S. LEWIS, professor of English literature, began a circuitous encounter with God on the day he read the *Hippolytus* of Euripides and was taken by its world's-end imagery. He introspected about the difference between the object of desire and the desire itself. This

Oxford don was moved to turn from his old "pursuit of Joy" to seek the "object of Joy itself." He found a road developing "right out of the self" toward objectivity itself.

He read Chesterton's *Everlasting Man*. The whole Christian outline of history began to make sense. A hardboiled atheist colleague remarked offhandedly that the evidence for the historicity of the Gospels is really surprisingly good. Lewis looked deep inside himself and discovered a "zoo of lusts," a "harem of fondled hatreds." He knelt in his room at Magdalen College and admitted that God is God. Then he applied his expertise in literary criticism to a fresh study of the gospel account of Word made flesh and began to see it as more than a myth. It became for the professor a history fulfilling all religion and philosophy. On the way to Whipsnade Zoo one morning he concluded that Jesus Christ is the Son of God.

Was this merely an intellectual gradually creating his own intellectually respectable God? C. S. Lewis, at least, felt strongly that something else was going on. He sensed God actively pursuing him through his mental meanderings. In the first place, he'd not really been in search of God at all. "To me, as I then was," Lewis recalled, " [you] might as well have talked about the mouse's search for the cat." Looking back, Lewis saw evidence of the "unrelenting approach of Him whom I so earnestly desired not to meet."

Lewis the cerebral academician had met his match, mind-on-mind.

Solesmes, France. 1938.

SIMONE WEIL was attending a ten-day series of liturgical services from Palm Sunday to Easter Tuesday. A mystic by nature, she enjoyed the majestic worship, but suffered from splitting headaches at the time. Every glorious sound in the cathedral hurt her like a physical blow.

Simone determined to rise above her "wretched flesh" and leave it to suffer by itself. She concentrated with all her might on the liturgy and somehow broke through the pain. She experienced a "pure and perfect joy in the unimaginable beauty of the chanting and the words." The possibility of "loving divine love in the midst of affliction" penetrated to her depths.

In the midst of this aesthetic and spiritual charm, Simone met God, heart to heart. She remembered it not as a vague emotion but as a distinct event: "Christ himself came down and took possession of me." It all came together so movingly that "the thought of the Passion of Christ entered into my being once and for all."

Western Illinois University. 1971.

SUNDAY MORNING Kathy woke up in her room at one of Western's high-rise dorms with a terrible hangover. Another wild party. As she tried to crawl out of bed, someone knocked on the door. It was Michelle, a girl on Kathy's floor who'd been bugging her about Jesus the last few weeks. Kathy didn't look good at all. And at the moment the "good times" weren't looking that good either.

Michelle again began talking about the alternative. A "personal relationship with Christ" could make things very different. Kathy's aching brain tried to sort through a mixture of urges: getting Michelle off her back, getting her act together, finding God—maybe, getting rid of her headache.

So she told the beaming girl sitting on her bed, "Look if Jesus can take this headache away, I'll accept Him." At least that would accomplish one or two of her objectives, she thought.

Michelle, a new believer of extravagant faith, took Kathy up on her challenge. The two knelt down amid the neighboring echoes of Led Zeppelin and Grand Funk and Michelle asked her Lord to remove Kathy's headache.

Her head stopped throbbing. The pain slithered away. Kathy realized she was stuck, psyche against psyche. So she knelt down again and asked Christ to come into her heart as Lord and Savior.

GOD EXPRESSES HIMSELF in physical encounters, mystical heights, intellectual profundities. He is all there, articulate of course to receptive hearts in the majesty of worship, but also making quick deals on the tenth floor of some dorm reeking of easy pot and throbbing with acid rock.

God reveals many different faces. Clearly they are all faces, not masks. Faces belonging to a person.

God flowed into each one of these four very different people—altogether as a Person. The condemned man spoke of someone there in his cell who had not left, would never leave. C. S. Lewis was dragged, kicking and struggling as he says, from Absolute to Spirit to God, and ended up with his sharp intellect pointed right at a very specific Person. Simone Weil encountered "a presence more personal, more certain, more real than that of a human being." And Kathy, during the time I knew her, lived very much convinced that a Person accompanied her to classes each day.

A person is not a statue. Change and growth are almost synonymous with being alive. The Hebrews made it a point to contrast immobile idols with their "Living God." Is the Eternal One static? I don't think perfection is a frozen state. Looking at the best in the world of nature one tends to think of it more as a continual blossoming. God certainly doesn't ever need to improve His forgiving ability or brush up on leadership skills, but He does create. He creates worlds in which to fashion new life. Surely He can create new experiences to venture into, even perhaps new qualities to express.

A person reacts to events, goes through emotions. What about God? He seems to me far more involved than untouchable (impassible, as the theologians used to say). Take a look at how God reacts in the Bible. He gets angry, is filled with jealousy, loves intensely, laughs, weeps, feels burdened down, exults, boasts, sorrows.

Scholars are usually quick to tell us these are only human ways of speaking about the inscrutable Absolute. They have a point. God's anger is not exactly the same as me kicking the TV when the Redskins score against Dallas. His emotions are not tainted and distorted by human frailty. But He does feel. He sorrows when people are hurt; He leaps for joy when someone turns toward Him. When we speculate about God in our ivory towers there's a tendency to draw God's emotions rather thinly. But the writers of Scripture paint Him in broad, thick strokes.

Samaria, Israel. c. 780 B.C.

NO ONE THOUGHT GOMER, a former prostitute, would make a fitting wife for the prophet Hosea. But he took her anyway, driven to act out a parable of his nation's apostasy. They had three children, two boys and a girl. Nice family. Unfortunately Gomer had trouble adjusting to diapers, small talk at the village well, and being there when Hosea came home at night.

The old ways came back to haunt; old customers started hanging around, and Gomer slipped back into promiscuity. Hosea pleaded with her to come back, shouting about the disaster she would bring on herself and her family, gently reassuring her of his love.

Gomer wasn't listening. She abandoned Hosea and the kids and began sinking lower and lower into that cycle of self-indulgence, guilt, and self-punishment. Finally the prodigal wife bargained her way down to slave status. She became the property of one of her customers.

He soon tired of the woman and put her up for sale. That's when husband Hosea showed up again. By Jewish law he should have come with rocks in his hand, leading a group of indignant male relatives to stone the adultress. Instead he came with fifteen shekels of silver and some barley grain. This honored prophet bought back his disgraced wife, took her home, and once again showed her his unconditional love.

Through all these events, as related in Hosea's book, one voice keeps calling out: "That's exactly what I'm going through." Remarkably, it's the voice of Jehovah. He tells wayward Israel that He feels like a jilted lover. When they bow down to those abominable idols he grows jealous. When they degrade themselves He experiences pain. No matter how far they stray, His love and longing remain unchanged.

Hosea shows us a God burning with emotion, heart-breakingly involved.

Brazoria, Texas. 1970s.

ONE CHRISTMAS I was sitting there in grandmother's living room enjoying another luscious piece of divinity candy when my brother the philosopher interrupted with one of his painful questions. Trying to answer Jerry's questions usually made my head hurt.

I had been talking enthusiastically about Don Richardson's missionary ventures in the book *Peace Child*, and he asked me why it was that people had to be saved by means of one particular gospel. "Let's take orange juice," he began, and I knew I was in trouble. "We know that the vitamin C it contains does some particular good thing for your body. But that vitamin can be synthesized and put in a pill. We can ingest it in many different forms."

"Yeah," I nodded, waiting for the punch line.

"So why can't it be the same with whatever 'saves' people. As long as the right chemistry is there to do the trick, why does it have to be labeled in a certain way? Can't God use all kinds of experiences to end up with this good result, without it involving Jesus, the 'gospel' or anything else in the Bible?"

I tried to think of an answer fast, and started babbling on about the difference between orange juice and Jesus and didn't get very far. In the end I offered Jerry some divinity and asked him who he thought was going to win the Super Bowl.

But his question stuck, and I kept groping for an answer. Months later it hit me: The bottom line is that God wants to be known. He's a person who wants to be known by other people. If God were some cosmic essence floating around out there, why not dispense salvation generically? We might expect an abstract deity to plain-wrap its formula for the masses.

But Jehovah has a face. He wants human beings to look at Him and recognize Him and love Him back. That's why He puts His good news in a brand-name package—with strings attached to Himself. Jehovah repeats one phrase over and over in Scripture as an explanation of His actions: "That you may know Me."

We don't know Him exhaustively of course. And we all know Him to varying degrees. The gracious God makes the most of our slivers of knowledge, and I think we can be assured He is merciful to those who know Him only as a tug on the heart.

But His one dominant purpose remains the same— getting people to know Him personally. That's part of being a Living God.

ON A FEW RARE OCCASIONS I've been able to put a finger on this "living" quality. It happens when I catch a glimpse of someone's whole personality crystallized in one gesture or expression. That's when life feels most precious to me. I see the miracle of an individual personality glow for a moment.

It's a little like kneeling down to capture those flowers on film. We're back to nature again. Each of those dashes of color that swarm over spring fields have their own hues, lines and contours. No two are duplicates. No two human faces either.

In my mind there's a gallery where friends and loved ones are pictured in ways that speak for the whole; I view scenes that tell me why each one is irreplaceable.

My father steps into a room, claps his hands, crosses his arms, and looks around with impish expectation. He does that when things get boring. That's him. All the warm humor and unfailing good will that have nurtured me through the years are there in his gaze.

My brothers and I have just teased Mom about something and she launches into her indescribable laugh. It fills the room and we curl around it like nesting robins.

Donovan turns to answer me. Slow, deliberate, brain churning earnestly, he "opens his mouth to speak" (as the gospel writers said of Jesus) and shares the latest from his spiritual journey.

Mark's face flashes into animation as we talk about our next pantomime film. Incurable zaniness built on a bedrock of spirituality. An outrageous straight arrow. It's there in the flailing of his rubbery arms.

Perry leans forward, eyes blazing, lifts his hands and shakes them, and I am swept up in the intensity of his convictions.

Jenny, my four-year-old, tells me she has divided the world into two groups: the slow-pokers and the fast-pokers. I stare into the treasure of her perfectly clear eyes.

Jason, my all-action six-year-old, decides to play

tackle with his sister in the bedroom away from Mom's disapproving eyes. He tells Jenny, "Don't cry when you fall cause it's gonna be an accident."

Kazko on the phone. Her mellow-sweet voice captures for me that generous, sensitive heart of gold.

Looking over my gallery I know this is what should be left when all else in the world is swept away. This is what it means to be alive, what makes it all worthwhile.

But let's take it one big step further. What if you could compress all the galleries that all human beings see into one portrait, one face? What a fascinating personality that would be. You'd begin to get a picture of the Living God, the livingest being around.

The Bible presents Jehovah as the creator of all the personalities in the universe. All the genes and chromosomes that encode those inimitable laughs, charming smiles and characteristic gestures go back to Him. He held them in His hands. Look around and see the incredible wealth, every person a glimmering masterpiece, a work of art one could spend a lifetime fathoming.

God is the fountain of all personality. How much of the richness of persons must lie in their source!

Eternal. Immutable. Absolute. We use these weighty categories to suggest God is more than human. But He is never less. God our Creator can never be less than a person. His fullness is evident from the way He deepens those who aren't fully human.

The road to Damascus. c. A.D. 31.

SAUL THE PHARISEE possessed a fierce singlemindedness. He prized only the meticulous observance of an elaborate religious tradition. Educated by the elite of Jewish society, he became a legalist of the highest order. God's love seemed infinitely qualified by a host of precepts.

In Saul's world, intolerance and bigotry found good soil.

So he became a grand inquisitor, scurrying about in search of Christians to persecute. But on the road to Damascus a flash of light and an inquiring voice knocked Saul off his high horse. Saul the zealous Pharisee became Paul the dedicated Christian apostle.

Most of us end the story of Paul's conversion at this point. I don't think that's quite the heart of the matter. Many people have radically altered their philosophy of life, apparently without divine assistance. Flaming communists become fiery capitalists. Pushy apple-pie-and-the-flag apologists become loud-mouthed feminists. Obnoxious John Birchers become offensive Moonies. A change in ideology doesn't necessarily mean something extraordinary has happened. So, in Paul's case, it could be asserted that an intolerant man simply found a new way to express his fanaticism.

I used to fear that this assertion might contain a great deal of truth. Then I decided to study "encouragement" in the New Testament. I wanted to find examples of how the writers of Scripture encouraged their readers. That topical study opened my eyes to the heart of Paul the Apostle.

I found myself writing down page after page of wonderfully encouraging texts—all from the epistles of Paul. The man had a marvelous gift for expressing love and faith in people. He tells Roman converts he is convinced they are "full of goodness, complete in knowledge." He tells the Thessalonians of "all the joy we have in the presence of our God because of you." He tells the Ephesians he cannot stop giving thanks to God for their faith and love.

I was deeply moved by the extent of this man's involvement in the lives of others. To Corinthian believers plagued by court disputes, immorality and even incest, Paul cries out, "You are in our hearts to die together and to live together." Chained to a dungeon wall, he exclaims to the Philippians: "Rejoice in the Lord always; again I will say, rejoice!"

Paul begins almost every one of his letters with a flood of encouragement. His run-on sentences are bursting with good news for people he so obviously loves. These words of grace are even more impressive when we remember they come from a late grand inquisitor, the hardnosed legalist. Now we're at the heart of the matter. Now we see how much really happened after Paul's dramatic encounter on the road to Damascus. This was one fanatic who came in out of the cold.

Toward the end of his ministry Paul is saying farewell to a group of believers in the port city of Miletus. They gather close about him on the dock as he reminds them of their life together: "Night and day for a period of three years I did not cease to admonish each one with tears." The Apostle gives a final message of encouragement and then the small group kneels to pray. They rise to their feet, look for the last time into the eyes of their father in Christ, and emotions break. Weeping loudly the believers embrace Paul and kiss him repeatedly. It is a difficult parting.

Paul moves off toward the ship, his friends follow, clinging to him, "grieving especially . . . that they should see his face no more."

I find this one of the most remarkable scenes in Scripture. I doubt any "Pharisee of Pharisees" could have inspired such devotion. Saul the Law expert would not have had such a wealth of affection at the end of his career. It was definitely someone else there on the dock tearfully embracing his children in the faith.

The Living God had been at work. He'd fashioned a whole human being out of a caricature. Paul, of course, did remain a passionate apologist. He could still be hardnosed on certain critical occasions. God did not turn an assertive person into a wimp. But He did mold gracious winsomeness out of self-righteous bigotry. From the arid ground of legalism He made a thirsty love blossom and bear much fruit.

Bucharest, Rumania. 1952.

RICHARD WURMBRAND began his adult life as a one-dimensional, zealous playboy in Bucharest, a place sleazy enough to be called "Little Paris." Doing well in business, he had plenty of money to spend on plenty of girls in flashy bars and cabarets. "I did not care what happened," Wurmbrand recalled, "as long as my appetite for fresh sensation was fed."

After his marriage he continued to chase women, breaking hearts, lying, asking of himself no questions about those he'd "seduced and slandered, mocked and bluffed."

So what happened? The same thing that happened to Saul of course. Flat on his back, Wurmbrand met the living God.

In a hospital fighting off tuberculosis, this atheist read a Bible and was overwhelmed by the personality of Christ. He could not help comparing his own pathetically confined life with the nobility of Jesus. This encounter proved decisive. The life that slid along in a narrow-rut of self-indulgence suddenly broadened. Wurmbrand decided to become a pastor.

Fast-forward several years to a Rumanian prison where Wurmbrand had been sentenced to a long term. There he failed both to be re-educated and to reveal any important Christian conspiracies against the government. The uncooperative went up against the wall. Everything imaginable was done to dehumanize such inmates. Deprivation. Paralyzing fear. Brutality at every turn. At times they endured tortures that drove strong men insane. Guards forced them to become animals feeding on excrement.

In this hell Richard Wurmbrand survived as something of a renaissance man, gifted in the art of deepen-
ing other people, all kinds of people. The pastor was
able to relate to a whole menagerie of human beings
passing through the dark of that prison.

There was Grecu the dedicated communist lieutenant swinging his truncheon, demanding that Wurmbrand confess to a list of crimes. Given paper and
pencil Wurmbrand confessed faith in Christ who bade
him love his enemies. Grecu read the confession and
began asking questions. Wurmbrand patiently and
skillfully weaned the lieutenant away from ideology
and into allegiance to a personal God.

Then there was Radu Mironovici, former leader of
the fascist Iron Guard, who claimed to be a Christian
but constantly vented his hatred of Jews. Wurmbrand
broke through his pride. He showed Radu that, according to his own orthodox beliefs, he was adding a few
drops of Jewish blood to his Aryan blood every time he
took communion.

Dionisiu, a young sculptor pressured into working
for the secret police, came to Wurmbrand. Torn
between survival and conscience, he would beat prisoners and then try to warn them of informants. For ten
nights the pastor talked Dionisiu through his maze of
guilt.

Wurmbrand gave hope to an impoverished woman
who'd been driven to stealing in order to survive. "I
was in your church, and now you're a martyr and I'm a
thief," she said. But the pastor lifted her up to common
ground, showing how both of them were sinners saved
only by the grace of God.

He made prayer real for "the Professor," a scholar-
ly inmate who'd despaired of ever finding God. He
managed to establish rapport with "Fingers" a calloused thief constantly talking of his exploits. Wurmbrand told him, "You've taught me a great lesson. If

beatings don't persuade you to give up your ways, why should I listen to those who want me to change mine? I must put at least as much thought into winning a soul as you do into pulling off your next coup."

The pastor found grounds for compassion even for the vilest offenders whom every prisoner despised. When fellow inmates abused a man who'd shot Jews by the hundreds, Wurmbrand interjected, "We don't know where he will spend eternity: If it's with Christ we're abusing a future citizen of Heaven; and if it's in hell, why add curses to his suffering?"

During seventeen years of mistreatment Richard Wurmbrand ministered to human beings narrowed and distorted by a myriad of hatreds and prejudices. He kept finding ways to open hearts and broaden minds. He had a remarkable gift for identifying with them all: sinners and saints, fascists and communists, clergymen and thieves, the broken and the proud. The one-dimensional playboy had met a Living God.

18

SHEPHERD WISE

DR. EJNAR LUNDBY drove up to the massive gray walls of the prison with great misgivings. He'd been asked to visit a prisoner named Kristian Himler, who was to be executed in a few days. During World War II the man had betrayed his country by helping plant a bomb in a building used by Norwegian patriots. An underground leader whom Lundby greatly admired had been killed.

Now he was supposed to minister to this assassin's spiritual needs. It seemed beyond his ability, but Lundby knew he had to go.

The doctor found Himler lying on his cell bed, staring at the ceiling. He asked, "Is there any way I can help you?"

Himler cursed his visitor.

Lundby stood silently a moment and realized his own emotions might be getting in God's way. He prayed for compassion and for Himler, then laid a Bible on the table. "Himler, you may not want to listen to my words," he said quietly. "That's all right, I'm only human. But I've brought you the words of One who is divine and who can help you because He cares for you in spite of all you've done."

The prisoner sat up in his bunk and stared at Lundby. He looked sullenly at the Bible, shrugged his shoulders and laid down again.

259

The following day a friend asked Lundby to accompany him to a conference in Switzerland. He was about to accept, when "to my astonishment I felt the strongest kind of inner guidance that I should go and see Kristian again."

Lundby had learned from members of a revival movement called the Oxford Group how to develop a sensitivity to God's leading by saturating his mind with Scripture and listening quietly during periods of prayer. He'd been skeptical about "guidance" at first, knowing how easily human desires can be projected as nudgings from heaven. But slowly he began to receive "communications" and gain confidence in their accuracy.

So when the inner voice urged him to return to the indifferent prisoner, he obeyed.

As soon as Lundby entered Himler's cell he saw something had come over the man. He'd washed and shaved himself and combed his hair. He greeted Lundby warmly and told him how grateful he was for the Bible. He'd been reading it avidly. The two had a long talk and Himler committed his life to Christ. After prayer, as they parted, he said, "I'm ready to die now for the crime I committed."

Lundby walked from the prison exhilarated by the conversion he'd just witnessed. But the inner voice stopped him cold. "Himler lied to you," it said clearly. Lundby wondered why on earth the man would lie just after becoming a believer. But the voice persisted and Lundby reluctantly returned to Himler's cell.

The prisoner was staring at his Bible. Lundby asked, "Why did you lie to me a few minutes ago?"

Himler looked up in shock and then back down at his Bible. "How incredible," he whispered, "that my lie should be exposed twice at the same time." He'd just read a verse in Job about "hiding counsel."

Pale and shaking, Himler explained that his acceptance of Christ had been sincere but that he'd lied about the bombing. He'd been forced only to drive the car; the actual killer had escaped.

"Why didn't you tell the truth at the trial?"

Himler explained that the bomber had a family to care for, "but I am single."

With three days left before the execution, Lundby began a frantic effort to free this man. After a few more choice directions from that inner voice, the doctor managed to slip through legal roadblocks and procure a postponement just before the execution. Eventually Himler was released.

DR. LUNDBY DID NOT regard his remarkable directives as "unexplained psychic phenomena." For him, they were simply the result of plugging into God, an all-knowing God. His inner voice was a part of God's omniscience.

The Bible speaks of a God whose eyes rove over the whole earth and pierce into our innermost secrets. Nothing is hidden from Him, not even the future. He gives names to all the stars and counts the hairs on our heads.

God knows everything. But "knowing" in the Bible is not quite the same as our English idea of knowing—a mental apprehension of something. For the writers of Scripture, to know X is to experience X, as when Adam "knew" his wife and she conceived.

God's all-knowing is all-experiencing. He does not cast an analytic, comprehensive glance from an ivory tower. He knows through experience. In this kind of omniscience, this deeper kind of knowledge, I see merging the Eternal Absolute and the Adaptable Person, the Rock and the Flowing Stream. Or at least I see a little of how they are combined to good effect.

God's knowing is eternal, absolute. He knows exhaustively because He is the objective observer, not submerged in the flow of things. He sees all things from that still point of peace. Yet His knowledge is experience—that of a person, rubbing up against things. God knows texture and emotion. He doesn't take it down in outline form. He's in touch with the pieces, the full uncontainable richness of life.

God is a rock of truth; His views are immovable, but He is not unmoved. His knowing is not that of a computer, gobbling up megabytes, churning all the data into mechanical formulas. He takes it all in as a person, mixing perfect knowledge with feeling, responding to us out of a wealth of experience.

This is what Dr. Lundby discovered. When he tuned in to God's kind of knowing he found an absolutely reliable source of information and also a Person caught up in the plight of a man wrongly imprisoned.

Eternal and experienced. That is why God's omniscience is so good. It's wisdom, not just exhaustive information. And so when it strikes us, the illumination goes deep; eternal principles strike us personally. God's kind of knowing often comes in strong doses.

FRANCES RIDLEY HAVERGAL longed to have God "say 'many things' to me." One Advent Sunday in 1873 the all-knowing One dropped a bit of wisdom on her about "the blessedness of true consecration." It went deep: "I saw it as a flash of electric light, and what you *see* you can never *unsee*."

John Bunyan agonized about how one could be sure of forgiveness and salvation. Out walking in the fields one day, a phrase from Scripture fell on him with liberating force: "Thy righteousness is in heaven." Everything became crystal clear. Bunyan felt as if chains had fallen off him and he was "loosed from my afflictions."

While laboring under religious despair in his youth, Charles Spurgeon wandered into a Primitive Methodist Chapel and listened as an unlearned layman worked one text to death: "Look unto me, and be ye saved, all the ends of the earth." The man kept harping on the fact that we must, "Look! Look! Look to Jesus Christ." And suddenly that one word unlocked the mystery of faith for Spurgeon. He did "look" and, thrilled by this bit of wisdom, felt he had "passed from darkness into marvellous light, from death to life."

Riverside, California. 1970.

SATURDAY MORNING I skipped breakfast and knelt by my bed. Burying my head in my hands I leaned hard into God: "You know what a mess I'm in. You know every blind alley I've been down in search of a clear mind. You are the One who put all the circuits together in my head. I need some rewiring. I need . . . I don't know exactly what. But I've got to get out from under this weight of doubt. It makes me see only the shadows when I know Your world is full of light and color. I believe You have an answer for me."

That prayer came after two years of painful struggle. (And another year would go by before reading Schaeffer's *The God Who Is There* would overwhelm me with the thoroughness of Christianity's answers to the big questions.) I had always taken doubts seriously and sought good reasons for my faith. But during my senior year in high school those doubts became obsessive. It was as if I had this sinister detective following me around, always asking pointed questions, never letting me really answer. He kept poking around for some loophole in my faith, always insinuating there was a fatal flaw somewhere. I just couldn't come up with a coherent defense all the time.

It wasn't that I lacked good answers. Christian apologetics seemed pretty sound to me. But I kept getting caught in circles, pushed into going over the same old ground again. I felt uneasy if I turned away from this "unsparing honesty."

In college those circles tightened. Sometimes it

seemed like my head was under attack. I couldn't think straight while the detective of doubt pressed me up against the wall and frisked me for "five good reasons why you believe." Finally, after a few intense interrogations I began to fear I was losing control of my mind. That's when I got desperate enough to try the old "fast and pray" all-purpose remedy.

After a long session of pleading with the Lord I began looking through the Bible for some potent word that might unknot my chronic tangle of reasons and rebuttals. Verses on faith caught my attention. "Faith . . . comes by hearing the Word of God." Yes I was listening as best I could. "Faith in His name . . ." Yes I was concentrating on Christ.

I read about the peace that passes all understanding, about setting our hearts and minds on things above and bringing every thought into captivity to Christ.

Rebounding between Scripture and prayer I kept after my goal. Paul's metaphor rang true. We *are* runners racing for a prize; we must persevere. It was all a matter of opening myself up to the Lord and hanging in there until something happened.

Only nothing happened. I was warmed and encouraged by the Word, but no clear answer popped out from its pages. I still had no alibi for my persistent detective.

In the afternoon I ran out of things to say to God and decided to go out with a group of students to sing at a local hospital. For some reason I felt benevolent after pleading with the Lord all morning on an empty stomach.

In the hospital we sang a few choruses and visited with patients. But gradually the smell of medicine, blood and urine started to get to me. Feeling weak already from my fast, I started getting light-headed. Hurrying out to the parking lot I found our van and collapsed on its carpeted floor.

SHEPHERD WISE

I lay there regaining my strength and watched a few slow clouds through the windows. Then, out of the blue, something struck me: "It's only a feeling." That concentrated bit of wisdom nestled into my brain for a few seconds and then exploded.

Yes, that's exactly right. It *is* only a feeling. All this hide-and-seek game of apologetics has been so disturbing because it's been so vague. It has little to do with the content of faith. It's just an altercation of feelings.

That explanation seemed perfectly obvious. Surely it had occurred to me before. I'm sure I'd tried to tell myself things like that many times. All my other efforts during the past two years, however, hadn't enabled me to stop fretting with the detective.

As I lay in the van, the message "It's only a feeling" had the freeing power of a precise exorcism; the demon had been named and captured by God's word of wisdom. Everything cleared. I was not in the same mental impasse and I knew it. The detective of doubt would never again return to haunt me.

GOD'S ABSOLUTE and personal way of knowing does have a penetrating quality to it. We are told the all-seeing God pierces human hearts with His gaze. He searches through every soul and understands every motive behind our thoughts. Nothing in all creation is hidden from His sight.

Shiloh, Judah. c. 910 B.C.

KING JEROBOAM, the man who sponsored two golden calf deities in the northern kingdom of Israel, wanted badly to gain a hearing with a prophet of Jehovah named Ahijah. Jeroboam's son was seriously ill and the king wondered whether the boy would ever be able to succeed him. What would become of his dynasty?

Jeroboam had been toying with idols and high

places for some time now but he still knew that there was only one source of absolute knowledge, Jehovah. So he wanted to get the bottom line from God's prophet. The problem was, Ahijah wouldn't give idolatrous Jeroboam the time of day. So the king came up with a brilliant alternative.

He gave his wife ten loaves of bread, some cakes and a jar of honey and had her dress down as your run-of-the-mill farmer's wife. She was to go to the prophet in this disguise, ask about the fate of a certain king's son and, they hoped, get a good answer.

Jeroboam's wife dutifully traveled from Samaria down to a little town called Shiloh. She located the prophet's residence, adjusted her convincingly tattered garments, walked up to the door and was just about to knock when she heard an old, cracking voice from the inside call out, "Come in, wife of Jeroboam."

Imagine how the queen must have felt, having come all that way in her careful disguise and suddenly finding herself exposed, without even the courtesy of receiving a curious glance.

As it turned out Ahijah could not have glanced. The aging prophet had lost his sight. But he remained very much tuned in to God's kind of knowing. He'd heard about who was going to drop by and why. God's wisdom had pierced right through all the layers—the prophet's blindness, the closed door, the disguise—and hit a bull's-eye.

Chicago to New York. 40,000 feet. 1980s.

A CALIFORNIA PASTOR—who had begun to believe God's active interventions in our lives are more prevalent than commonly believed—settled into his seat after takeoff, hoping for a relaxing flight. He glanced over at the middle-aged businessman across the aisle . . . and then did a double-take. In that split-second he'd spotted "in very clear and distinct letters" the word "Adultery" written across the man's face. The pastor rubbed his eyes and glanced over again. There it was, plain as day, "Adultery."

Now the man became aware he was being stared at. "What do you want?" he asked with some irritation.

Just then a woman's name flashed into the pastor's mind. He leaned across the aisle awkwardly and asked, "Does the name Jane mean anything to you?"

Immediately the man's face turned ashen and he whispered, "We've got to talk."

The two went upstairs to the jumbo jet's cocktail lounge. As they were climbing the stairs, the pastor got another message: "Tell him if he doesn't turn from his adultery, I'm going to take him."

This made the pastor even more uncomfortable. How was he supposed to drop that on a total stranger?

As they sat down, the man asked suspiciously, "Who told you that name?"

The pastor blurted out, "God told me." He was too rattled to think of a way to bring it up gracefully. Then he delivered the rest of the message, bracing himself for what he was sure would be an indignant, defensive reaction.

Instead the man crumbled and began to weep. In a choking voice he asked, "What should I do?"

The pastor had some suggestions. Before the plane landed, the stranger had repented, turned his life over to God, confessed his unfaithfulness to his wife (who was accompanying him) and watched as the pastor led her to faith in Christ.

GOD LOOKS INTO the secret places of the heart. But when He does so, it's with a surgeon's care, a personal touch. He doesn't overdo His exposés, forcing people indiscriminately into public confessions. We rarely have to worry about our latest sin coming out in red letters on our forehead. He usually employs more subtle means of making our sins find us out. But God does know when a revelation will have the most impact for good. And he does, on occasion, go for the bull's-eye.

The omniscience that peers into our souls also looks into the future. God the all-experiencing One somehow experiences that too; His unsearchable wisdom sees the end from the beginning.

Pharaoh's Palace, Egypt. c. 1700 B.C.

SEVEN SLEEK, FAT COWS walked right up out of the Nile and began grazing in the tall marsh grass on its banks. Then seven other cows arose from the river, ugly and gaunt. These seven skinny cows ate up the seven fat ones. End of dream.

Pharaoh couldn't get it out of his mind. He concluded, according to the prevailing orthodoxy, that the gods must be trying to get through. So the monarch summoned his magicians and wise men and commanded them to divine some sense out of his cow vision. For some reason these court advisers, skilled in the art of creative interpretation, couldn't come up with a good caption for the dream. None of their usual tag lines about coming prosperity and Pharaoh's future greatness made sense.

It was then that the ruler's chief cupbearer remembered Joseph, a Hebrew youth down in the royal dungeon who'd endeared himself to everyone by his cheery helpfulness. He had once interpreted two prisoners' dreams. He predicted that one would be hanged and one would be restored to office. And that's exactly what happened.

Pharaoh was interested. Guards brought Joseph out of his cell, had him cleaned up and stood him before mighty Pharaoh. After hearing about the dream, Joseph said, "God has told to Pharaoh what He is about to do."

The seven good cows signified seven years of plenty, seven years of abundant harvests in Egypt. The seven tubercular cows stood for seven years of famine when Egypt would suffer, "scorched by the east wind." The point of it all was this: if Pharaoh didn't do something to prevent it, the years of famine would eat up the years of abundance. Food would disappear; the people would starve.

Joseph suggested that grain be stored during the seven good harvests and held in reserve for the coming lean years. Pharaoh agreed. And he thought this Hebrew, gifted with a "divine spirit" was just the man to oversee the great task. In fact he was so impressed by this sliver of omniscience he'd just experienced that he gave Joseph his signet ring, placed a gold necklace about his neck, clothed him in fine linen and had him paraded around the palace as his viceroy.

The next fourteen years unfolded just as Joseph had predicted. Rich harvests gave way to severe famine. But Egypt had been prepared. Thousands were spared starvation because the all-knowing One had a man in place who could convey His wisdom.

Armenia. 1850s.

EFIM WAS KNOWN as the "boy prophet" in Kara Kala, a village of cattle herders nestled amid the rocky foothills of Mount Ararat. He'd shown a gift for prayer and fasting from early childhood. At the age of eleven, Efim was "called" to one of his long prayer vigils; this one lasted seven days and seven nights. And this one produced a vision.

Sitting in his little stone cottage he saw before him charts and a message in beautiful handwriting. Efim asked for pen and paper. His parents wondered why; the boy could neither read nor write. But he proceeded to copy down the letter shapes and the diagrams that passed before him. He wrote it all down sitting on the rough plank-table where the family ate.

When the village readers looked at the finished manuscript they discovered the illiterate child had written out in perfect Russian a series of instructions and warnings. At some future time every Christian in Kara Kala would be in terrible danger. Thousands of men, women and children would be murdered. At that time everyone must flee to a land across the sea.

The boy also indicated exactly where they were to go. Although he'd never seen a geography book, he drew a recognizable outline of the Atlantic ocean and the east coast of the United States.

Fifty years later, just after the turn of the century, Efim the aging "boy prophet" announced that the time had come. "We must flee to America. All who remain here will perish."

Not everyone in Kara Kala wanted to pull up roots from their ancestral lands. But some heeded Efim's word, packed up their belongings, and began the long journey to America.

In 1914 the time of horror came. Turks drove two-thirds of the Armenian population into the Mesopotamian desert. Over a million men, women and children perished during these death marches. Half a million more were butchered in their villages.

Those from Kara Kala who'd escaped the holocaust wept for their slain countrymen and thanked God they'd listened at that critical moment when the all-seeing One shared His wisdom.

GOD'S OMNISCIENCE comes close to us. It's not just a great data-bank in the sky; it's that "lamp to my feet and a light for my path." Eternal truths and personal insights make the Lord a trustworthy guide, a wonderful counselor. Dr. Lundby, the pastor on the airplane, Joseph, and many others have enjoyed a taste of His omniscience, in sync with superhuman knowing for a while, sailing along in an eternally significant wind.

The image of a good shepherd also comes to mind. I think of a weather-beaten face out there on the hills peering out from deep-set eyes. Winter's cold wind, spring's dewy breezes, sunsets, starlit vigils, dangers, tranquil meadows—they're all etched in a countenance rock-steady, looking out over the flock, counting every lamb. The wisdom of the shepherd comes close. It's experience; he knows every stand of good grass, every rocky precipice, every spot where streams flow slow and deep. It's good to have a guide like that.

Wilderness of Zin. After the Exodus. c. 1260 B.C.

THE PEOPLE were panicking again. Their water jars poured dry, they could see no way of replenishing the supply out there in that trackless wasteland. The familiar litany of complaints arose again: We should have stayed in Egypt. We wish we were dead. We're all going to die. The Israelites at this point had a gift for overdramatizing their plight.

Moses, as usual, took the matter to the Lord. The Lord sent him to a rock. He was to give a command and water would gush forth from the stone. Moses, who had seen just about everything, believed this also.

He gathered the Israelites from their tents and, looking out over their whining faces, lost his temper. Instead of commanding the water to come forth in the name of the Lord, he shouted at the "rebels" around him and struck the rock twice with his rod.

Water gushed out anyway. The people and their livestock drank their fill.

NEW TESTAMENT WRITERS were quite taken with this picture of water gushing out of the rock. It became one of the Bible's great metaphors. God is the eternal Rock, and through Him pours the water of life, flowing everywhere.

I like the image too. It suggests that God can be simultaneously an immovable point of peace and a torrent of passion. And it's also a way to put many other divine attributes together. God, the Rock of power, sovereignty, justice, and transcendence, also flows close by as a merciful, adaptable Servant.

The Most Holy Place. Always.

TWENTY-FOUR ELDERS approach the great white throne on a sea of glass. Dressed in white garments, wearing golden crowns, they fall down at the feet of Him who lives forever and ever and throw their crowns at His feet, declaring that He alone is worthy of glory and honor and power.

Lighting flashes. Thunder peals. An emerald rainbow around the throne pulsates. Then four symbolic creatures, full of eyes, stare at Him: Arms and feet of burnished bronze. Garments whiter than any launderer on earth could bleach them. Voice like the sound of a multitude, like the sound of many waters. Eyes flaming fire. Face like the sun in its strength.

They call out ceaselessly, "Holy, Holy, Holy, is the Lord God, the Almighty, who was and who is and who is to come."

TAKING IN THIS SCENE of heavenly worship described in Revelation 4, I always wondered what it would be like to repeat that refrain over and over. Was, is, is to come. It has a nice ring at first, but wouldn't it get old after a while? I couldn't quite get the point of what seemed to be a rather monotonous adoration.

The Sahara. 1920s.

ANTOINE DE SAINT-EXUPÉRY, a French aviator flying the mails across the Sahara, was anxious to talk to the three Moslem chieftains returning from the trip of their lives. They'd been flown to France for a visit. Since the day of their birth these nomads had seen only sand and desert scrub stretching from horizon to horizon. What was it like for them to tour Paris, see the Eiffel Tower and the Palace of Versailles?

Saint-Exupéry asked. The tribesmen seemed rather indifferent. They granted that the Louvre was "very big." But technical progress had not impressed them. Locomotives, automobiles, telephones—they were curiosities to be sure, but not curious enough to break the composure of Allah's proud warriors.

Then the three chieftains recalled a trip into the French Alps and they could not speak for a moment. The memories moved them too deeply. Slowly Saint-Exupéry coaxed the story out. A guide had led the three to a tremendous waterfall, a braided column of water that thundered over the rocks. The Sahara tribesmen tasted it. It was sweet.

Water! A thing worth its weight in gold. How many times had they marched for days to reach some well where they had to dig deep for a few cupfuls of muddy liquid. When a little rain fell in the Sahara, tribes might ride two hundred miles toward a bit of grass springing up in the sand.

The men stood transfixed. The guide tried to lead them away to the next scenic spot. They wouldn't budge: "Leave us here a little longer." Here roaring out of the belly of a mountain was the life-blood of man. Here God was manifesting Himself and they did not want to turn their backs.

"That's all there is to see," the guide said.

"We must wait," they insisted.

"Wait for what?"

"The end."

It was inconceivable that this torrent of water could just flow on and on. How could it never stop? The Sahara tribesmen were shaken to their roots. They wondered how Allah could possibly pour such unfathomable blessings on infidels.

Then the guide delivered a final blow: "But that water has been running for a thousand years!"

SOME TIME AFTER reading Saint-Exupéry's story I began to see how we fit into that heavenly worship, calling out praises with the symbolic creatures.

We're staring at a waterfall, rushing from the Rock. We can't believe how such mercy can go on and on. Doesn't God ever get fed up with us? We can't fathom holiness going on and on. With heroic effort we manage to scratch out a few minutes of virtue in the self-centered rush of our days on earth. But here's someone whose goodness never misses a beat.

His passion for justice rolls on, undiluted, uncompromising. He is a servant always there for us, the water of eternal life flowing on and on to be soaked up by many rags. His patience, faithfulness and compassion form an endless stream splashing down around us.

Nothing in our morally barren world has prepared us for this sight. We stand transfixed before such an abundant Life; we gape at a Person eternally demonstrating His excellence. Nothing can make us budge.

‖ PART VII ‖

Clear and Present Picture

THE FATHER, SEEING HIS
PRODIGAL SON, RAN
TO MEET ME.

Sergius Bulgakov

19

MANCHILD

HER FOREHEAD WET, her cheeks flushed, she lies wrapped in white, reminding me of Lazarus writhing out of the cave with a new life. I stand by the bed feeling like a gawky appendage.

The labor room would look odd with rustic paintings or bright wallpaper I admit, but the fatigued green paint hovering about us seems excessively solemn.

It is 10 P.M. All the carefully memorized contraction sequences flow together indecipherably, like so much static. Beside a silver pitcher of water on the night stand, a machine resembling a seismograph steadily rolls out lined paper. The ink jerks jagged and erratic. The peaks cut higher and higher on the graph. I know they only measure Kazko's contractions, but as I keep staring at the slow, steep crescendo and feel her hand grip mine hard, the machine begins to seem almost volitional, as if it were the cause of these abdominal assaults.

A few times during the long night there are lulls in the struggle. My wife rests. I retreat to a couch in the fathers' waiting room and try to sleep. At 2 A.M. I am alone. A row of amiable ferns and the homey sofa can't overcome the eerie emptiness of the place.

My mind fastens on another, distant scene. I wonder: How did Jehovah feel while Mary labored in that Bethlehem barn? Surrounded by adoring angels and the

279

glories of heaven, what did He think about delivering His babe into the quagmire of this earth? I can almost picture Him pacing back and forth among the cherubim.

Back in the labor room a little electric dot jogs around its track. Fetal heartbeat they say. I prefer not to understand. The signs I do know about are unnerving enough.

I continue rubbing her back, counting and breathing rhythmically, and lifting her up. Still I can't get into where the blows strike. I'm in another world.

The Sovereign God had to wait too—as if helpless, staring at His palms, taking a back seat to cows and shepherds. He was no amateur attendant. His hands had not lost their skill since fashioning the orchids, gazelles, and DNA of this planet. Yet He must remain hidden. Disarmed.

The nurses have been kind and firm through the sluggish early morning hours. But my winded mate has long ago given up being gutsy. She takes all the medication her groans can squeeze out of them.

Finally our infant makes a telling move. They roll one body of pale flesh (soon to be made two) into a delivery room full of stainless steel. I sneak in behind a green gown and am surrounded by an ominous array of instruments and pale green sterility. While I wipe her forehead, she is spread-eagled and harnessed for the big push. I can't help thinking of an experimental aircraft buzzing over a cliff on its first attempt.

I imagine the suspense that must have hung over Bethlehem. God was to become man—the once-in-eternity event. Everything depended on that tiny, frail life struggling in the womb. The fate of the human race hung in the balance.

Before my tense senses the doctor grabs steel forceps. Great claws they are, looking like something from Joe's Garage. He inserts them (blindly it seems) around those tiny eyes, lips, nose—gets a good grip and pulls hard, grunting like a stevedore. The baby doesn't budge.

Suction. They crank it up. The machine rattles like a Model T. There's no smooth professional-sounding hum to comfort the rookies here awaiting our firstborn. The doctor slips the suction cup in. He plants his feet, grasps the tube and leans back, face turning red. I squirm miserably. The suction cup pops off, sending our physician flying backwards. Any other time a touch of Keystone Cops would have been amusing, but this is nerve-racking.

Then I remember the Father and the clumsy hands that seized His Son. A sensitive, guileless youth given up into the hands of hardened men—what more foolhardy thing could this God have done? His heavenly character is lost on us. We fumble and grab rudely at a treasure grossly misunderstood.

And Pilate delivered Him up to the will of the mob. Their voices prevail. When Christ's arms are yanked across the wood I see the Father involuntarily stretch out His arm, cringing. The cry pierces.

Suddenly a manchild is plopped down warm on my wife's stomach. He is there. I don't know how. He still grimaces from the violence of his arrival. My heart stops. His cry pierces. He gasps in the cold, arms waving helpless as those of a man falling through black, featureless space.

Could the Christ have been like this? God Almighty smudged with dark blood, squinting in the strangeness, head distended, limbs unwieldy as crowbars.

A nurse gently wipes the newborn's face. I nonchalantly rush over and count fingers, arms, eyes . . . everything is there. A son without blemish. And yet when the nurse brings his face close to us he is surprisingly like no one in particular, nothing recognizable, someone you'd bump into on the street.

And the Father saw Jesus made flesh. He became

Another. The Godhead had been joyously one in the womb of heaven for all eternity. Now that womb must be broken. Souls indivisibly intertwined must bear the deep ripping.

After our child is bathed, measured and clothed, I run from nursery window to Kazko's bedside reporting each momentous event—his tongue is moving; he's staring at his left hand.

There in the recovery room we need to release our exhilaration heavenward. Fluid with the miracle that has just passed through us, we pour out a prayer of thanksgiving to God. The weariness of the long night is gone.

The Father too rejoiced in the Messiah's birth, though knowing every detail of Jesus' coming sacrifice. It was a potent love welling up in Jehovah that opened His hands and delivered the Infant into our calloused ones. To draw us to Himself, he became vulnerable. He saw many other sons, twice-born, emerging from the dark like Lazarus, writhing with a new life.

THE GIFT of the Manchild climaxes all the biographical data about God that went before and looms over all that has come after. God-in-the-flesh has come into our living room and sat for a portrait. He is the clear and present picture of what everyone from Egyptian priests to Philo to Alfred North Whitehead has speculated about.

No human being looking upward can ignore this revelation. I have a sense that any attempts, however contemporary, to take notes on God while ignoring Jesus are giant steps backward. Nothing I have seen comes close to the wealth of illuminating data that emerges from four slim, overlapping Gospels.

To a certain extent Christ demonstrates one side of God more heavily than another. Obviously He is more down here than Most High while walking the sheep-trails of Galilee. The itinerant Rabbi strikes us as more servant than sovereign. And of course we see in Jesus more of a Person than an Eternal Absolute. That was the point. God came here in part to fill out a misunderstood part of the picture.

It's also true that Christ lived encumbered with the limits of human nature. He did not come in full glory—no one would have survived His appearance. But in His three-and-a-half-year career we do see glimpses of God in all His fullness. The divine opposites mesh. Living water flows from the Rock.

We see a miracle-worker who makes it look so easy. A touch, a word, and it's done. "Tabitha, rise." "Be still." "Rise and walk." He's confident, this minimalist of form. Jesus is so unobtrusive in His work that one wonders if anything has happened at all. But the results persuaded witnesses that they were beholding a skill qualitatively different from anything they'd seen before.

Here He is driving the merchants and money-changers out of the temple. A bustling, lucrative business melts away before the consuming fire in Jesus' eyes. And here He is eating with publicans and prostitutes, rescuing the woman taken in adultery, scandalizing the upright with His wide gestures of mercy.

Watch Him confronted by a leper. The crowd shrinks back in horror. They stare at Jesus—will the Master touch the untouchable? Yes, He places a hand firmly on the diseased man's shoulder. God is with man. But He remains transcendent, more than. Jesus is not defiled by the leper, He cleanses the disease. The outcast's decayed flesh reverses to ruddy health. Joy bursts out as the Most High shows Himself very present.

This Jesus commanded with authority. With a quick rebuke He made a raging storm calm down like a naughty child brought suddenly to its senses. He once ordered a funeral procession to stop, summoned a young man from stone-cold death and turned the trail of mourners into an ecstatic parade. But in all His wonder-working He remained a servant. He spent most of

His time out in the countryside, patiently ministering to the clamoring crowds. Each and every miracle met a genuine human need. Skeptics could never provoke Him into showing off His powers.

Here was a Man who grew tired and thirsty, who longed for sympathetic companionship. Yet He became a rock upon whom others depended. The disciples were schooled by His consistent example. He never let them down, remaining a faithful friend to the end.

Christ's life reaches the height and depth, the breadth and width of God—all of it acted out in a dusty, backward Roman province. His short life was packed so full that there's always more to discover. Jesus is the antithesis of a black hole; His compacted biography explodes with light. Even looking at just one day, we contemplate a dazzling whole.

Jerusalem. A.D. 31.

GOD COLLAPSED. Somewhere in the narrow, winding street leading out of the city, His bloodied back gave way under the weight of a large wooden cross. He dropped to His knees on the stone pavement; the crown of thorns jarred deeper; blood mingled with His sweat; He gasped for air. The accused had stood courageously silent during an abusive trial the previous night. He would suffer heroically in the hours to come. But here in the narrow street He hurt as a common criminal kicked about toward execution. He was humiliated, unable to bear the load, unable to walk tall and straight toward His fate.

Nowhere can we see God more with us, more immanent. In this day of extremes, the grim procession pushed ahead a Man closed in by suffering, seeing only cobblestones, the butt of spears, gray walls, tramping feet. Bent almost double, He tried to stagger on, someone very much with us, hurting just as we hurt, walking by our carpentry shops, vegetable markets, front porches, as pathetic as any street urchin trampled by the harsh world.

Roman soldiers grabbed a stranger from Cyrene and placed the cross on his back. Jesus stumbled along behind, leading a vast funeral procession of the weeping, the wondering, the mocking.

The criminal passed by a row of women and recognized something familiar in their heartfelt lament. Looking up at their faces He recognized several who had supported Him throughout His ministry. They had watched this Man heal paralytics with a touch and sway multitudes with His "Verily, verily . . ." To see Him so abased was more than they could bear.

They had much to mourn about, staring at the incomprehensible climax of a glorious career. And Jesus had much to think about. He faced the slow torture reserved for the worst of Rome's offenders, and the prospect of entering hell—utterly cast off by God.

An ordinary man facing agony can be admired for keeping his sanity. It takes all one's strength and more to brace for the ordeal ahead. But Jesus somehow looked right through it. He turned to His weeping friends and asked them not to cry for Him but for themselves. A day of terrible trial was coming. A day when people would pray for the mountains to fall on them.

The accused stood there bleeding and heaving and worried about the trial these believers would face, as if they, not He, were the center of cosmic conflict. This man wasn't there in the narrow street; He stood far above looking over the horizon at events decades away, preparing His followers for their moment of truth: A.D. 70, the destruction of Jerusalem.

How much He transcended Himself—the pathetic, exhausted figure pushed about by Roman soldiers. It was the Most High they goaded on, One who rose far above the cruelty around Him and painted a bright streak of compassion along the enclosing gray.

THEY MOVED ON through the East Gate and up toward a hill called the Skull where the bodies of rapists, extortioners, and murderers had breathed their last. In an act of mercy strangely out of place on that terrifying hill the executioners offered Jesus wine mixed with gall. He declined the anesthetic, choosing to walk into hell with eyes wide open.

The soldiers lay their prisoner down on the cross and tied His arms to the crossbeams. Working quickly and efficiently they pounded spikes into His hands and feet, trying to avoid looking at the Man's face. To survive work as executioners, they must make it impersonal. They lifted up the cross with the accused impaled on it and heaved it into a hole.

Thud. Into the Earth. Deep. God nailed to the fate of the planet. He had said so clearly. Even though the soldiers had avoided Jesus' eyes they had heard His words: "Father forgive them. They don't know what they are doing."

God again was manifested in the extreme. It is one thing to forgive after time heals the wounds and mutes the memory. It is one thing to forgive the trembling penitent bowing at your feet. But forgiving the spikers in the act. Being lifted up as a jarring spectacle and then pleading grace for the whole miserable world. That is extravagant mercy. That's too much—holy ointment wasted on those at the foot of the cross who see only a few shekels to be made off a seamless garment.

Jesus hung suspended above a crowd of spectators, His shoulders slowly pulled out of joint; soon He would begin to suffocate. A few passersby saw irony. This distended victim was the same presumptuous rabbi who they heard had boasted he could destroy the temple and rebuild it in three days. They suggested that if he were the great Son of God he should come right down from the cross. All Christ's claims seemed summarily disproved there on the Skull.

His arch-rival priests took up the mockery. "He's the big savior but he can't even save his own neck." They taunted Jesus, "Come down from the cross and we'll believe in you."

Surely this would come as an irresistible challenge to the man who had raised the dead and quieted a raging sea storm with a three-word reprimand. How easily He could have made those gloating priests in their dignified robes choke on their words. All it would take was a bit of the power that had stopped violent demoniacs dead in their tracks.

But the omnipotent miracle-worker restrained Himself. He did absolutely nothing (it seemed). He appeared—for all the world—as the weakest, the most powerless, allowing His enemies to go away boasting that He had proved their point by His silence.

Here was evil at its most flagrant. Unmasked. A mad tragedy. The destruction of the best. And God didn't move a muscle.

AT NOON THE SKY suddenly darkened. The blazing sun was obscured. What appeared to be a violent storm filled the sky and threw an end-of-the-world eeriness over the terrified spectators crowded on the Skull. The darkness lasted an eternity of three hours during which many flippant souls gave up hope of ever seeing blessed daylight again. Toward the end the earth itself began trembling. Huge rocks tore into pieces. Tombs were shaken violently until they gave up their dead.

The God of the storm had arrived on the scene. Silent, yes. But all heaven and earth convulsed when He shook with grief over the death of the spotless Son. Every spectator felt to the bone the elemental force of His sorrow.

In His most powerless stance, God became the Victorious Warrior. Christ acted as more than a meek Lamb led to the slaughter. He was also an aggressive participant in the Passion. When spineless Pilate threatened Jesus, He replied: "No one takes my life from Me, unless I give it up."

The cross was a weapon Christ wielded. He attacked the darkest heart of evil. He walked into hell as a man swinging wildly, laying people out with His stunning sacrifice. He still uses it to pierce hearts. People are moved from evil to good by those blows.

And so God becomes skillful creator, the transformer of human life, doing nothing but doing everything. Passive but endlessly active. Creating righteousness through the spectacle of Himself overwhelmed by evil.

In the midst of that noonday darkness, Jesus was overwhelmed to the point of crying out, "My God, My God, why have You forsaken Me?"

Here He had reached another extreme: God's passion for justice taken to its end. Christ had taken on the hideous cloak of human sin. From the horror of Assyria's skinned captives to the gassed human pyramids of Auschwitz, it all came together on the shoulders of the accused.

God turned away in revulsion. His whole being cried out against the terrible wrongs done. The seamless bond of Father and Son tore apart. That separation ripped so loud in Christ that it muffled all the other sounds of agony. He could take the humiliation before His own chosen people. He could take betrayal by His closest friends. He could stand up under the beatings and the mockery. He could even endure the jagged pain of dying impaled on a cross.

But He could not endure the Father's face turned away. Anything but that. Christ knew why it had to be. He knew He'd been given as a Manchild for this hour. But when the awful moment came, everything but anguish was blocked out. He could see and feel only the abyss of eternity without God.

Alone, cast off by heaven and earth, the derelict

showed His greatest courage. When every fiber of His being demanded that He flee from the dark, He hung on stubbornly to His weapon. Not even the ultimate terror of eternity apart from God could make Him let go.

So the Son died with a shattered heart. When the soldiers pierced His side for good measure, out flowed water and blood.

Justice asked so much. Behind the mercy that flows so extravagantly towards us lies an extravagant cost. After Jesus' gracious words of forgiveness comes the price. On the cross Christ displays the fire of justice, the warmth of mercy, melded into one act of atonement.

IN THE MIDST OF THIS HELL, Jesus looked down and saw His mother standing nearby, sobbing uncontrollably. How was she to recover from the ordeal of watching her Son die as a criminal? Who would take care of her in the future when He was gone?

The focus of the whole universe centered on Jesus' ordeal. Nothing as important had ever happened or ever would happen. Yet Jesus, again, looked beyond. He spotted His disciple John, the one who'd been most affectionate and most receptive to His teachings. That was the answer. Who better to keep Mary comforted with his memories as a beloved disciple? John was also the one best able to benefit from Mary's cherished recollections.

Jesus fought for a good breath and called out hoarsely: "Woman, behold your son!" Looking at John He said, "Behold, your mother."

Done. Their needs taken care of. Jesus remained the irrepressible servant, still helpful in hell.

Servant and Sovereign. At the very end He drew Himself up on His spiked feet and shouted loudly, "It is finished!" Christ was not finished off. He had finished off every obstacle and completed His sacrifice. Everything accomplished according to plan. The lamb led to the slaughter had been in control all along. When the gospel writers looked back on those scenes they saw with amazement how much happened precisely "in order that Scripture might be fulfilled."

Even sworn enemies unwittingly spoke the truth on behalf of the Sovereign sufferer. When a priest argued, "It's better for one man to die than for the whole nation to perish," he never dreamed he was arguing for the atonement. Every scene had its point and place: The mob calling for the release of lowlife Barabbas instead of the noble Christ as they stood side by side on Pilate's portico. Pilate washing his hands of responsibility. The Romans placing on the cross an inscription reading, in three languages, "King of the Jews." Christ crucified between two thieves. Even the worst mockery— "He saved others, but can't save himself"—strikes us now with its terrible, beautiful truth.

All these details served to amplify the theater of the cross. The Sovereign Lord had planned this drama down to the props. It would say what He willed it to say. Every participant would echo, wittingly or unwittingly, the great scenario planned from ages past.

There was one man there who got the point. One of the crucified thieves read the play as it was happening around him and turned to Christ with a request: "Remember me when you come in your kingdom."

He'd seen something of the Eternal in this Man who suffered so nobly, who didn't exist solely in this moment of numbing cruelty. He lived in touch with compassion and moral clarity, qualities patently unavailable on a cross.

This dying thief had heard rumors of a Messiah's eternal kingdom before. Now it seemed very real. So he called out from the dark. And Jesus promised that he would be with Him in paradise.

Snatched from time to eternity. Here was God promising absolutely, certainly. Welcoming the first unworthy applicant to fall into His arms.

Jesus spread-eagled on the cross embodied Everlasting Arms. They were stretched out unconditionally. Friends drifted away in embarrassment or terror. The arms stretched out. Israel mocked. The arms stretched out. The Father Himself turned away. The arms stretched out.

Jesus' welcome is carved in granite. Immovable. Nothing in heaven or hell can make Him fold the Everlasting Arms.

But it's more than a great statue up there welcoming us into eternity. It's someone who calls out from parched lips, "I thirst." His dying body craves water. He longs for physical relief.

And more. He'd made His cross into a weapon that pierces hearts. His call pierces also. He thirsts for people. The eternally open arms long for an embracing. It's isolation, after all, that's killing Him. God the Person is thirsty for face-to-face reconciliation. He longs for eternal relationships with the personalities He has created. And so Christ's passion crescendoes with a passionate call: "I thirst."

THIS ONE DAY in the dying of Jesus puts a capstone on His claim: "If you've seen Me, you've seen the Father."

20

FATHERLOVE

DR. PIA SANTIAGO took a few moments to visit with the Moslem noblewoman who'd brought her grandson in for an ear examination. She kept glancing curiously at something Bilquis Sheikh was holding. Finally she asked, "Madam Sheikh, what are you doing with a Bible?"

The stately woman with luminous eyes replied that she was earnestly searching for God and had been studying the Bible and the Koran. She was intrigued by Christianity but found it somewhat confusing: "You seem to make God so . . . I don't know . . . *personal.*"

The doctor, who was also a nun, suggested that Bilquis find out for herself why Christians felt this way. "Why don't you pray *to* the God you are searching for? Talk to Him as if He were your friend."

Bilquis smiled. It was like being told to talk to the Taj Mahal.

But then the doctor leaned closer, took Bilquis's hand, and said, "Talk to Him as if He were your father." For some reason those words shot through the Moslem woman like electricity.

In Pakistan the idea that God was a father, that He had children, was blasphemous. How could the Great One be brought down to a human level?

But what if God really were like a father? On the way home, Bilquis couldn't get the thought out of her

293

mind. Hours after going to bed it kept her wide awake. She fondly recalled her own father who would put aside everything to listen to his beloved child. Suppose, just suppose, God were like that . . .

Finally, sometime after midnight, Bilquis got up and knelt on the rug by her bed. Trembling with excitement and uncertainty she looked up toward heaven and spoke aloud, "Oh Father, my Father . . . Father God."

She was not prepared for the surge of confidence that followed. Suddenly Bilquis didn't feel alone; God was present. "He was so close," Bilquis recalled "that I found myself laying my head on His knees like a little girl sitting at her father's feet. For a long time I knelt there, sobbing quietly, floating in His love. I found myself talking with Him, apologizing for not having known Him before. And again came His loving compassion, like a warm blanket settling around me."

THOSE WHO COME into God's house are usually swept off their feet by a Father's love. That divine quality, in Scripture, seems to envelop all the others. The Psalms repeatedly celebrate Jehovah's love. His lovingkindness is everlasting. It fills the earth, reaches the heavens, stands firm forever. Priceless and unfailing, God's kind of love is better than life.

God's love better than life? I often wondered what the psalmist meant by that. Lately I've come to think he was declaring that if given a choice between experiencing fully God's love for a few moments and living the usual seventy-or-so years, the former would be preferable. Sound a bit farfetched? Granted, the Psalms speak with a certain poetic enthusiasm. But there are also many other witnesses of God's love who can identify with those exaggerated sentiments.

Charles Finney recalled a life-changing encounter with God's Holy Spirit in this way: "No words can express the wonderful love that was shed abroad in my heart. I wept aloud with joy and love. . . . These waves came over me, and over me, and over me, one after the other, until I recollected I cried out, 'I shall die if these waves continue to pass over me.' I said, 'Lord, I cannot bear any more'; yet I had no fear of death."

When Oswald Chambers found God's "special blessing" after years of agonized search he exclaimed: "Glory be to God, the last aching abyss of the human heart is filled to overflowing with the love of God. Love is the beginning, love is the middle and love is the end."

Another spiritual pilgrim, Samuel Logan Brengle of Salvation Army renown, found that "my heart was melted like wax before fire; Jesus Christ was revealed to my spiritual consciousness, revealed in me, and my soul was filled with unutterable love, I walked in a heaven of love." One day he told a friend: "This is the perfect love about which the Apostle John wrote; but it is beyond all I dreamed of; in it is personality; this love thinks, wills, talks with me, corrects me, instructs and teaches me."

THAT IS GOD'S Fatherlove. It animates all His actions and permeates all His thoughts toward us. Every divine attribute is molded by that quality.

It is love that impels God to be intensely present. Love enlarges His heart to omnipresence. And He is most transcendent precisely in that alien love that sacrifices itself so completely.

The Father's love cries out for justice: "How can you do this to my children!" And His love finds ingenious ways to zap the most unworthy with an overdose of mercy.

Love moves God to humble, unassuming acts of service. And love injects His sovereignty with an irresistible charisma. He compels allegiance by His willful compassion.

God's love stands constant and immovable, an eloquent call into His everlasting arms. And of course it's a Person who does the loving, and longs in His depths for love in return.

The Father's awesome attributes are seen most sharply through the prism of love. But those attributes also help define the word. The human experience we call "love" isn't a summary of God. Rather, His qualities fill out the meaning of that frail word. The human experience of fatherhood is no complete summary either. God has none of the typical male limitations. As is evident from the witnesses quoted above, He's not short on expressing affection. Rather, His qualities define what it means to be Father in Heaven.

God's Fatherlove surpasses human categories. It's not something one comes to know casually. It's usually encountered through experience, from the inside. We grasp it best not by observation but by doing. Our own acts of compassion sometimes open an unexpected window into His.

Macomb, Illinois. McDonough County Hospital. 1981.

JERRY AND I WALKED into Room 311 at the worst time. Barbara, our step-mother, was trying to suction Dad, holding his restless tongue flat with a suppressor, wiggling the tube gingerly down his congested throat. "If only I could keep him suctioned for one day," she explained reflexively in greeting, "maybe the pneumonia . . ." and then paused to thank us for flying out from California. Her drawn face made it clear she'd been fighting a losing battle for some time.

I had come with anxious expectations. After the stroke, how pale and emaciated would his face be? I did not want to see those familiar ruddy features wasting away. But it wasn't his face, still holding a bit of color, that shocked. It was his terrible struggle for breath, chest and abdomen heaving, never a moment's rest. I wasn't ready for suffering.

Then Barbara broke down. The frustration of struggling alone was too much. She'd promised herself she wasn't going to cry, but helpless, grateful tears come in our presence. Jerry and I, white-faced, jumped into the fray. Trembling, we tried to get the tube down deeper to the deadly, ever-forming mucus, and watched his eyes roll and his head shake in vain. His limbs were weak, his moans strong.

It was Saturday, a cold autumn day in Illinois. Jerry had to go pick up Dan, who was flying in from Colorado, at the airport in Moline. Outside the room he began weeping uncontrollably and stumbled toward the car. He continued sobbing on the interstate past miles of broad, flat farmland full of dead leaves.

Jerry remembered. Dad had been a man of few fears. We three boys grew up under the umbrella of his steadfast moral courage. But he had expressed one apprehension: He didn't want to die in a hospital—life taken away in small clinical pieces. Jerry remembered and wept.

Back in 311 Barbara talked to Dad incessantly. She wiped his forehead, smoothed the sheets, suctioned, adjusted the oxygen tube, and poured out hopeful, devoted words on her husband of three months. Every groan became a sentence she completed. She repeated his name, nodded yes, yes, encouraged every breath. By sheer force of will she created conversation in that brain flooded with sinister blood.

But I grew weary with the struggle and imagined Dad was too. If only he could sleep a little.

Barbara said the doctor had left instructions with the floor nurses not to resuscitate Dad should he stop breathing. I wanted to know why.

Out in the hall the doctor outlined the damage caused by a ruptured artery in the brain.

"So what are his chances of recovering?"

"I would say almost none."

"You're saying his brain is dead?"

"Well even if he recovers from the pneumonia . . . you must think of what you are going to have left. In order to recover, your father must regain basic functions. He must be able to swallow, to eat, he must be truly alert, recognize people. Otherwise he will just be a vegetable I'm afraid."

"What about words, talking? Barbara has heard him say a few."

"Well on occasion a patient may say a word, or move a limb, but it could just be some reflex action; it doesn't really mean the brain is functioning adequately."

I still wanted to know how the doctor was making his evaluation. "Okay, you did a brain scan. Can you tell exactly how and where the brain is damaged?"

"Well a brain scan doesn't really tell you about the future. Some people with minor damage will never recover. There are other people with half their brains gone who are functioning normally. The key is still function—the ability to eat and be alert."

The doctor left us with the suggestion that at some point the family might start thinking about when it would be appropriate to stop artificial support systems.

So we stood numbly in the hallway as visitors walked by. Finally Barbara sobbed, "I just wish I could have known him longer." I embraced her awkwardly and thought, Yeah, that's the rub; three months together and zap. I mumbled a few words about heaven. It was the first time in my life I had referred to it as a present consideration.

For some reason they moved Dad to 309. I couldn't decide whether that was good or bad. After he was settled in, Barbara wiped his forehead, smoothed the sheets, suctioned, adjusted the oxygen tube, and poured out her hopeful devoted words. She told me the pastor planned to come at three for an anointing service.

I wondered how I should pray. It seemed to me that

an "if it be Thy will" petition was very near to no petition at all. I was quite willing to wield some hard-hitting promises and pound on the Lord's door like that persistent widow in Jesus' parable. But I didn't want to see Dad go on suffering pointlessly. I was also willing to cooperate passively and give him up into God's hands. Should I fight in petition or should I rest in submission?

For some reason, looking at Dad's heaving thorax in Room 309, I wasn't willing to settle for a safe medium. I wanted to go one way or the other. After praying about how to pray I recalled the doctor's words concerning function. Maybe that could be a sign. We could ask God to give us an indication about how He wanted us to pray. And it wouldn't be something arbitrary.

Yes, there are two specific things: swallowing and recognizing people. If we see some bit of progress in these areas then we would know to petition for recovery all the way in earnest. If not, we would rest in prayer.

Barbara and I had a long talk about this and we agreed that our part in the anointing would be to ask for these particular signs.

The pastor and an elder arrived, old friends of the family. The pastor took out his tiny bottle of oil and rubbed a little on Dad's pallid forehead. He placed a hand on his numb shoulder and began to pray quietly. It was a very mild petition, just laying things out before the will of the Lord.

Suddenly Dan walked in the room, the firstborn, tall and broad-shouldered. Everyone looked up and saw his face white as a ghost. He strode over to the bed, bent down to kiss Dad and said, "I love you."

It turned out he and Jerry had just walked into Room 311 and found an empty bed, newly made. For a moment Dan thought he had arrived too late. After the relief of finding the right room, he wanted to make sure he got the good word in.

There were polite hugs all around, clumsy words

of encouragement for all present. My brothers said they would stay with Dad and urged me to go out for some food. I persuaded Barbara to take a break too.

Driving up the gravel road to Dad and Barbara's country house I spotted the red barn he had built for his horses. While Barbara fixed a bite I walked over to take a look.

Beneath a covering of leaves the grass looked terribly green, green as the tall stands I'd seen at Dad's boyhood farm near Texarkana. I stepped inside the barn and smelled the pungent hay. The horses were gone. But every beam stood sturdy as ever. Solid oak. He'd put up most of it by himself.

Dad built well. I remembered all the times I relied on him. I remembered well. . . . I was five, and slipped off his back while he was climbing out of the swimming pool. I couldn't swim, but they say I just lay in the water calmly (sinking), sure that Dad would fetch me out again. And of course he did. . . . I was twelve, walking with him in the woods he loved. It was always easy to talk. I had so many questions about right and wrong. And he lived the answers. . . . I was twenty, coming home from college on vacation. We would sit out on the porch looking at the sunset. When I shared how my faith was growing, his eyes would sparkle.

It was getting late. Shadows settled over the cornfields bordering Dad's place. I took a last look up at the sturdy oak rafters, breathed deeply the fragrance of wood and hay, and walked out into the dusk, grateful for good shelter.

Back at the hospital Jerry and Dan reported that Dad had slept awhile, breathing rather restfully for the first time. It was exhilarating news.

That night the three of us kept a vigil in Room 309, watching over the helpless man who had changed our diapers. He still heaved sometimes, but was definitely sleeping more than struggling. On occasion he snoozed very quietly. His shallow but regular breathing sounded wonderful.

We didn't talk much. But our night watch felt good. We changed his position at regular intervals, fiddled with the blankets, and jumped up whenever he groaned.

Slowly I began to understand why Dad always got up around 2 A.M. to check on us and smooth our blankets—even after we were older. This was the only time I had been up in the night for the one who was up so many nights for me. This was unexplored territory. In its strange stillness I came face to face with the power of his love for me. I knew then that I would love my children with the same unquenchable desire.

About ten on Sunday morning, Dan, Jerry and I returned to the hospital after a few hours of sleep. Nurses had disconnected the oxygen. Dad was breathing just fine on his own. They believed he'd licked the pneumonia. One said, "A miracle is just what we needed around here."

I walked over to the bed; Dad saw me and smiled. I grabbed on to the faint twinkle in his eyes for all I'm worth. A good sign. Then he asked for water. I held a paper cup to his lip; he gulped, and swallowed, yes, swallowed twice. We were jubilant. Two signs. I remembered that I could now pound on the door without reservation. But of course I'd jumped the gun and had already been petitioning very pointedly.

We spent the day congratulating Dad on his imminent recovery and exercising the languid limbs on his paralyzed right side. Each of us spotted more signs of recognition in his eyes. That night my brothers and I took turns keeping watch at the hospital. Dad slept like a baby.

Monday it was time to fly back to our other homes. Dad was making gains by the hour. We said goodby in good spirits. At the airport the three of us reminded each other how fortunate we were to have arrived right at the critical time. We were glad we had been there to witness and participate. Our farewell embraces were strong and sure, no longer those of awkward, self-conscious children. We clutched at roots, almost torn up, that now bound us more visibly together within the miracle of a Father's love.

FATHERLOVE IS DISCOVERED from the inside. We are given a moment of recognition, and our hearts respond: Yes that's the way God is. In my night watch at the hospital I was privileged to see a Heavenly Father rescue the one who had showed me what He is like.

But what about people who have no father to suggest such a being, or worse, have a father who models a terrible distortion of the heavenly one? How are they supposed to get a hold on Fatherlove?

A house on Crown Haven Court.
Southern California. 1980s.

DARRYL KNEW it was time for the kids to go to bed. His wife had reminded him for the second time. But their cries of delight and the pure joy in their eyes were too much. They promised to play more quietly. The game went on. It was Jimmy's turn to throw a paper wad across the room to the trash basket in the corner. Suzy tried to knock it down with one hand before it got there. Somehow they had hit on one of those games that are SO much fun for a few unrepeatable hours.

Darryl's turn to throw. The kids laughed at six-foot-four Dad winding his long arms up for the "pitch." But his throws are hard to intercept. One more try for Suzy.

Every house on Crown Haven Court darkened and fell quiet except for one home where the muffled squeals and snickers flowed on until almost midnight. "Just this time."

When Darryl finally crawled into bed and tried to sleep he could remember vividly other voices late in the night. Very different ones. His own father's voice, ragged-edged, booming over his brother Joey in the next room: "You WILL play in that church next week. Don't you dare disobey me."

Years before Joey had been taught by their fanatical father that walking into a Catholic church was equivalent to dropping into the fires of hell. Joey, the most sensitive and conscientious of the children, had accepted wholeheartedly the harsh black-and-white lines his father laid out on the world.

But now Joey had become a budding organist. People were noticing his talent; even the big Catholic church in town noticed. They wanted the boy to play at services. The proud father, abruptly forgetting his previous tirades, thought that would be wonderful—and ordered his son to do it.

Joey believed it was terribly wrong. From his bed in the dark he begged, "I just can't Dad, I can't. Please, please don't make me do it."

"So you're going to disobey your father?" the man thundered down. "I'll make you eat your own vomit, boy."

"Please, Dad. Please."

Darryl would never forget that wrenching struggle. It went on for weeks. The father threatened and berated, jabbing at his son's tender conscience. The boy agonized between two terrible sins: disobeying his father and playing music for the "antichrist."

Finally this gifted child-musician, who longed so much to do only good in this world, broke under the strain. Taken to psychiatrists, he was pronounced a hopeless case. The doctors recommended that he be committed to an institution. After that the father bitterly complained about the "mental case" in the family.

Fortunately the mother did not abandon her son.

Finally separated for good from Dad, she nurtured Joey back to health. But the damage went deep. The boy would never fulfill his potential as a musician. From then on Darryl saw his brother as a shadow of what he could have become.

ANGER. THAT'S WHAT Darryl remembered. And fear of that man with creased forehead and heavy eyebrows who conducted regular bullying sessions in the guise of religious instruction. Darryl would never be able to erase the long night of his childhood in the hands of a monster who consumed his own kind.

He became the angriest of the sons, the most bitter, though these emotions were well hidden. He'd seen his own flesh-and-blood destroyed. How was it possible to forgive that?

Predictably, Darryl turned against everything his father stood for—and ended up reflecting him. He adopted his mother's religion, but served his father's God, an endlessly demanding Lord. Darryl tried so hard to please Him. An easy prey for fanaticism, he went off to a small school in the West Virginia mountains to cut himself off from the world and serve God every minute, every second.

At one point it became a 24-hour-a-day effort. Darryl concluded that if Jesus prayed all night and came away refreshed, he should too. So he denied himself sleep in order to pray and study Scripture, night after night. As his body and mind weakened, he kept hoping against hope that he could somehow achieve that supernatural refreshment with the Lord.

Finally, a few verses in the Psalms interrupted Darryl's ordeal. He read of God as a Father who has compassion on his children. A Father of the fatherless. Someone who would care for us even if our parents forsake us.

Darryl realized that if He were a compassionate Father He wouldn't put His kid through this. He wouldn't demand this kind of abuse. Darryl began listening to friends who were both sane and pious, and fanaticism began to loosen its stranglehold on him.

Then he ran head-on into something called Justification by Faith. He found Scripture loudly declaring that God accepts the ungodly on the basis of Christ's accomplishments, and that He cherishes the believing sinner as if he had all the perfection of His own Son.

God forgave. God was gracious. He was not endlessly demanding, but endlessly giving.

This discovery rose like a dazzling sun in Darryl's life and he walked right out of the long night. God's graciousness illuminated everything. His Fatherlove seeped down deep. That's why Darryl could play that silly game with Jimmy and Suzy until almost midnight.

Darryl is one of my closest friends. I like watching him with his children. Like most parents I yell at my kids too much (instead of talking to them). I have to struggle against getting uptight and impatient. Darryl seems different. He has high standards; a lot of people might consider him strict. But he disciplines with such grace. He wins his children over to goodness. When little missteps threaten to blow up, my friend's good humor eases the family out of a showdown. I find in him much to learn from.

I had a father who mirrored a heavenly one. Darryl could envy an orphan. But what a Father he discovered! And what a difference He has made! One day Darryl told me about a little incident in his home that illustrated for him what our Father God can mean to us.

BEDTIME HAD ROLLED AROUND again with that stolid finality that energetic children instinctively distrust. The kids wanted "cozy time" with Dad: "Please, just a few minutes."

Darryl gave in. Jimmy and Suzy piled into bed on either side of Dad and snuggled up. Darryl told them a story and then turned out the lights. "Time to be quiet. Try to go to sleep now."

Then a little ritual began. Suzy slowly reached a hand out, felt Dad's face, and gently pulled it around toward her. Now she could sleep.

Jimmy had heard something suspicious. He quietly reached out his hand and turned Dad's face back toward his side of the bed.

This little game went on for a while until both were sound asleep. It was pitch dark, the kids couldn't see a thing; but both wanted that familiar countenance looking their way as they drifted off into the mysterious night. Both wanted Fatherlove beaming in their direction.

Darryl saw a picture of God in all this, of course. And I saw more. This was more than just a symbol. This was Fatherlove made flesh and dwelling among us. It had appeared right in the midst of that abuse and suffering which breed their own kind, generation after generation. Grace had disrupted the inevitable cycle. Somehow, out of an angry, bitter wasteland, a compassionate father blossomed and bore fruit.

I thought of two immeasurably different night scenes. A child listening in terror to threats and abuse raining down on his fragile brother. And two kids nestled against the rock of Fatherlove.

VICTORIOUS Warrior. Wise Shepherd. King of Kings. Consuming Fire. These are not absolute categories. They're more like nicknames we have for our God. Nicknames aren't used officially. We can't speak of God authoritatively or exhaustively; we can't manipulate Him by our definitions. But a nickname often describes accurately some quality we've observed in a person close to us. And we do have many divine qualities to describe—many great names—because God has acted so eloquently in our world.

Immutable. Omnipotent. Omniscient. They are best seen as terms of endearment, special names we call out to the Father who cherishes us.

And in the end, all that matters is that His face is turned toward us in the dark.

‖ SOURCES ‖

Most Scripture quotations in this book are from *The Holy Bible: New International Version,* copyright 1973, 1978, 1984 by the International Bible Society, and published by Zondervan Bible Publishers.

Chapter 1: Elemental Force

(page)	(reference)	(source)
17	atomic bomb	*Brighter than a Thousand Suns,* Robert Jungk, translated by James Cleugh (New York: Harcourt Brace, 1958), pages 199-203. *Day One,* Peter Wyden (New York: Simon and Schuster, 1984), pages 208-216.
18	wields nature	Psalms 77:5, 77:14-18, 89:9, 107:25.
21	Barton Stone	*Conversions—The Christian Experience,* Hugh T. Kerr and John M. Mulder, editors (Grand Rapids: Eerdmans, 1985), pages 93-94. *An Endless Line of Splendor,* Earle E. Cairns (Wheaton, Ill.: Tyndale House, 1986), pages 100-101.
23	Charles Finney	*Memoirs of Rev. Charles G. Finney* (New York: Fleming H. Revell, 1903), page 74.

Chapter 2: Victorious Warrior

28	Warrior	Psalms 24:7-8, 45:3-4, 74:14.
27	captives taken	Isaiah 50:25.
27	victorious	Zephaniah 3:17.
28	Mount Carmel	1 Kings 19.
29	Watchman Nee	*Against the Tide,* Angus I. Kinnear (Fort Washington, Penn.:Christian Literature Crusade, 1976), pages 70-75.

Chapter 3: Skillful Creator

37	whistled	Isaiah 7:18-19.
37	nothing too hard	Jeremiah 32:17.
39	creator	Psalms 13, 33:9, 65:6, 104:2, and 146:6; Isaiah 40:26; Jeremiah 27:5.
40	human eye	*Light and Vision,* Conrad G. Mueller, Mae Rudoph, and the Editors of Time-Life Books (New York: Time-Life Books, 1969).
42	effectual working	Ephesians 3:7,16,20; John 1:12.
43	Nicky Cruz	*The Cross and the Switchblade,* David Wilkerson with John and Elizabeth Sherrill (Spire Books, 1963), pages 86-95.
44	Harold Hughes	*The Honorable Alcoholic,* Harold E. Hughes (Grand Rapids: Zondervan, 1979).

Chapter 5: Carefully Restrained

60	sin separates	Isaiah 59:2.

63	*Lucifer*	Ezekiel 28:12-19, Revelation 12:7-9, and Isaiah 14:12-15.
66	*gentle whisper*	1 Kings 19:11-13.
67	*Why will ye die?*	Ezekiel 18:31.
67	*bruised reed*	Isaiah 42:3.
67	*Maximillian Kolbe*	*A Man for Others: Maximillian Kolbe, Saint of Auschwitz—in the Words of Those Who Knew Him,* Patricia Treece (San Francisco: Harper & Row, 1982.

Chapter 6: The Saboteur

76	*Peter's escape*	Acts 12.
79	*anything too hard?*	Jeremiah 32:27.
79	*all things possible*	Matthew 19:26.
82	*perfect in weakness*	2 Corinthians 12:9.
84	*Gandhi*	*Freedom at Midnight,* Larry Collins and Dominique Lapierre (New York: Avon Books: 1976).
86	*F. Nietzsche*	*The Story of Philosophy,* Will Durant (New York: Simon and Schuster [Pocket Books], 1961), pages 445-447.

Chapter 7: Consuming Fire

91	*Merlin Carothers*	*Prison to Praise,* Merlin Carothers (Plainfield, N.J.: Logos International, 1979).
93	*mountains—ocean*	Psalms 36:6.
93	*too pure*	Habakkuk 1:13
94	*Wilhelm Boehme*	*Among the Mystics,* William Fairweather (Freeport, N.Y.: Books for Libraries Press, 1968), page 97.
94	*Teresa of Avila*	*Among the Mystics,* page 47.
94	*sold for sandals*	Amos 2:6-7.
94	*let justice roll*	Amos 5:24.
96	*Tex Watson*	"Today's Student" (May 8, 1978), pages 1,4.
100	*heart followed my eyes*	Job 31:7-8.
100	*chosen you*	1 Thessalonians 1:4.
101	*Ahab*	1 Kings 21.

Chapter 8: Tender Heart

105	*Manasseh*	2 Chronicles 33.
109	*God's ability to forgive*	Psalm 51:1, Isaiah 1:18, Jeremiah 31:34, Micah 7:19.
109	*Leroy*	*Soul on Fire,* Eldridge Cleaver (Waco, Tex.: Word Books, 1978), pages 211-212.
109	*Thomas Tarrants*	"Christianity Today" (September 22, 1978), pages 13-16.

111	*I revealed myself*	Isaiah 65:1.
113	*banished*	2 Samuel 14:14.
113	*John Newton*	"The Amazing Grace of John Newton," Alex Haley, "Readers Digest" (October 1986), pages 138-142; *Conversions, The Christian Experience* (as cited above), pages 88-91.

Chapter 9: Holy Encourager

118	*Charles F. Andrews*	*Conversions, The Christian Experience* (as cited above), page 176.
118	*Paul Stookey*	"Christianity Today" (May 19, 1973), pages 12-17.
120	*Abraham and Sodom*	Genesis 18.
122	*led them safely*	Genesis 19:16
125	*great encourager*	Psalms 40:2 and 3:3; 2 Thessalonians 1:11.

Chapter 10: Most High

131	*Rabi Maharaj*	*Escape into the Light,* Rabindranath R. Maharaj (Eugene, Ore.: Harvest House), pages 107-108.
132	*Jeroboam*	1 Kings 13.
134	*second commandment*	Exodus 20:4-6.
134	*wind and emptiness*	Isaiah 41:29.
134	*scarecrow*	Jeremiah 10:5.
134	*lifeless stone*	Habakkuk 2:19.
135	*lift up your eyes*	Isaiah 40:26.
136	*David—the heavens*	Psalms 19:1.
136	*Walt Whitman*	*The Protestant Mystics,* selected and edited by Anne Fremantle (Boston: Little, Brown and Company, 1964), pages 252-253.
137	*Michael Pupin*	*Man Discovers God,* Sherwood Eddy (Freeport, N.Y.: Books for Libraries Press, 1968), pages 174-175.
139	*Most High*	Job 22:12, Psalms 97:9, Isaiah 57:14, 1 Timothy 6:16.
140	*Solomon*	2 Chronicles 6:18.
140	*Plotinus*	*Man Discovers God* (as cited above), pages 31-32.
141	*Gregory of Nyssa*	*From Glory to Glory—Texts from Gregory of Nyssa's Mystical Writings,* selected and with an introduction by Jean Danielou (New York: Charles Scribner's Sons, 1961), page 118.
141	*John of the Cross*	*Among the Mystics* (as cited above), page 58.

Chapter 11: Close Companion

147	*Thomas Traherne*	*The Protestant Mystics* (as cited above), pages 98-99.

147	*e. e. cummings*	*The Protestant Mystics,* page 348.
147	*Francis of Assisi*	*Man Discovers God* (as cited above), pages 91-92.
147	*George Fox*	*The Protestant Mystics,* pages 86-87.
147	*very near*	Psalm 145:18; Matthew 6:6; Psalms 16:8, 89:15, and 27:4; Acts 17:27-28.
148	*Hagar*	Genesis 16:8 and 16:13.
150	*Peter Marshall*	*A Man Called Peter,* Catherine Marshall (New York: Avon Books, 1971), page 24.
151	*image and likeness*	Genesis 1:26 and 5:3.
151	*invisible*	1 Timothy 1:17.
156	*Brother Lawrence*	*Man Discovers God,* page 104.
156	*Julian of Norwich*	*Showings* (The Classics of Western Spirituality), Julian of Norwich, translated and with an introduction by Edmund Colledge and James Walsh (New York: Paulist Press, 1978), page 288.
156	*Dwight L. Moody*	*Moody,* J. C. Pollock (New York: Macmillan, 1963), page 90.
156	*Ethel Waters*	*Conversions: The Christian Experience* (as cited above), pages 221-222.

Chapter 12: Surpassingly Present

161	*Don Richardson*	*Peace Child,* Don Richardson (Ventura, Calif.: Regal Books, 1976).
163	*Dwight L. Moody*	*Moody* (as cited above), pages 185-186.
165	*the magi*	Matthew 2.
167	*Brother Andrew*	*God's Smuggler,* Brother Andrew (Old Tappan, N.J.: Fleming H. Revell, 1980), pages 181-184.
170	*every sparrow*	Matthew 10:29.
170	*numbered hairs*	Matthew 10:30.
170	*Al Kasha*	"Charisma" (July 1987), pages 37-40.
173	*Malcolm Muggeridge*	*Jesus Rediscovered,* Malcolm Muggeridge (Garden City, N.Y.: Doubleday, 1969), pages 49-50.
173	*in Thy presence*	Psalm 16:11, *New American Standard Bible.*
174	*Norman Vincent Peale*	"Leadership" (Spring 1986), page 62.

Chapter 13: King of Kings

179	*Robert Meeler*	"Guideposts" (May 1982), page 62.
181	*I will teach you*	Exodus 4:11-12.
182	*King of Kings*	1 Timothy 6:15; Psalms 99:1, 80:1, 96:6, 93:1-2 and 68:4.
182	*Rameses II*	Exodus 5—15.
184	*Nineveh*	Jonah 1—4.
184	*Nebuchadnezzar*	Daniel 1—4.

| 187 | *Viggo Olsen* | *Daktar: Diplomat in Bangladesh,* Viggo B. Olsen (Old Tappan, N.J.: Revell, 1975), pages 186-187 |
| 189 | *Corrie and Betsie ten Boom* | *The Hiding Place,* Corrie ten Boom with John and Elizabeth Sherrill (Minneapolis: World Wide Publications, 1971), pages 197-208. |

Chapter 14: Burden Bearer

196	*Alan*	This story appeared originally in *Take Five,* Steven Mosley (Boise, Idaho: Pacific Press, 1987).
198	*Hebrew complaints*	Exodus 16, Numbers 11 and 13.
199	*watched over*	Deuteronomy 2:7.
200	*satisfy every*	Psalm 145:16.
201	*Aunt Lana*	"Guideposts" (August 1977), pages 6-9.
205	*Helmuth James*	*The Protestant Mystics* (as cited above), pages 358-360.
206	*Joy Swift*	*"They're All Dead, Aren't They?",* Joy Swift (Boise, Idaho: Pacific Press, 1986), pages 73-74.
208	*weighted down*	Amos 2:13.
209	*carry you still*	Isaiah 46:4.

Chapter 15: Lowly Lord

211	*Beatrice church choir*	*More of Paul Harvey's The Rest of the Story,* Paul Aurandt (New York: Bantam, 1980), pages 3-5.
213	*David*	*A Man Called Mr. Pentecost,* David du Plessis as told to Bob Slosser (Plainfield, N.J.: Logos International), pages 123-129.
216	*Elijah, ravens*	1 Kings 17.
217	*Joshua*	Joshua 10.
217	*Elijah's farewell*	2 Kings 2.

Chapter 16: Ageless Rock

225	*Peter in court*	Acts 4.
227	*Treena Kerr*	"Radix" (Fall 1985), pages 21-22.
229	*Rock of Ages*	Psalms 18:12, 30:1-12, 90:2, and 111:3.
229	*not consumed*	Malachi 3:6.
230	*George Mueller*	*George Mueller—Delighted in God!,* Roger Steer (Wheaton, Ill.: Harold Shaw Publishers, 1981).
233	*word stands forever*	Isaiah 40:7.
234	*Polycarp*	*The Ante-Nicene Fathers,* Alexander Roberts and James Donaldson, editors (New York: Charles Scribner's Sons, 1899), Volume I, pages 39-44.
237	*David*	Psalm 23:1-4.
237	*Rock eternal*	Isaiah 26:4.
237	*perfect peace*	Isaiah 26:3.

237   *Paul, the Philippians*   Philippians 4:12-13.

238   *Chrysostom*   *Butler's Lives of the Saints,* edited, revised and supplemented by Herbert thurston (New York: P. J. Kenedy and Sons, 1962), Volume I, pages 178-182.

239   *John Wesley*   *John Wesley,* Basil Miller (Minneapolis: Dimension Books, Bethany Fellowship, Inc., 1943), pages 46-48.

240   *Merrill Womach*   *Tested by Fire,* Merrill and Virginia Womach (Old Tappan, N.J.: Fleming H. Revell), pages 18-19.

Chapter 17: A Thousand Faces

244   *death row*   *God Ventures,* compiled by Irene Burk Harrell (Plainfield, N.J.: Logos International, 1970), pages 102-104.

244   *C. S. Lewis*   *Surprised by Joy,* C. S. Lewis (New York: Harcourt, Brace and World, 1955), pages 212-238.

245   *Simone Weil*   *Waiting for God,* Simone Weil (San Francisco: Harper and Row, 1973), pages 68-69.

248   *Hosea and Gomer*   Hosea 1—3.

252   *Road to Damascus*   Acts 9:1-30, 26:12-20

254   *Paul's farewell*   Acts 20.

255   *Richard Wurmbrand*   *In God's Underground,* Richard Wurmbrand (New York: Bantam Books, 1977).

Chapter 18: Shepherd Wise

259   *Ejnar Lundby*   *God Ventures* (as cited above), pages 34-40.

262   *Frances Ridley Havergal*   *They Found the Secret,* V. Raymond Edman (Grand Rapids: Zondervan, 1976), page 74.

262   *John Bunyan*   *They Found the Secret,* page 32.

262   *Charles Spurgeon*   *Spurgeon,* Arnold Dallimore (Chicago: Moody Press, 1984), pages 18-20.

265   *searches hearts*   1 Kings 8:39, Hebrews 4:13.

265   *Jeroboam's wife*   1 Kings 14.

266   *California pastor*   *Power Evangelism,* John Wimber with Kevin Springer (San Francisco: Harper and Row, 1986), pages 32-34.

268   *Joseph*   Genesis 41:25.

269   *Efim, Kara Kala*   *The Happiest People on Earth,* Demos Shakarian as told to John and Elizabeth Sherrill (Old Tappan, N.J.: Fleming H. Revell, 1975), pages 19-22.

271   *water from a rock*   Numbers 20.

272   *heavenly worship*   Revelation 4.

273   *Sahara tribesmen*   *Wind, Sand and Stars,* Antoine de Saint-Exupéry (New York: Time, Inc., 1965), page 96.

Chapter 19: Manchild

279   *Dad in hospital*   This story first appeared in *Take Five* (cited above).

         Christ's passion   Matthew 27, Mark 14-15, Luke 22-23, and John 18-19.

Chapter 20: Fatherlove

293   *Bilquis Sheikh*   *I Dared to Call Him Father,* Bilquis Sheikh (Waco, Tex.: Word Books, 1980), page 52.

294   *lovingkindness*   Psalms 36:5, 36:7, 33:5, 57:10, and 63:3.

294   *Charles Finney*   *They Found the Secret* (as cited above), page 55. *Conversions—The Christian Experience* (as cited above), page 110.

295   *Oswald Chambers*   *They Found the Secret* (as cited above), *page 47.*

295   *Samuel L. Brengle*   *They Found the Secret* (as cited above), page 25.

296   *Dad in hospital*   This story first appeared in *Take Five* (cited above).

304   *God as Father*   Psalms 27:10, 68:5, 89:26.

INDEX

Abraham (Abram), 120f
Abram, 148f
Adam, 64f, 151
Ahab, 28, 101f, 216
Ahijah, 265f
Alan, boy at camp, 196f
Amio, 160f
Amos, 94f
Andrew, Brother, 167f
Andrews, Charles F., 118f
angels, 122
Annas, 225f
Aquinas, Thomas, 37
Aunt Lana, 201f
Beatrice, Neb., Baptist church
    choir, 211f
Bill (friend of author, killed in
    boating accident), 56f
Boehme, Wilhelm, 94
Borgorwiec (prisoner), 69f
Brengle, Samuel Logan, 295
Bunyan, John, 262
Caiaphas, 225f
California pastor, a, 266f
Carothers, Merlin, 91f
Chambers, Oswald, 295
"Chestie," Japanese business-
    man, 194, 219f
Chrysostom, John, 238f
Cruz, Nicky, 43f
cummings, e. e., 147
Daniel, 150, 185f
David (boy from Chicago), 32f
David (in London), 213f
David (king), 53, 172, 237
David (London),
de Foucald, Charles, 143
death row convicts, 247
Dodie (woman), 32

Donne, John, 47
Edwards, Jonathan, 23
Efim (Armenia), 269f
Elijah, 28, 66, 102, 216f
Eudoxia, Empress, 238
Eve, 64f, 151
Ezekiel, 67
Finney, Charles, 23, 294f
Foss, Robert, 201f
Fox, George, 147
Francis of Assisi, 95f, 143, 147
Gale, Robert, 31f
Ghandi, Mahatma, 84f
Gomer, 248f
Gregory of Nyssa, 141
Habakkuk, 134
Hagar, 148
Hans, 167f
Havergal, Frances Ridley, 262
Hebrews, the, 198
Herod Agrippa, 76f
Hezekiah, 105
Himler, Kristian, 259f
Hosea, 67, 248f
Hughes, Harold, 44f
Hurip, 159f
Isaiah, 23, 37, 110f, 134, 237
Ishmael, 149
James, Helmuth, 205f
Jeremiah, 37, 39, 55f, 134
Jeroboam, 132f, 265f
Jezebel, 101f
Job, 56, 100
John Mark, 76
John of the Cross, Saint., 141
Jonah, 150, 184
Joseph (patriarch), 268f
Joseph of Nazareth, 165f
Joshua, 217

Juanita (schoolgirl), 98
Julian of Norwich, 156
Junko, 80
Kasha, Al, 170f
Kerr, Treena, 227f
Kolbe, Maximillian, 67f
Lawrence, Brother, 156
Leroy E. (Black Panther), 109
Leviathan, 27
Lewis, C. S., 244f
Lot, 122
Lucifer, 63f
Lundby, Ejnar, 259f
Luther, Martin, 48
magi, 165f
Maharaj, Baba Jankhi, 131
Maharaj, Rabi, 131f
Manasseh, 105f
Manson, Charles, 96
Marshall, Peter, 149f
Mary, mother of Jesus, 165f
Meeler, Robert, 179f
Mexican Indians, 141f
Mironovici, Radu, 256
Moody, Dwight L., 156, 163
Moses, 19, 134, 181, 182f, 271
Mosley, Jerry (author's brother), 171f, 249f
Mosley, Kazko (author's wife), 153f, 170f
Mosley, Ramon (author's father), 19f, 296f
Mountbatten, Lewis, 84
Mueller, George, 230f
Muggeridge, Malcolm, 173
Naboth, 101
Nebuchadnezzar, 184f
Nee, Watchman, 29f
Nellie, Miss, 244
Newton, John, 113f

Nietzsche, Friedrich, 86
Olsen, Viggo, 187
Oppenheimer, Robert, 18
Paul, 82, 237f, 252f
Peale, Norman Vincent, 174
Peter, 76f, 225f
Plotinus, 140f
Polycarp, 234
Pupin, Michael, 137
Rameses II, 182
Richardson, Don, 160f
Sahara tribesmen, 273f
Saint-Exupéry, Antoine de, 273
Samuel (car thief in Chile), 107f
Sarai, 148f
Satan, 64f
Schaeffer, Francis, 207f
Sheikh, Bilquis, 293f
Singh, Sundar, 234f
Sinyavski, Andrei, 62
Solomon, 140
Solzhenitsyn, Aleksandr, 62
Sonya (English teacher in Japan)79f
Spurgeon, Charles, 262f
Stone, Barton, 21f
Stookey, Paul, 118f
Sunday, Billy, 151f
Swift, Joy, 206f
Tarrants, Thomas, 109f
ten Boom, Betsie, 189f
ten Boom, Corrie, 125, 189f
Teresa of Avila, 94
Traherne, Thomas, 147
Turner, Ruthie, 227f
Waters, Ethel, 156
Watson, Tex, 96f
Weil, Simone, 245f
Wesley, John, 239

Whitefield, George, 23
Whitman, Walt, 136f
Wilkerson, David, 43f
Wittgenstein, Ludwig, 171f

Womach, Merrill, 240f
Wurmbrand, Richard, 255f
Zephaniah, 27